Palgrave Studies in Classical Liberalism

Series Editors
David Hardwick
Vancouver, BC, Canada

Leslie Marsh
Department of Pathology and Laboratory Medicine,
Faculty of Medicine
University of British Columbia
Vancouver, BC, Canada

This series offers a forum to writers concerned that the central presuppositions of the liberal tradition have been severely corroded, neglected, or misappropriated by overly rationalistic and constructivist approaches.

The hardest-won achievement of the liberal tradition has been the wrestling of epistemic independence from overwhelming concentrations of power, monopolies and capricious zealotries. The very precondition of knowledge is the exploitation of the epistemic virtues accorded by society's situated and distributed manifold of spontaneous orders, the DNA of the modern civil condition.

With the confluence of interest in situated and distributed liberalism emanating from the Scottish tradition, Austrian and behavioral economics, non-Cartesian philosophy and moral psychology, the editors are soliciting proposals that speak to this multidisciplinary constituency. Sole or joint authorship submissions are welcome as are edited collections, broadly theoretical or topical in nature.

More information about this series at
http://www.palgrave.com/gp/series/15722

Filipe Nobre Faria

The Evolutionary Limits of Liberalism

Democratic Problems, Market Solutions and the Ethics of Preference Satisfaction

palgrave
macmillan

Filipe Nobre Faria
Nova University of Lisbon
Lisbon, Portugal

ISSN 2662-6470 ISSN 2662-6489 (electronic)
Palgrave Studies in Classical Liberalism
ISBN 978-3-030-31495-8 ISBN 978-3-030-31496-5 (eBook)
https://doi.org/10.1007/978-3-030-31496-5

This Palgrave Macmillan imprint is published by the registered company Springer Nature Switzerland AG
The registered company address is: Gewerbestrasse 11, 6330 Cham, Switzerland

It is of the nature of desire not to be satisfied, and most men live only for the gratification of it.

—Aristotle, Politics

This book is dedicated to my family, a group like no other.

Preface

I wrote *The Evolutionary Limits of Liberalism* to analyse the sustainability of liberal institutions and of their political philosophy. This analysis is no easy task. The subject matter is complex and has overwhelming importance. After all, liberalism has been the dominant political and moral force in the West for some centuries now. Although communitarian, scientific or religious forces continue to challenge liberalism, this philosophy keeps defining the western paradigm. Some authors even thought of liberal democracy as embodying the end of history. Yet, my analysis suggests that liberalism presents numerous limitations. When analysed from a scientific, naturalist and evolutionary perspective, liberalism reveals striking unsustainability. To explain why that is so is the reason I wrote this book.

Analysing the sustainability of any institution requires some conceptual tools with predictive power. In positive political theory, these tools are models. I chose the evolutionary model of multilevel selection to achieve my aim, contrasting it with more standard rational choice models applied to political analysis that one finds in public choice theory. Many discussions by public choice theorists aim at discerning which liberal institutions can best satisfy individual preferences, if free markets or current liberal democracies. Here, the classical liberal tradition of James Buchanan and Gordon Tullock identifies the shortcomings of current liberal democracies regarding preference satisfaction and shows how a shift towards market liberalism can rescue the liberal paradigm. But my research reveals that the problem runs deeper. By looking at the problems of liberal institutions from an evolutionary perspective, I conclude that it is the liberal satisfaction of preferences itself which is problematic. Liberal institutions aiming at maximising the preference satisfaction of individuals are potentially too fragile in terms of evolution.

When I started writing this book at the beginning of my Ph.D. at King's College London, I was more optimistic about liberal robustness. However, like the Frenchman Tocqueville in America, I was a Portuguese living in London. The amazement of living in cosmopolitan London prompted questions about the moral underpinnings of a liberal society. Evolutionary ethics was already a main interest of mine and I was aware that culture and morality are under natural selection. So I asked myself what the evolutionary consequences of liberalism are for those who embrace it. This question became part of my Ph.D. thesis, which in turn became this book.

My initial optimism about liberalism gave place to scepticism. Yet, the conclusion of my research is not disappointing. On the contrary, it opens avenues through which to tackle pressing contemporary challenges in western societies. I believe that with more and better information about the limits of liberalism it is possible to find suitable alternatives to our social problems.

Lisbon, Portugal Filipe Nobre Faria

Acknowledgements

The making of *The Evolutionary Limits of Liberalism* took around seven years, a task that I carried out in London, Bonn and Lisbon. Throughout this time, I had the financial support of the Foundation for Science and Technology, both during my Ph.D. years at King's College London and also later as a postdoctoral researcher at Nova University of Lisbon. Without this financial support, for which I am thankful, it would have been impossible to write the book.

I would like to thank my colleagues and friends for contributing directly and indirectly to the birth of this monograph. I thank José Pedro Zúquete, André Santos Campos, Riccardo Marchi, Susana Cadilha, Gabriele de Angelis, Luís Miguel Simões and Jonathan Anomaly for their support and for the continuous exchange of ideas. They create a stimulating academic environment that aims at excellence. I would also like to thank Prof. António Marques, João Constâncio, Nuno Venturinha and Giovanni Damele for welcoming me to the Nova Institute of Philosophy (Ifilnova). They made me feel at home. To work at Ifilnova allowed me to develop my work and to be in regular contact with some of the best philosophers in Portugal, which is an invaluable experience.

I am grateful to John Meadowcroft, my Ph.D. supervisor at King's College London, who gave me the liberty to pursue unorthodox ideas throughout my doctoral studies, even when such ideas were contrary to his own. He is an example of academic liberty. The book owes a lot to him and his support. I want to thank, too, my colleague Paul Graham for his comments on earlier drafts. Paul's insights have made this monograph more solid in terms of scholarship.

I also want to thank my non-academic friends, from whom I receive wisdom and camaraderie across the years. To single them out would not make justice to all those who made a difference. In the end, and it couldn't be otherwise, I am deeply thankful to my family. In particular, I am indebted to my partner Sandra for all her encouragement and constructive feedback, to Ina and Jörg for their ready assistance and to my parents António and Maria, as well as to my late grandmother Francisca, for all their perpetual support. Finally, I thank my daughter Helena and my son Tristan for being a constant inspiration.

Praise for *The Evolutionary Limits of Liberalism*

"This book not only challenges the dominant model of preference-satisfaction in economic and political theory, but unlike much work in behavioural economics it provides an alternative framework for assessing whether individual choices are adaptive: Darwinian multilevel selection, which gives a central role to intergroup competition. As such, it is an important contribution to the field."

—Paul Graham, *Senior Lecturer in Politics, University of Buckingham*

"Faria sets out a provocative analysis of the implications of evolutionary theory for liberalism. Liberal thinkers have often argued that liberal institutions have evolved as a solution to the challenges that face advanced societies, but Faria argues that there are reasons to believe that liberal values and institutions are weaker in evolutionary terms than many of the alternatives. Accordingly, liberalism faces an existential challenge that it is not well-placed to overcome. Whether or not one agrees with Faria, this is an important book that addresses issues all of us living in contemporary liberal democracies should take seriously."

—John Meadowcroft, *Reader in Public Policy, King's College London*

"With falling birthrates and a crisis of self-confidence, liberal political societies in the West are facing an existential crisis. Dr. Faria deploys concepts from economics and evolutionary biology to investigate whether liberal societies are, over the long run, stable and adaptive. This is one of the most important questions of the twenty first century, and political philosophers who ignore it may become as obsolete as a poorly adapted primate."

—Jonathan Anomaly, *Associate Director of the Philosophy, Politics and Economics Programme, University of Pennsylvania*

Contents

CHAPTER 1

Introduction

Liberalism rests on the liberty to pursue individual preferences. In this sense, the success of liberal institutions depends on their institutional capacity to maximise the preference satisfaction, utility or happiness of individuals. While much literature aims at fulfilling the utility-based *telos* of liberal institutions, there is less inquiry on the evolutionary consequences of such institutions. This work uses evolutionary theory to assess two central aspects of liberalism. First, the monograph appraises the capacity of liberal democracy and free markets to maximise preference satisfaction. In particular, it re-evaluates public choice theory's claim that free markets are a suitable alternative to the shortcomings of western liberal democracies regarding the satisfaction of preferences. Second, and most importantly, the monograph assesses the desirability of the liberal satisfaction of preferences concerning its institutional sustainability.

Altogether, *The Evolutionary Limits of Liberalism* scrutinises the sustainability of liberal institutions. By appraising the liberal satisfaction of preferences from the standpoint of evolution, this work focuses on evolutionary fitness as the object of maximisation. Such an approach contrasts with the standard focus on the maximisation of preference satisfaction taken by rational/public choice approaches.

The monograph asserts that both liberal democracy and markets have a high potential to maximise the preference satisfaction of individuals. Public choice approaches are correct in emphasising the good performance of markets regarding preference satisfaction, although these approaches underestimate the good capacities of liberal democracy in

F. N. Faria, *The Evolutionary Limits of Liberalism*, Palgrave Studies in Classical Liberalism, https://doi.org/10.1007/978-3-030-31496-5_1

that regard. Yet, to maximise individual preferences does not mean to maximise the evolutionary fitness of individuals and their groups. After analysing the evolutionary impact of the liberal satisfaction of preferences, the book argues that such a practice reveals maladaptive tendencies which impact negatively on the fitness of the groups that promote it. From an evolutionary point of view, the liberal satisfaction of individual preferences is not particularly desirable. Therefore, the free market is an unsuitable alternative to liberal democracy's shortcomings because both institutions operate under a liberal meta-morality that potentially weakens groups in the evolutionary process of inter-group competition. Whether in market or democratic liberalism, it is the ethic of the liberal satisfaction of preferences that leads to maladaptiveness and thus to institutional unsustainability.

This book represents a unique research that uses the evolutionary model of multilevel selection to reassess the classical claims of public/rational choice theory regarding preference satisfaction in markets and liberal democracy. It also constitutes a novel biopolitical evaluation of the evolutionary desirability and sustainability of the liberal satisfaction of preferences. Within political theory, no extensive and consistent research has utilised contemporary multilevel selection theory to analyse the theoretical underpinnings of liberalism. In particular, this research suggests the adoption of a more realistic account of social behaviour than the one offered by standard rational/public choice theories to build a robust political theory. While the cognitive sciences have already been demonstrating that the assumption of universal rational egoism is unverified, multilevel selection theory offers explanations for why moral and behavioural pluralism is present in society. By integrating behavioural and evolutionary science within political theory, this work develops an evolutionary political theory of preference satisfaction which operates in the tradition of scientific realism and that represents a more accurate explanation of public choice.

The study of the impact of liberal morality on the evolutionary fitness of social groups is another essential contribution to knowledge. Because morality is a collective phenomenon under selection, to research the impact of morality on group fitness is of high importance to understand institutional sustainability. The monograph contributes to the deepening of this important research in relation to liberal morality, which is of high relevance for contemporary liberal societies. Ultimately, this work specially interests all of those who want to understand the desirability and the limits of liberal institutions in our increasingly challenging times.

1.1 The Outline

The book focuses on the nature of preferences and their social impact. The academic fields of economics (Samuelson, 1938; Sen, 1986; Sunstein & Thaler, 2006), psychology (Lichtenstein & Slovic, 2006; Tversky & Simonson, 1993) or philosophy (Brennan & Lomasky, 1993; Goodin, 1986) have studied preferences from various angles. However, when comparing the satisfaction of individual preferences in markets and politics, public choice theory is the classical framework of study. Such a framework is the comprehensive body of theory that applies the tools of economic reasoning to the study of politics and markets. Public choice theory, in the classical liberal tradition of James Buchanan and Gordon Tullock, asserts that largely unrestricted markets are a possible and probably better-suited institutional mechanism to satisfy individual preferences than current western liberal democracies (Buchanan, 1999a, 1999b; Buchanan & Vanberg, 2001). These authors claim liberal democracies suffer from intrinsic structural shortcomings (e.g. rent-seeking, rational ignorance, etc.) and that free markets reveal comparative advantages. Put differently, this classic public choice tradition postulates that the aim of fulfilling the liberal satisfaction of individual preferences is better achieved by reforming/limiting current liberal democracies and instituting a classical liberal market-oriented society. Such public choice theorists reveal disappointment with current liberal democracies. They believe that only market liberalism and politics "as exchange" can provide a good basis for fulfilling the liberal satisfaction of preferences.

Based on this argument, the monograph employs evolutionary theory to reanalyse if free markets[1] are truly a suitable alternative to the shortcomings of liberal democracy[2] in respect of preference satisfaction. Above all, the monograph aims at understanding how desirable

[1] A "free" market is hereby regarded as a market economy which is directed by market prices and that results from an institutional political arrangement that, through the general absence of government economic intervention, aims at conserving market prices.

[2] In this book, unless stated otherwise, liberal democracy is defined as a form of democracy that respects the principles of liberalism (i.e. the defence of individual freedom and equality). It is a democracy operating under constitutions that protect individual rights and minorities from the abuse of power of autocratic regimes or from the tyranny of the majority. It upholds human or natural rights, the rule of law, universal suffrage and political and civic freedoms.

the liberal satisfaction of individual preferences is from an evolutionary perspective. It assesses the impact that the morally liberal aim of satisfying/maximising individual preferences has on the evolutionary fitness of individuals and groups that embrace this aim. The assessment of the positive or negative impact of liberal morality on fitness is fundamental in determining the sustainability of such an ethic. In sum, the book analyses the capacities of democratic and market liberal institutions to satisfy individual preferences and assesses if the liberal satisfaction of preference is sustainable in terms of evolution.

To achieve the proposed aim, this work introduces the main arguments in public choice literature about free markets being a suitable alternative to liberal democracy's shortcomings. In particular, the work introduces the shortcomings of liberal democracy and the institutional market-enhancing solutions, as well as public choice's main behavioural assumptions, which rest on rational choice theory.[3] Afterwards, the monograph puts forward the evolutionary framework. The evolutionary perspective that reanalyses the claims of public choice theory relies on the model of multilevel selection theory—a group selectionist model which asserts that natural selection takes place not only at the level of individuals but also at the level of groups (Sober & Wilson, 1998; Wilson & Wilson, 2007). Based on the insights and logic of multilevel selection theory, the monograph proposes a new set of behavioural assumptions as an alternative to the ones used by public choice theory. This new set of assumptions is pluralistic and make up the "pluralism of types" approach.[4] Such a new set will become the basis to discuss the potential for preference satisfaction in markets and politics, reanalysing the

[3] Classic public choice theory assumes that individuals are the same (i.e. rationally self-interested/egoist) in all institutional contexts. It rejects the pluralistic or bifurcated vision that sees individuals as self-interested/egoist in markets while at the same time considering that they can be publicly interested in politics. Thus, it assumes that the motivation of behaviour is unified and universal (Tullock, Seldon, & Brady, 2002, p. 4).

[4] This "pluralism of types" postulates that natural selection generated different types of individuals with different behavioural tendencies (i.e. altruistic, self-interested/egoist, pro-group, anti-group, etc.) and that this pluralism of types should be taken into consideration when analysing and comparing social/political institutions (like markets and liberal democracy).

postulates found in public choice theory. Furthermore, the monograph discusses the role of morality in shaping preferences and in providing group cohesion under inter-group competition to understand the impact of moral institutions on group evolutionary fitness. Such an understanding is important to assess the desirability of a liberal morality that aims at satisfying individual preferences. Ultimately, after presenting this comprehensive evolutionary framework, the book assesses the main claims of public choice theorists and answers the work's main questions from this evolutionary perspective.

In more detail, the chapters have the following content. After the general introduction, Chapter 2 introduces the key definitions and methodology, focusing on the behavioural assumptions of rational/public choice theory and on the rational/public choice methods for comparing preference satisfaction in politics and markets. This chapter also introduces the evolutionary model of multilevel selection theory along with important clarifications of key concepts like preferences, fitness and morality. Chapter 2 revises public choice theory's behavioural assumptions, presenting a new set of assumptions based on multilevel selection theory with which to compare preference satisfaction in markets and politics (i.e. "the pluralism of types").

Chapter 3 presents the public choice account of the main shortcomings of liberal democracy and the potential market solutions proposed therein. In particular, it assesses how those shortcomings prevent individuals from satisfying their preferences. This chapter also assesses if a market autocracy is a viable public choice solution to maximise individual preferences. In addition, Chapter 3 reveals the liberal-contractarian market solution put forward by public choice theorists, especially focusing on the acknowledged market advantages over democratic choices.

Chapter 4 builds the evolutionary theoretical framework that the last chapters will use to reanalyse the public choice claims. Chapter 4 explains how one can apply multilevel selection theory to social groups and asserts the vital importance of group forces for social understanding. It also explains the role of group morality in shaping individual preferences and explicates how such a morality can be adaptive or maladaptive for groups that internalise moral norms under inter-group competition. Overall, the fourth chapter highlights the strict interdependence of moral/cultural evolution and genetic evolution. It also emphasises the importance of punishment mechanisms, which groups use to maintain moral/group cohesion. Another important point is how morality is produced and internalised, a procedure that this fourth part explains through the logic of the "pluralism of types". Finally, Chapter 4 examines the process of moral and political framing to show how preferences are highly dependent of moral and political contexts and are not well defined a priori.

Chapter 5 reanalyses public choice theory's account of the shortcomings of liberal democracy and of their potential market-enhancing institutional solutions from the evolutionary perspective. Based on multilevel selection theory, Chapter 5 utilises the new set of pluralistic behavioural assumptions to re-evaluate the conclusions that public choice theory offers in terms of preference satisfaction in markets and liberal democracy. In particular, this chapter assesses if markets truly have a higher capacity to satisfy preferences and if liberal democracy is as problematic at satisfying individual preferences as classic public choice theorists claim. Chapter 5 will then answer a central question: what is the capacity of both liberal democracy and market liberalism to maximise preference satisfaction? While doing so, this chapter also appraises public choice's general claim that markets are a suitable alternative to the shortcomings of liberal democracy regarding preference satisfaction.

Chapter 6 discusses the impact of a liberal market society on the evolutionary fitness of groups to assess if market liberalism is indeed a sustainable and viable alternative to the shortcomings of liberal democracy. Notably, this chapter discusses F. A. Hayek's (1979, 1988) defence of market liberalism, which he considers to be evolutionarily superior to collectivist modes of social organisation, and reassesses his defence. The sixth chapter examines the evolutionary consequences of the liberal satisfaction of preferences as a meta-morality to understand its desirability for social groups.

1.2 On Liberalism

By focusing on the liberal satisfaction of preferences, the monograph focuses on liberalism. Like with most political philosophies, it is difficult to craft a precise definition of liberalism that satisfies everyone. However, it is not the aim of this book to explore all the possible ways to understand this philosophy. Yet, regardless of how we may understand liberalism, the liberal satisfaction of preferences is a key and irreducible component of liberal normativity. While liberalism varies in its conceptions of freedom, which may be positive or negative, and in its conception of equality, which may be formal or substantive, liberal theory must uphold the freedom for individuals to pursue preferences, provided no direct harm is done to others. It is the centrality of the liberal satisfaction of preferences in liberalism that justifies equating the two. In this sense, removing the liberal satisfaction of preferences would mean to remove liberalism.

Liberalism came out of the Enlightenment as a dominant political philosophy. This ideology postulated three radical thoughts. First, political society is an artificial construct, rather than organic. Second, the individual is the locus of value, and not the group or society. Third, individuals differ in their values, preferences, interests and goals, and there are many irreconcilable conceptions of the good that may lead to different, yet fulfilling lives. Unlike communitarians, liberals give moral primacy to the individual. If there is a tension between the group and the individual, the moral primacy rests on the individual. While liberals may not ignore the anthropological importance of communities, they believe that individuals should choose their political institutions, which in turn should serve the individuals. In this way, liberals have an instrumental conception of normative justification. Still, liberalism is not merely about the political choices made by individuals. Before liberal doctrine, Hobbes had already proposed a popularly chosen leviathan. Liberalism only arises when one joins its instrumental conception of politics with the moral recognition of value pluralism. At heart, liberal philosophy is about asserting the legitimacy of different conceptions of the good life. Only by having the liberty to pursue their preferences and goals can individuals lead fulfilling lives, which are free from unchosen communal or state authorities (Dimock, 2000).

At the institutional level, liberal democracy is the most common expression of political liberalism in the West, while markets express economic liberalism. This monograph compares preference satisfaction in liberal democracies with preference satisfaction in free markets or market liberalism. But can liberal democracy be contrasted with free markets? After all, liberal democracy seems to include relatively free markets. In this sense, one normally thinks that liberal democracy already acknowledges private property rights and contract law as fundamental to achieve liberal democratic aims (e.g. individual liberty, formal equality). Yet, liberal democracy can be more or less market oriented to the point of two liberal democracies being radically different in practice. One liberal democracy may have high taxation and redistribution while another may have low taxation and redistribution, potentially leading to dissimilar outcomes in terms of happiness, preference satisfaction, etc.

It is the claim of classic public choice scholars (i.e. Tullock and Buchanan) that existing liberal democracies have structural problems that prevent a desirable satisfaction of preferences. Their solution is to ensure people make most choices via the market and only the strictly necessary choices through politics. Although both Tullock and Buchanan present free market solutions within what we may still understand as liberal democracy, i.e. with political power being constitutionally restricted to the maximum, a market-based solution that can truly maximise the satisfaction of preferences may very well be a free market autocracy. This market autocracy would already not be a liberal democracy, at least in the way we commonly acknowledge democratic liberalism. Even if we consider a market autocracy to have a liberal nature because of attempting to maximise preference satisfaction, we cannot straightforwardly consider it democratic. Yet, in theory, such an autocracy could be better at allowing markets to work and hence at satisfying preferences than any liberal democracy. For instance, Tullock (2005, p. 41) is sympathetic towards eastern regimes like the one of Singapore, which combines broadly free markets with autocratic rule. Hence, although free markets can operate within a framework of liberal democracy, they can also work outside of it. In this sense, liberal democracy and free markets are distinct at the conceptual level and also in practice, which makes them comparable.

For the likes of Tullock and Buchanan, the comparison made between liberal democracy and free markets regarding their institutional capacity to satisfy preferences is of utmost importance to preserve liberalism and its institutions. They worry that without substantial revision in favour of free markets, liberal democracy may not survive or may not achieve liberal values at all. In contrast, the monograph argues that the problem of liberal democracies is not that these institutions do not leave more choices to the market. In fact, upon analysis, liberal democracies can properly satisfy preferences even without a very strong market orientation. The main problem of liberal democracy is that its intrinsic liberal satisfaction of preferences is problematic from an evolutionary perspective. Institutions underpinned by a liberal meta-morality have considerable problems in being sustainable and they are likely to give way to more sustainable moral institutions through a process of biocultural selection.

1.3 Towards an Evolutionary Political Theory of Preference Satisfaction

The study of preference satisfaction in markets and liberal democracies is a central point of public choice theory, with an abundant literature already produced on the topic (Brennan & Buchanan, 2000; Buchanan, 2000; Buchanan & Tullock, 1999; Tullock et al., 2002). In addition, there have been several attempts to analyse preferences, behaviour, morality and social institutions through an evolutionary perspective (Alexander, 1995/1985; Boyd & Richerson, 2005; Haidt, 2012; von Hayek, 1988; Rubin, 2000; Wilson, 2002; Zywicki, 2000). Yet, until now, no extensive and consistent research has utilised the evolutionary model of multilevel selection to reanalyse the public choice approach to preference satisfaction in markets and liberal democracy. This monograph therefore introduces the logic of multilevel selection to the analysis of preferences in social/political institutions, generating an evolutionary political theory framework with which to assess social phenomena, particularly in relation to preference satisfaction in these institutions. The insights from public choice theory are the point of departure because public choice theory is the traditional theoretical framework that compares preference satisfaction in markets and politics.

Classical public choice theory relies on the rational choice-based assumption that all individuals are self-interested egoists (knaves). This happens even though some of its prominent scholars doubt that such an assumption is empirically accurate. For instance, James Buchanan clearly states that the egoism assumption is probably not an accurate representation of reality, but still proposes such an assumption as a method to limit government and prevent knaves from achieving power (Buchanan, 2008, p. 290). Buchanan's logic reveals a fusion of the public choice methodological approach with a normative desire to achieve moral liberalism. Yet, fields like experimental psychology and behavioural economics have empirically tested such an assumption and found it to be wanting. Individuals reveal non-selfish behaviour even in situations of high costs (Kliemt, 2004, p. 241). Analysing the consequences of the misguided assumption of universal rational egoism in public choice, philosopher Hartmut Kliemt wrote:

> From a philosophical methodological point of view it seems even more doubtful that without major revisions of the underlying behavioural model Public Choice theory can in fact lead to true explanations of public choice. (…) Psychology and cognitive science, as well as experimental economics, are knocking at the door of Public Choice and political philosophy. Once this door opens in full, new insights into Public Choice and how it might be improved in theory and practice will emerge. (Kliemt, 2004, pp. 241–242)

The Evolutionary Limits of Liberalism attempts to advance the study of public choice by incorporating the insights of cognitive and anthropological sciences in an evolutionary framework of political theory/philosophy. To achieve this aim, it is of high relevance to reanalyse the main postulates of classic public choice theory on preference satisfaction in markets and liberal democracies. The monograph suggests that political theorists/analysts should pay more attention to competing groups and their moralities when analysing individual behaviour and preferences. At the individual level, theorists must assume behaviour to be plural, even if bounded by a pluralism of types (e.g. altruistic, egoist, pro-group, anti-group, etc.). These revisions can take the study of public choice to higher levels and provide more solid postulates both at the public policy level and at the level of political philosophy. Finally, by assessing the impact of liberal morality on evolutionary fitness through the lenses of multilevel selection, the book aims at contributing towards the wider discussion on the role of morality in evolutionary theory (Alexander, 1995/1985; Boyd & Richerson, 2005; Haidt, 2012; de Waal, 2006).

It is important to stress that this is a non-normative work. It is an exercise in positive, interpretative, realistic or non-ideal political theory and not one in ideal normativity. The monograph does not support particular actions, although its conclusions can be used to shed light on the consequences of particular normative approaches to public policy and political theory (e.g. the liberal satisfaction of preferences). This is a relevant point given that group selectionist evolutionary models can arouse images of outright group conflict and devastating wars. In this sense, it is significant to acknowledge that group selection can take place in different forms and that it is not the purpose of this work to support any particular form. Further, not all forms of group selection imply significant hostility towards out-groups. Some forms can operate through differential birth rates or through maladaptive practices that lead some groups to be naturally selected against. Religion as a mechanism for cooperation within groups can also have an important role in the group selection process, as one can infer from the cases of the Amish or the Hutterites. These are groups that keep expanding in relation to their surrounding populations because of having particular religious beliefs and cooperation mechanisms (Bowman & Kraybill, 2001; Hostetler, 1993; Kraybill & Olshan, 1994; Peter, 1987). Another potential form of group selection is what is known as middle-man or market-dominant minorities, a phenomenon made up by skilled groups who operate in professional fields between producers and consumers (e.g. money lenders, traders). These groups are usually characterised by their clannishness, common moral/religious understanding and economic aptitudes. An example of such "middle-man" groups would be Chinese merchant minorities operating in the economies of Southeast Asia. Chinese merchant minorities achieve considerable competitive advantages over other groups (e.g. the larger receiving populations) by using Confucian ethics and codes of mutual reciprocity among kinsman (Landa, 1999). Lastly, the group selectionist model of multilevel selection does not imply that groups have to be genetically related to be adaptive. It merely implies that groups with more altruists and that are better able to act as adaptive units will succeed in the process of inter-group competition. Still, genetic relatedness can have an important role in the formation of groups because of altruistic genes being more likely to concentrate in closely related groups than on random samples. Notably, genetic relatedness seems to be an empirically verified source of group identity (Shaw & Wong, 1989) and it can allow individuals to pass on more of their own genes to the next generations. Still, the question of genetic relatedness remains a secondary point for the purpose of this book.

In the end, it may be objected that reproductive fitness is not something we would want to maximise because, unlike other living organisms (cockroaches, bacteria, etc.), we have widely shared normative standards, which go beyond simple fitness maximisation. However, the book's central focus on reproductive fitness is not an attempt to demonstrate how only reproduction has value. It is rather a way to show that liberal institutions are eroding the biological ground that underpins the continuity of liberal values. The values undermining reproductive fitness are likely to be selected out of the evolutionary system, making them unsustainable and thus undesirable for those concerned with the continuity of life and institutions.

References

Alexander, R. (1995/1985). A Biological Interpretation of Moral Systems. In P. Thompson (Ed.), *Issues in Evolutionary Ethics* (pp. 179–202). New York: State University of New York Press.

Bowman, C., & Kraybill, D. (2001). *On the Backroad to Heaven: Old Order Hutterites, Mennonites, Amish, and Brethren*. Baltimore: John Hopkins University Press.

Boyd, R., & Richerson, P. (2005). *Not by Genes Alone: How Culture Transformed Human Evolution*. Chicago: The University of Chicago Press.

Brennan, G., & Buchanan, J. M. (2000). *The Reason of Rules: Constitutional Political Economy*. Indianapolis, IN: Liberty Fund.

Brennan, G., & Lomasky, L. E. (1993). *Democracy and Decision: The Pure Theory and Electoral Preference*. Cambridge, UK: Cambridge University Press.

Buchanan, J. M. (1999a). Individual Choice in Voting and the Market. In *The Logical Foundations of Constitutional Liberty* (Vol. 1, pp. 75–89). Indianapolis: Liberty Fund.

Buchanan, J. M. (1999b). Politics Without Romance: A Sketch of Positive Public Choice Theory and Its Normative Implications. In *The Logical Foundations of Constitutional Liberty* (Vol. 1, pp. 45–60). Indianapolis: Liberty Fund.

Buchanan, J. M. (2000). *The Limits of Liberty: Between Anarchy and Leviathan*. Indianapolis: Liberty Fund.

Buchanan, J. M. (2008). Constitutional Political Economy. In C. K. Rowley & F. Schneider (Eds.), *Readings in Public Choice and Constitutional Political Economy* (pp. 281–295). New York: Springer.

Buchanan, J. M., & Tullock, G. (1999). *The Calculus of Consent: Logical Foundations of Constitutional Democracy*. Indianapolis: Liberty Fund.

Buchanan, J. M., & Vanberg, V. (2001). Constitutional Choice, Rational Ignorance and the Limits of Reason. In *Choice, Contract, and Constitutions* (pp. 127–148). Indianapolis, IN: Liberty Fund.

de Waal, F. (2006). *Primates and Philosophers: How Morality Evolved* (S. Macedo & J. Ober, Eds.). Princeton: Princeton University Press.

Dimock, S. (2000). Liberal Neutrality. *The Journal of Value Inquiry, 34*, 189–206.

Goodin, R. (1986). Laundering Preferences. In J. Elster & A. Hylland (Eds.), *Foundations of Social Choice Theory*. Cambridge: Cambridge University Press.

Haidt, J. (2012). *The Righteous Mind: Why Good People Are Divided by Politics and Religion*. London: Allen Lane.

Hostetler, J. (1993). *Amish Society*. Baltimore: Johns Hopkins University Press.

Kliemt, H. (2004). Public Choice From the Perspective of Philosophy. In C. K. Rowley & F. Schneider (Eds.), *The Encyclopedia of Public Choice* (Vol. 1, pp. 235–242). New York: Kluwer Academic Publishers.

Kraybill, D., & Olshan, M. (1994). *The Amish Struggle with Modernity*. Hanover: University Press of New England.

Landa, J. (1999). The Law and Bioeconomics of Ethnic Cooperation and Conflict in Plural Societies of Southeast Asia: A Theory of Chinese Merchant Success. *Journal of Bioeconomics, 1*(3), 269–284.

Lichtenstein, S., & Slovic, P. (2006). *The Construction of Preference*. Cambridge; New York: Cambridge University Press.

Peter, K. (1987). *The Dynamics of Hutterite Society: An Analytical Approach*. Edmonton: University of Alberta Press.

Rubin, P. (2000). Group Selection and the Limits to Altruism. *Journal of Bioeconomics, 2*(1), 9–23.

Samuelson, P. (1938). A Note on the Pure Theory of Consumers' Behaviour. *Economica, 5*(17), 61–71.

Sen, A. (1986). Behaviour and the Concept of Preference. In J. Elster (Ed.), *Rational Choice*. New York: New York University Press.

Shaw, P., & Wong, Y. (1989). *Genetic Seeds of Warfare: Evolution, Nationalism, and Patriotism*. Boston: Unwin Hyman.

Sober, E., & Wilson, D. S. (1998). *Unto Others: The Evolution and Psychology of Unselfish Behavior*. Cambridge, MA: Harvard University Press.

Sunstein, C., & Thaler, R. (2006). Preferences, Paternalism, and Liberty. In S. Olsaretti (Ed.), *Preferences and Well-Being* (pp. 233–265). Cambridge, UK: Cambridge University Press.

Tullock, G. (2005). *The Social Dilema of Autocracy, Revolution, Coup D'Etat and War*. Indianapolis: Liberty Fund.

Tullock, G., Seldon, A., & Brady, G. L. (2002). *Government Failure: A Primer in Public Choice*. Washington, DC: Cato Institute.

Tversky, A., & Simonson, I. (1993). Context-Dependent Preferences. *Management Science, 39*(10), 1179–1189.

von Hayek, F. A. (1979). *Law, Legislation and Liberty* (Vol. III). London: Routledge.

von Hayek, F. A. (1988). *The Fatal Conceit: The Errors of Socialism*. Chicago: University of Chicago.

Wilson, D. S. (2002). *Darwin's Cathedral: Evolution, Religion, and the Nature of Society*. Chicago: The University of Chicago Press.

Wilson, D. S., & Wilson, E. O. (2007). Rethinking the Theoretical Foundation of Sociobiology. *The Quarterly Review of Biology, 82*(4), 327–348.

Zywicki, T. (2000). Was Hayek Right About Group Selection After All? *Review of Austrian Economics, 13*, 81–95.

CHAPTER 2

From Public Choice to Evolutionary Theory

2.1 Introducing Rational/Public Choice Theory

Public choice theory is the application of economic tools or economic reasoning to the analysis of politics. In this application, rational choice theory's behavioural assumptions are conceptual tools with which to analyse political actors and the political systems designed by the actors' actions. Most public choice studies assume individuals to be rational and self-interested. Here, individuals pursue their own self-interest rather than being interested in public welfare. Gordon Tullock, one of the main figures in the field, claims this view of politics is relatively new and that, for most of western civilization's history, analysts assumed that political actors aim at the public interest. In his own words: "From the time of Plato and Aristotle political science was viewed simply as a matter of producing morally correct policies" (Tullock, Seldon, & Brady, 2002, p. 4).

In this book, I will account for the existence of altruism, public interest and political cooperation. Yet, the self-interested or rationally egoist side of humans also exists, and that is the side classical public choice theory relies on. Because classical public choice utilises the methodological assumptions of rational choice theory (i.e. that individuals are universally and rationally self-interested), it becomes important to explain the standard methodological assumptions of rational choice theory.

F. N. Faria, *The Evolutionary Limits of Liberalism*, Palgrave Studies in Classical Liberalism, https://doi.org/10.1007/978-3-030-31496-5_2

2.1.1 *The Standard Methodological Assumptions of Rational Choice Theory*

Rational choice theory has been one of the most relevant methodologies in the social sciences. Regardless of having its origins in economic thought, it has become prevalent in several other fields like political science or philosophy. Rational choice's general focus on rationality and individual preferences seems to be in accordance with the current moral framework of liberalism and, in particular, with liberal democracy. The philosophical idea that one can rationally and purposefully act on our preferences and that they are in a process of maximisation fits well with current liberal democracies, where each individual should rationally choose his/her own legal laws according to inner preferences. The liberal framework is also a moral context where the preferences of individuals are sovereign, provided that people do no harm to others. This preoccupation with individual preferences would probably be less fitting in traditional moralities that are less individual or reason centred.

It is not my goal to give an in-depth account of rational choice theory; others have done this analysis before (Elster, 1986; Green & Shapiro, 1994). Instead, the aim is to present a general vision of what rational choice means and to highlight its diverse relevant interpretations, especially the ones that have a direct impact on moral philosophy and public choice theory. It is not always clear if rational choice theory is a theory or a family of theories. Still, the rationality assumption is the one that prevails. There is a classical assumption that action is the product of a conscious social actor who engages in purposeful calculative strategies. In this sense, individuals calculate the costs and benefits of any choice before choosing. The actions of people are hence a direct product of this process of calculation and of their correspondent choices. But rational choice theorists do not necessarily assume that actors are conscious. Theorists often use rational choice models to study bacteria or plants and all they assume is that the organism has goals and applies strategies to achieve such goals. These models work *as if* people consciously pursued their aims, thus being an approximation of reality for modelling and prediction purposes, yet rational choice scholars need not hold that people are in fact conscious and calculative in all their actions.

Even though one may defend rational choice theory from criticism with the claim that it is not a simple and defined theory, there are certain assumptions that those dealing with rational choice generally assume and share. Such assumptions are utility maximisation, the structure of preferences, decision-making under conditions of uncertainty and the centrality of individuals in the explanation of collective outcomes.

The assumption of utility maximisation refers to the idea that rational action will invariably involve the maximisation of utility (i.e. preferences); rational behaviour is then the result of maximisation of some kind (Arrow, 1951, p. 3). However, this maximisation does not have to specify goals or objectives. Namely, it does not imply selfishness or the more ambiguous term "self-interest", it simply means that people will try to maximise whatever they feel they should attain.

The structure of preferences is another defining point of rationality. This structure requires some degree of consistency to be a rational framework. The two most widely accepted assumptions within this structure are the assumptions of connectedness and transitivity. Connectedness assumes that it is possible for an agent to always rank preferences; that is, to always prefer one option to another (unequal) or at least to be indifferent to options (equal). Rational actions will therefore require respect for connectedness. Still, respecting transitivity means that when an agent or actor prefers A to B and B to C, it follows from logic that the same actor will not prefer C to A. The respect for these two assumptions is what Kenneth Arrow defined as the weak ordering of preferences, which in turn constitutes what rational choice theories usually see as the axiom of rationality.

Because most decisions take place under conditions of uncertainty, the utility that rational choice theories often mention is the expected utility that each agent tries to maximise, and not actual utility. This expected utility has been the standard concept used in models that represent preferences in decision-making under conditions of risk (Fishburn, 1988, p. 1). Finally, the practitioners of rational choice theory tend to work under the individualistic assumption. They assume that the individual is the central unit of choice and therefore the central unit of reasoning. Yet, rational choice does not require this methodological individualistic assumption, given that rational choice theorists have used Marxist classes, political parties or countries to analyse social realities (Przeworski, 1991). Still, even when theorists use these collective units, the units are simplified and countries or classes end up "acting" like an individual unit, which does not seem to do away with the individual as the central unit of choice, it is just that theorists exchange the human individual for the entity-individual. The idea that only human individuals choose, as James Buchanan (1979, pp. 280–282) and Gordon Tullock claim (Buchanan & Tullock, 1999), became one of the central tenets of classic public choice theory and became common in rational choice theory analysis. Hence, the notion that a country or that society may choose on the basis of a rational and autonomous will is beyond the limits of methodological acceptability. To be sure, methodological individualism is distinct from rational choice, even though they usually come together. Ultimately, it is important to point out that rational choice theory, at least in current practice, seems to have universalist claims, in the sense that its assumptions apply to all people in all times (Becker & Stigler, 1977, p. 76). This stands on the grounds of theoretical parsimony, but it is likely that, as our knowledge of human behaviour increases, some may rethink these assumptions. In particular, this book contributes to a more complex behavioural approach, arguing in favour of evolutionary behavioural pluralism while rethinking rational choice's classic "homogeneity" assumption.

2.1.2 Different Perceptions of Rational Choice Theory

Scholars divide rational choice theory into two categories that reveal how demanding we should be with its explanatory power. The two most common visions of rational choice theory are "thin" and "thick". The "thin" version is one that mainly implies rationality but not much more; and it simply means that agents will try to achieve their ends in the most efficient possible way (Ferejohn, 1991, p. 282). The "thick" version already implies a more complete psychological framework of the agent's mind. This version often assumes that agents will rationally pursue material wealth, power, status, income, etc. It assumes not only rationality and self-interest but also a well-defined concept of self-interest. A common example is the assumption that entrepreneurial economic agents want to maximise profits.

Rational choice theorists often prefer one version to the other. For example, in defence of the "thin" version, William Riker (1990, p. 173) claims that, as long as we respect the weak ordering of Kenneth Arrow, any choice is rational. Critics of the "thin" version may claim it is tautological, explaining everything and therefore nothing. An additional criticism is that it makes rational choice theory impossible to test empirically, making it unfalsifiable. Still, the criticisms of "thick" versions of rational choice are perhaps more famous, given that these versions' main problem is to make self-interest (i.e. the maximisation of income, power or status) compatible with selfless altruism. Critics exploit such a problem. Yet, most rational choice theory literature relies on a "thick" version, given that rational choice theorists often assume that agents of political parties try to maximise votes, rent-seekers try to maximise rents, bureaucrats attempt to maximise their benefits, etc. (Green & Shapiro, 1994, pp. 17–19). This "thick" version seems to be the norm, particularly within public choice theory.

When trying to assess the impact of rational choice on morality, J. N. Hooker postulated that rational choice theory rose to prominence because of the shift from a medieval economy to a market one, which shifted from a value system based on honour and loyalty to the self-interested *Homo economicus*. Hooker also divides rational choice theories in two ways:

> One identifies rationality with rational self-interest, the traditional motivator for *Homo economicus*. On this definition, rational choice theories subscribe to some form of psychological egoism (at least in economic matters), which is the view that humans act solely out of self-interest. Despite the widespread popularity of psychological egoism, the evidence for it is unclear. (…) A second interpretation of rational choice does not presuppose self-interest. It assumes only that choices reflect the agent's preferences in a rational fashion, preferences that could be altruistic as well as self-interested. (Hooker, 2012, p. 2)

Hooker's taxonomy is not much different from the "thick"/"thin" one, given that the first way belongs to the "thick" version while the second way belongs to the "thin" one. However, it is important to emphasise that rational choice theory does not have to rely on self-interest, even though it usually does. This is relevant for this book when articulating evolutionary altruism and egoism with rational choice assumptions. Furthermore, even when we assume self-interest, it is possible to claim that self-interest already includes altruism, since one might be altruistic because it makes one feel good (i.e. increases our utility or happiness). One might also say that, because of rational choice's potential for tautological explanation, this semantics or conceptual plasticity ultimately undermines the scientific validation of rational choice theory. Still, at least for the moment, the rational choice framework survived such critical points, probably because of its non-consensual precise meaning.

2.1.3 *Public Choice Theory: Analysing Markets and Politics*

Even though public choice theory is a methodological program of positive analysis (what is), its insights are also useful for normative purposes (what should be), of which the field of constitutional political economy is an example (Rowley & Schneider, 2008). I deal with this field in Chapter 3; but for now, I will expose the general method of classical public choice theory for analysing markets and politics.

The standard school that set the basis to compare politics and markets under a unified criterion is public choice theory. Comparing choices and their outcomes in two different contexts like the political process and the market is a traditionally difficult enterprise. Yet, public choice theory has been doing it via certain assumptions of welfare maximisation and human behavioural homogeneity, more explicitly present in the postulates of self-interest and rationality. This school relies on rational choice theory as a proxy for human nature and human behaviour. Notably, it rejects a dual vision of human nature, one that assumes that individuals in the market do not behave in the same way as when they are operating in the political realm; it rejects the idea that when people go into politics they do it out of public interest while remaining self-interested in the marketplace. For public choice theorists, one should assume that the self-interested individual performing in the market is the same as the one acting within politics. If an individual wants to maximise his/her welfare in the market, there is no reason to assume that he or she will act differently in government. Hence, one should assume that politicians and bureaucrats pursue their own self-interest and not the public interest, leading to the standard public choice argument that individuals mostly want power to redistribute wealth and advantages. This unitary vision of human behaviour relies on a parity of assumptions, both in the market and in politics. As F. S. McChesney and W. F. Shughart put it:

> Homo politicus and homo economicus are the same. The critical implication of this assumption of universal self-interest is that the observed differences between public choices and private choices emerge not because individuals adopt different behavioural objectives in the two settings, but rather because the constraints on behaviour are different. Different outcomes emerge not because public choices are guided by motives different from those guiding private choices, but rather because in private markets self-interested voters and politicians make choices that mainly affect themselves, while in political markets self-interested voters and politicians make choices that mainly affect others. (McChesney & Shughart, 1995, pp. 9–10)

Or like Gordon Tullock explains it: "Given that the same people engage in market activities and in politics, assuming that their behaviour has the same motivation in both of these areas seems simpler" (Tullock et al., 2002, p. 5).

In classic public choice theory, there is a rejection of what Tullock called "a bifurcated vision of human behavior" (Tullock et al., 2002, p. 4). This is the notion that individuals have different motivations when operating in the market and in politics. By rejecting this longstanding idea, public choice theorists use what we may call "parity of assumptions", which is the idea that we should consider the person operating in the market to be the same as the person operating in politics. If one assumes that the person going to the supermarket is inherently pursuing her self-interest, the voter or the politician should be no different. By establishing this unified vision of behaviour, it became possible to compare politics and markets under the same standard of measurement. Hence, in *The Calculus of Consent* (1999), a classic of public choice theory, Buchanan and Tullock defy the common perception created by the welfare economics of Paul Samuelson and Kenneth Arrow that governments should always intervene to correct market failures. According to these public choice theorists, when one applies the same behavioural standard to politics and to markets, one can identify all kinds of government failures; which reveals that any government intervention may produce worse results than the identified market failure that the government tries to correct. In particular, Keynesian and Pigovian economists, as well as Arrovian social choice theorists, identified countless and endemic situations where markets supposedly fail and offered government interventions as the solution to those failures. These solutions assumed that governments would be benevolent, democratic and impartial. Buchanan and Tullock challenged this solution. They showed that problems afflicting markets, like monopolies, externalities, public goods or bounded rationality are equally present in politics, thereby identifying "government failures" (Rowley & Schneider, 2008, p. 10). It is the discovery of "government failure" that allows public choice theorists to compare the failures of the market with the ones of the government and the efficiency of both contexts in relation to each other. This is how these theorists compare preference satisfaction in both backgrounds.

The rational choice assumptions applied to the study of politics gave origin to several schools of analysis. According to Charles K. Rowley, one can identify four schools: Rochester, Chicago, Virginia and Political Economics. For a discussion of all of them, see Rowley and Schneider

(2008, pp. 6–11). What is important to note is that the Virginia school is the one that scholars usually identify with the field of classic public choice, often becoming synonyms. Rowley explains why by emphasising the plasticity of the methods in Virginia:

> Virginia, unlike Chicago, does not assume that individuals are always price takers in political markets; significant discretionary power is recognized. Virginia does not assume, as generally as Chicago does, that political markets clear instantaneously and completely. Virginia does not assume that decision-makers in political markets are always fully informed about the present or that they are capable of forming rational expectations over the future. Virginia does not excise human error or voter stupidity from its theory of political markets, and does not ignore institutions in favour of the black-box theory. (Rowley & Schneider, 2008, pp. 10–11)

In this book, unless explicitly stated, public choice theory will refer to this more "plastic" and "open" method of the Virginia School.

As Tullock postulated, assuming the motivation of behaviour is one and universal (regardless of context) is indeed simpler (Tullock et al., 2002, p. 4). Still, this simplicity might obscure important tendencies about human nature and behaviour, regardless of the accuracy of these assumptions. In the same way, the classic public choice theory adherence to methodological individualism, which explains social phenomena from the perspective of the individual, might also obscure human aspects that are important when analysing economic and political outcomes in the realm of choices.

2.1.3.1 The Mind Is Not a Blank Slate

This book discusses public choice assumptions by crossing their postulates with the insights of evolutionary theory; namely, by rejecting what evolutionary psychologists John Tooby and Leda Cosmides defined as "The Standard Social Science Model". This model postulates that the mind is a blank slate and that all knowledge and content within minds come through information, education, culture, etc. Differently put, that nurture and not nature is the primary driver of human behaviour (Barkow, Cosmides, & Tooby, 1992).

Yet, it is debatable if rational choice theory can be part of this "Standard Social Science Model". The assumption of self-interest seems to be an innate feature of the human brain, which drives behaviour in a self-interested direction. Hence, it is reasonable to assume that, if for rational choice theorists the mind was a blank slate, it would then be possible to educate individuals to be altruistic or publicly interested, which would nullify the assumption as a basis of scientific analysis. Even assuming rational individuals who calculate costs and benefits when making choices seems to depict an innate biological predisposition of the mind or an evolved psychological mechanism. Once again, if for rational choice theory the mind was a blank slate, one would assume that humans are rational or not according to environmental nurture. If so, rational choice theory would be invalid, so it makes sense to assume that its postulates require some form of innateness.

Evolutionary biology and psychology tell us that the mind is far from a blank slate like Steven Pinker illustrated in *The Blank Slate: The Modern Denial of Human Nature* (2002). The mind resulted from a process of biological natural selection that predisposes humans to act in ways that maximised the fitness of our ancestors in the environment where they evolved. The following hypothetical example seems illustrative: two different people in exactly the same situation, under the exact same incentives, can act in different ways. Let's imagine a scenario where an individual must choose whether to save another person drowning. Some individuals would try to save her and some would not, regardless of the incentives. Even if all the incentives were in place to save another person, it is not likely that we would get 100% of people engaging in that act. Ultimately, innate features like lack of empathy or even sadistic pleasure can trump incentives. With the rejection of the blank slate, ceteris paribus, innate predispositions make the difference. And there is considerable empirical evidence showing the effects of genes. For instance, through the analysis of numerous studies, behavioural geneticist Robert Plomin (2018) has demonstrated the importance of genetic predispositions for social outcomes, from divorce rates to educational achievement.

This psychological nativism is better expressed in the famous words of Arthur Schopenhauer: "Man can do what he wills but he cannot will what he wills" (Zucker, 1945, p. 531), which means that our innateness, our biology precedes individual will, since whatever we can do with it is already a consequence of the existence of those genetic underpinnings. This, of course, does not mean that culture, environment or incentives do not play a role in human behaviour. It rather means that innate human pre-dispositions will always process and produce these incentives, culture or environment.

2.2 Introducing the Evolutionary Approach

After having presented the tenets of rational/public choice theory, it is time to introduce the group selectionist evolutionary model of multilevel selection theory. I describe and use the model's logic to review the main assumptions of public choice theory with which to compare preference satisfaction in politics and markets. My evolutionary perspective revises the standard behavioural assumptions of public choice, which rely on motivational uniformity, self-interest/egoism and parity of assumptions, considers the assumptions incomplete, and proposes an alternative set of behavioural assumptions based on pluralism: the pluralism of types.

2.2.1 Multilevel Selection Theory as a Framework for Public Choice

Regardless of the context (markets or politics), the social analysis of choices and preferences requires a framework that explains certain observed forces while attaining predictive power. In the following pages, I explain how we can combine the evolutionary model of multilevel selection with standard models of public choice theory to compare different social contexts like politics and markets. To do that, it is important to illustrate what multilevel selection is.

Eminent biologists like David Sloan Wilson, E. O. Wilson, or psychologists like Jonathan Haidt, propose multilevel selection, breaking from the old paradigm based on strict gene/individual selection argued by Richard Dawkins in his book *The Selfish Gene* (2006). The goal of this approach is not to engage in a detailed debate over these two paradigms, but to understand how the forces that operate under multilevel selection theory can enlighten other models of social analysis (like public choice theory).

The main question behind multilevel selection tries to understand how altruism can evolve in a world of competitive natural selection. If the biological world is such a competitive place where every individual strives to maximise her fitness, why do we observe acts of altruism (i.e. acts that decrease the fitness of the actor but that increase the fitness of others)?

Multilevel selection theory postulates that altruism evolves because it benefits the group of a given set of individuals when that group competes with other groups. In other words, when groups are competing against other groups, the most cohesive and internally altruistic one trumps less cohesive and altruistic groups in this competitive race towards fitness maximisation. Multilevel selection relies on the classic idea of group selection, to which Darwin had hinted in the following way:

> It must not be forgotten that although a high standard of morality gives but a slight or no advantage to each individual man and his children over the other men of the same tribe... yet that an increase in the number of well-endowed men and advancement in the standard of morality will certainly give an immense advantage to one tribe over another. (Darwin, 1871, p. 166)

Still, multilevel selection is not simply group selection, it represents selection at all levels: gene, individual and group. Genes are replicators, but the individual organism (e.g. person) constrains them. Even though individual genes would like to replicate themselves regardless of the destiny of other genes inside the same organism, the fact is that they can only replicate if the organism survives, so they have to replicate as a group. Hence, for genes, the individual is the "group". We may regard these genes trying to achieve an advantage over other genes within the organism as outlaw genes. Although often maladaptive, these outlaw genes can be adaptive if some beneficial genes for the individual organism can successfully gain an advantage over other genes (Okasha, 2006, pp. 149–154). An example would be antagonistic genes. This is a gene that when present in females increases fecundity while reducing it in the other sex. Because these genes in females tend to increase the overall fertility of the group, they can be beneficial in the group selection process (i.e. at the group level).

Individual selection is the classic level at which the evolutionary system naturally selects individual actors on the basis of their fitness. It serves the interests of the individual regardless of the group of individuals he/she belongs to. Finally, group selection takes place when groups of individuals compete against other groups to maximise their fitness, like tribes against other tribes. Here, just like the genes depend on the fate of the individual, the individual depends on the fate of the group. Whatever happens to the group directly affects the individual. E.O. Wilson and David Sloan Wilson famously described the logic of multilevel selection: "Selfishness beats altruism within groups. Altruistic groups beat selfish groups. Everything else is commentary" (Wilson & Wilson, 2007, p. 345).

What this means is that when an altruistic individual interacts with a selfish one, the latter benefits at the expense of the former, but when two groups of individuals interact, the one with more altruists beats the one with fewer altruists. Yet, by default, altruism cannot win against selfishness within groups. Altruism can evolve only if group members can successfully suppress selfishness within groups. For example, groups can suppress egoism by using second-order punishment mechanisms. The exact process of how this happens is an important point of discussion in evolutionary theory.

Still, this creates the main logic of multilevel selection: selfishness evolves within groups when groups are not in strong competition with other groups, but altruism evolves within groups when they are competing against each other and group members efficiently suppress within-group selfishness. Therefore, it is possible to observe these two forces at work: group forces, with strong suppression of within-group selfishness, and individual forces, with a weak suppression of within-group selfishness. Population dynamics will be more group-oriented or individual-oriented depending on the strength of these forces; producing more altruists when group competitive forces are stronger and more selfish individuals when group competitive forces are weaker (Wilson & Wilson, 2007). This explains how humans have the natural tendency to operate through the logic of in-groups (the object of altruism) and out-groups (the object of antagonism).

As a theoretical framework, multilevel selection explains why some individuals selfishly try to weaken their own groups (within-group selection), why some individuals altruistically strive to benefit their own groups (the supposedly radiant side of between-group selection) and why altruistic individuals work on behalf of their groups to tear down other groups (the supposedly gloomy side of between-group selection) (Wilson, 2004, p. 203).

The presence of altruism in a group is especially important for the provision of public goods. Groups with more public goods providers (altruists) would be in a better position to beat other groups that have few individuals willing to pay a private cost to serve their group. Between-group selection implies mechanisms of social control within the groups that cause them to function adaptively. These social controls imply "policing" costs (e.g. like the costs of enforcing the local rules) that are far from being always successful. Hence, if selfish individual forces are stronger than altruistic group forces, selfishness will weaken the adaptiveness of a group in relation to others.

Like two boats with rowers competing in a race, each boat needs to make sure that everyone is striving to achieve success. If some free riders or cheaters exist, that will hurt everybody in the boat. Policing mechanisms and ways to punish cheaters and free riders are fundamental in every single group. As a result, because of the presence of these rules within successful groups, "groupish" altruism evolves. Another example is the competition of two firms in the market, in which each firm is a group that strives to punish cheaters and inefficient individuals within the group to compete for profits against other groups (firms).

Having evolved in tribes, and with the natural tendency to take part in family groups, political groups, sports groups, among many others, humans evolved "groupish" characteristics partly because to be alone usually meant to have no means of protection for survival. In this sense, we have evolved the capacity to increase the relative fitness of the individual in relation to other individuals but also the capacity to increase the relative fitness of our group in relation to other groups. Evolution gave us the behavioural tendency to limit the self-serving attitudes of others in order to maintain the adaptability of the group. To optimise that tendency, individuals developed certain cultural markers, like language, rituals, religion or social norms.

Humans learned to control the selfishness of others within groups. Free riders and dominant individuals that took advantage of their positions were often victims of punishment by the collective action of subordinates. Hence, humans have been eternally vigilant against abuses of power. Through punishment, they reduced the opportunities to benefit at the cost of the group (Wilson, 2004, p. 205).

Before multilevel selection theory's approach to the evolution of altruism, biologists postulated other theories to explain altruistic acts by humans. For instance, William Hamilton (1963) developed his theory of inclusive fitness. Hamilton postulates that altruism can evolve when one is altruistic towards closely related individuals because these individuals are more likely to share genes for altruism above the population average. This focus on genetic relatedness can also be a way of maximising our own fitness (i.e. it helps to pass on a higher degree of our own genes), which makes altruism apparent. In this sense, altruism becomes another expression of self-interest. An additional form of explaining the existence of altruistic acts came through Robert Trivers's (1971) theory of reciprocal altruism. He based this theory on the idea that altruism, especially altruism that goes beyond kin and close genetic relatedness, existed because people will cooperate and pay a cost to themselves to get some advantage in return. This idea relates to “tit for tat” strategies and evolutionary game theory. Together with Richard Dawkins’ (2006) explanatory logic of the “selfish gene”, where individual selection is the only type of natural selection and where individuals are the only vehicles for the replicators-genes, inclusive fitness or reciprocal altruism did not require group selection. Yet, Elliot Sober and David Sloan Wilson consider that these theories are simply different perspectives of the same phenomenon, so they are compatible and already included in the logic of multilevel selection. In their own words:

> We believe that a legitimate pluralism is possible and that it will lead to a unified evolutionary theory of social behaviour. The theories that have been celebrated as alternatives to group selection are nothing of the sort. They are different ways of viewing evolution in multigroup populations. In most cases, the behaviours that are called “apparently altruistic” entail lower relative fitness for individuals within groups and evolve only because they increase the fitness of some groups relative to others. (Sober & Wilson, 1998, p. 57)

Another important point for the use of multilevel selection as an analytical framework is the definition of group and the criteria to identify one. Darwin (1871) straightforwardly defined a group as a tribe. Still, for multilevel selection theory, a group is a set of individuals who mutually influence each other and that influence affects their fitness directly but not the fitness of individuals outside the group. An example given by Sober and Wilson (1998, pp. 92–97) is a study group: if someone in a study group did not read the required material, all members of that group would be affected negatively; while if someone else outside the study group did not read the material, it would not affect the members. In multilevel selection theory, fitness effects are the ultimate objects of study. This does not imply that group organisms need spatial proximity to work as a group. In the same way that people in the library can group around tables, this does not mean that they all belong to the same study group. Individuals might join a group and then disperse while still maintaining the interactions that allow them to be a group. Hence, individuals belong to the same group because of their interaction. Defining these collectives based on interaction allows for the study of traits that make them act as adaptive organisms. Therefore, studying traits of genetic or cultural nature on a case-by-case basis is the best way to identify our objects of analysis. It is also important to mention that even though the capacity to process culture is a genetically evolved characteristic and the production of culture depends on specific genetic traits, this capacity has the power to pass on diverse culturally acquired traits.

In summary, multilevel selection is an evolutionary theoretical framework that assesses fitness at all levels of selection, postulating that evolution results from these two opposing forces: group selection and individual selection. We are the descendants of people who were good at banding together and winning battles against other groups. So evolution selected our in-group/out-group instinct through the same process it selected the selfish instinct. These two opposing forces are, in a way, what David Hume (2005, pp. 373–387) described as the two main characteristics of the human mind: self-interest and sympathy.

2.2.2 *Pluralism of Types*

When comparing markets and politics, classic public choice theory postulates that there should be parity of assumptions about the type of individuals that work in the marketplace and in politics (Tullock et al., 2002). For example, if one considers humans to be self-interested and rational when operating in the market, one should consider political actors (politicians, bureaucrats, voters, etc.) to be the same. Thus, if humans pursue their own self-interest when buying and selling, they will do the same when acting in the political realm. The common dual assumption that individuals are self-interested in the market but altruistic (or public-interested) in government is then a clear fallacy since we are talking about the "same" individuals.

It makes perfect sense to embrace this parity of assumptions postulated by public choice theorists because the individual engages in both markets and politics while having the same innate pre-dispositions. Still, from an evolutionary perspective, the traits that evolve are diverse and depend on selective pressures. Biodiversity makes human beings vary substantially (Cochran & Harpending, 2009). Hence, it should be clear that this parity of assumptions means that individuals have different behavioural predispositions, both in the marketplace and in politics. Put another way, we should assume parity of assumptions in both contexts, but in practice, this means people might all be different in both contexts because individuals evolved different behavioural traits. This behavioural pluralism recognises the different personality types that can operate in markets and politics (e.g. some people are more altruistic than others).

It is also important to clarify that institutions expect certain behaviours and therefore impose constraints on action. For instance, evidence shows that individuals behave much closer to the *homo economicus* when they operate in the market (Ariely, 2008, p. 72) regardless of their altruistic dispositions. Hence, politics can manifest a stronger plurality of potential behaviours because it is a more open-ended process, with a higher capacity to create goals, change constraints (e.g. constitutions) and shape institutions. One could then expect to find more pluralism in politics than in markets. Either way, we should revise the public choice view that motivations are common across individuals and across institutions.

From a psychological perspective, we can see self-interest as utility maximisation and that can mean virtually everything, including the wish to act altruistically. Still, within public choice theory, it is usually simplified and interpreted as material maximisation, where more material goods are better than fewer goods. This view, of course, is not necessarily true and there is a need to account for behavioural pluralism, namely from an evolutionary perspective.

Experimental economics can offer insights about this behavioural pluralism. For example, from "public good games" experiments, Peter Turchin identified 3 types of behavioural archetypes: the knaves, the saints and the moralists. These games are cooperation games where the best individual strategy is to cheat while others bear the costs of public goods, but, if everyone cooperates, every person will be better off than if nobody cooperates. Purely self-interested and rational individuals would then choose to cheat as an optimal individual strategy. Still, this is not what happens. As Turchin shows: "people started halfway between being fully cooperative and fully self-interested positions" (Turchin, 2006, p. 98). In the subsequent rounds of the game, cooperation decreased to very low levels when individuals realised that some group members were free riding and taking advantage of other group members. The ones that started by cooperating and then stopped, justified their change of attitude by claiming that they changed their cooperative behaviour as a way of punishing the free riders in the only possible way: ceasing to contribute to the common pool. To understand if this was in fact the cause, scientists changed the rules of the game in a way that at the end of each round every person could fine the cheaters by 3 dollars at a private cost of 1 dollar. Thus, "for every dollar forked out by the punisher, the punished was fined three" (Turchin, 2006, p. 98). Because punishment does not force rational agents to cooperate due to being a second-order collective good, it is then "irrational" to punish others for no personal gain; especially because if benefits occur, they come dispersed. Hence, one should expect self-interested people to not engage in the punishment of cheaters. Yet, they did. This time participants started by contributing around half of what they could and at the end of each round they could punish cheaters, so the result was that cooperation increased and reached nearly its maximum. In his own words, Peter Turchin explains the 3 behavioural archetypes we can take out of these public good games:

> What these experiments, and many others like them, reveal is that society consists of several types of people. Some of them—perhaps a quarter in experiments with American students—are self-interested, rational agents—"the knaves". These will never contribute to the common good and will choose free riding, unless forced to do so by fines imposed on them. The opposite type, also about a quarter, are the unconditional cooperators, or "the saints". The saints continue to contribute to the common pool, and lose money, even when it is obvious to everybody that cooperation failed (although most of them reduce the amount of their contribution). The largest group (40 to 60 per cent in most experiments) is the conditional cooperators or "the moralists". The preference of moralists is to contribute to the pot so that everybody would be better off. However, in the absence of the mechanism to punish noncontributors, free riding proliferates, the moralists become disgusted by this opportunistic behaviour and withdraw their cooperation. On the other hand, when the punishment option is available, they use it to fine the knaves. To avoid the fines, the knaves grudgingly begin contributing. Once free riding has been eliminated, the saints and the moralists can follow their prosocial preference of contributing the maximum. The group achieves the cooperative equilibrium at which, paradoxically, the moralists do almost as well as the knaves, because they now rarely (if ever) need to spend money on fining the free riders. (Turchin, 2006, pp. 98–99)

The general results are always the same. Still, the percentages of each type (knaves, moralists and saints) vary according to the social group in question. According to Turchin: "College students, for example, tend to be more cooperative than subjects coming from less-educated and poor social strata" (Turchin, 2006, p. 99). Garett Jones (2008) revealed a similar finding. He found that intelligence (IQ) correlates positively with cooperation. In this sense, intelligent individuals tend to cooperate more than less intelligent ones. Revealing the principles of biodiversity and cultural pluralism, it is not surprising to know that results on cooperation levels differ considerably across different countries in the world. The strength of cooperation and the composition of those three behavioural archetypes differ according to place, culture and group/population (Turchin, 2006, p. 99). One can conclude that different societies contain different amounts and percentages of knaves, moralists and saints. Therefore, when comparing contexts like markets and politics from an evolutionary perspective, the parity of assumptions means that different behavioural (evolved) types will exist within both contexts. This behavioural plurality is the "pluralism of types".

In conclusion, for the past decades, the analysis of markets and politics relied on behavioural assumptions based on rationality and self-interest to assess the most efficient way to discover, understand and satisfy the preferences of agents. Public choice theory, the standard research tool to compare markets and politics, often used these same assumptions. Yet, recent empirical testing of these assumptions cast doubts on them and creates incentives to refine their meaning. Experimental psychologists like Daniel Kahneman have thoroughly tested human decision-making and found that humans often reason in illogical ways (Evans, 2002), they can miscalculate simple situations and probabilities (Kahneman & Tversky, 1983) and, of course, reveal irrational biases (Kahneman, Slovic, & Tversky, 1982). As a step forward, it is possible to enlighten the plurality of behaviours observed in individuals by incorporating evolutionary theories in behavioural assumptions. Adding to rational choice theory, we can use the evolutionary model of multilevel selection to better understand not only the choices of individuals in society but also their interests and preferences. Still, in order for this to happen, one must take the definition of rational self-interest in a broad sense, meaning every individual preference from egoist to altruism, and not in the narrow materialistic sense that culminates with simple egoism.

Acknowledging the central role of groups in human affairs is important to understand not only politics and war conflicts (i.e. which seems to be more explicitly about groups), but also markets and how group formation can affect the development of market institutions. Yet, as I argued before, to reject a universal monolithic assumption of behaviour means to assume pluralism of behaviour, in which individuals can vary from being extremely cooperative, self-sacrificing and altruistic to being egoistic and merely focused on material or institutional gains. This seems to complicate the methodological framework I here use to analyse the social realm, but evolutionary theories can help to enlighten these differences of behaviour and to produce more accurate explanatory tools.

The study of choices, preferences, markets or democracy depends on these behavioural insights. What this pluralism of behaviour means to public choice theory and to the comparison of markets and politics is that the traditional parity of assumptions should not mean that individuals are the same, but that they are equally different in both contexts. Pluralism means that, both in politics and in markets, we should assume agents to be equally different (e.g. altruists, cooperators and egoists operate in both contexts). To do so, one has to take the notion of rational self-interest in a broader sense to accommodate this new conception of parity of assumptions. With this caveat, we are open to explore the innate behavioural tendencies of agents in politics and markets and to provide normative positions that stand on solid ground. For this purpose, I suggest the use of a "pluralism of types".

2.3 On the Meaning of Preferences, Fitness, Self-Interest and Morality

I will now discuss and clarify some fundamental concepts to achieve the aim of this book. These are the concepts of preferences, fitness, self-interest and morality. I will present them through the construction of bridges between the evolutionary and the rational/public choice perspectives.

2.3.1 Preferences

Like with most concepts, scholars dispute the precise meaning of the concept of preference. Hence, it is important to clarify how this book articulates it, especially in relation to the origin of preferences, that is, in relation to how far preferences are innate or shaped by environmental context. The more traditional approach to preferences, which theorists developed in the twentieth century, relies on the idea that rational individuals articulate preferences and that the expressive logic of these preferences obeys to the aforementioned assumptions of connectedness and transitivity. Economists from this tradition (Becker & Stigler,

1977) tend not to worry too much about the preferences themselves, but mostly about their structure and their expression revealed through choices. Hence, by equating choice with preference, for them the question of the real nature of preferences becomes less important. The standard paper that influenced this agnosticism about the origin and nature of preferences is Gary Becker and George Stigler's *De Gustibus Non Est Disputandum* (1977). They famously postulated that economists should not worry about explaining preferences but only about the constraints that impact on choices. In the words of the evolutionary theorist Satoshi Kanazawa:

> They wanted to leave preferences and values exogenous to the economic models, rather than endogenous to them. (Endogenous means within the model of explanation whereas exogenous means outside of such models. (…) exogenous factors are left unexplained). (…) They focus on money (…) because money is fungible; people can use money to buy virtually anything they want. (…) Whatever they [individuals] want, they all want more money because money will allow them to have more of whatever they want. (…) The focus on the fungible resource of money obviates the need to know what individuals really want. (Kanazawa, 2012, pp. 4–5)

Scholars of this rational economic tradition often consider that to know about the nature and origins of preferences is irrelevant because individuals can exchange almost everything through money. To know why and what people want is irrelevant. Conversely, Kanazawa (2012, pp. 4–5) follows an approach that aims at endogenising preferences and values to models of human behaviour by applying evolutionary theory, which is something that this book also does.

Also in the rational economic tradition, Paul Samuelson (1938) was a pioneer in the development of the "revealed preferences" model, which produced a behaviourist approach to preferences. These days, behavioural economists and experimental psychologists empirically criticise this approach, but, before these appeared, Amartya Sen (1986) had already criticised the idea that preferences can be accurately revealed through choices. By using the prisoner's dilemma as an example, Sen shows that a decision to cooperate by both prisoners (non-confession) can happen because they want to maximise their own welfare or because they want to maximise the welfare of the other prisoner. By only observing their choice, one cannot know the real preference behind it, which shows, according to Sen (1986, p. 72), that the revealed preference theory is deeply flawed.

More recently, empirical findings in behavioural economics and psychology reveal that individuals do not seem to have preferences which are well defined a priori from experience (Lichtenstein & Slovic, 2006). Hence, individuals construct preferences as they are elicited. The context and the experience of the moment deeply influence preferences. This contradicts the standard economic assumption of preferences being given. By "given", it means that people have a menu of internal preferences, which individuals properly rank, and that their decisions will reflect the consultation of such a menu. Empirical testing revealed that preferences are shaped or constructed by the framing of the context. For example, in the words of Cass Sunstein:

> If people are told, "Of those who undergo this medical procedure, 90% are still alive after 5 years", they are far more likely to agree to the procedure than if they are told, "Of those who undergo this procedure, 10% are dead after 5 years". Framing matters for ordinary consumer choices as well as for unusual medical decisions. Most consumers might prefer a small television to a medium-sized one when choosing among the two, but if a large television is added to the set of options, many consumers will favor the medium-sized one over the small one. (Sunstein, 2006, p. xv)

The default rules decisively influence the preferences of people. As scientists observe, when employees are put on an automatic program that devotes a certain percentage of their wages to a retirement plan but with the option of opting out, more employees choose to stay in that program than if the employer simply asks the employees if they want to join. Yet, it is important to state that there are limits to this process of preference construction, given that, to quote Sunstein, "some televisions just won't sell; most of the time, people are unlikely to want 80% of their wages to go into savings", among countless other examples (Sunstein, 2006, p. xvi). According to these insights, it is not possible to claim that no inner preferences exist whatsoever, but it is possible to understand that, to a large extent, they are more malleable and less fixed than some scholars assumed in traditional economic theories of rationality.

Given that this book approaches preferences not only from a rational choice theory perspective but also from an evolutionary one, it is important to understand what this malleability of preferences might mean in evolutionary theory. After understanding that preferences are not well defined a priori from experience, the following question arises: "Do we have innate or given preferences prior to experience?". Many studies seem to confirm that we do, or at least studies confirm that we have tendencies that are hard to change via context. For example, in the field of gender, a study with infants ranging in age from 3 to 8 months reveals that boys tend to choose "masculine" toys like trucks while girls tend to choose feminine toys like dolls; which shows, according to the researchers, that preferences are at least partly in-built (G. Alexander, Wilcox, & Woods, 2009). Another study of what one may call an innate taste for sweets, not only shows that humans reveal a disposition to like the sweet taste, but that preferences for sweet tastes are, at least in part, genetically determined (Keskitalo et al., 2007). Even in more traditional areas of economics like savings behaviour, a study by Cronqvist and Siegel (2013) shows that, based on classic identical twin studies, twins who share 100% of their DNA, at least 1/3 of the variation in savings behaviour comes from innate, genetically defined traits. Similarly, using identical methods, Cesarini et al. (2009, 2010) show clear evidence that a disposition towards risk-taking is genetic and heritable, with Barnea et al. (2010) equally showing that one can attribute around one-third of risk-taking behaviour to innate preferences. Even in the study of political preferences, scientists show that the individual's brain structure seems to influence political preferences (Feilden, Firth, Kanai, & Rees, 2011). The brain structure, together with environmental factors, generates one's political adherence.

This brings us to the evolutionary notion that social outcomes are the product of dual evolution. Social outcomes are the products of the interactions between innate biological tendencies (nature) and culture/environment (nurture). This duality might lead us to think we are dealing with two independent variables, when in reality they are two sides of the same coin. Behavioural economics or psychology shows that preferences are malleable, at least to a certain extent. But how can the evolutionary system select this malleability if evolution is a long process and relies on a stable environment for traits to be fixed? That cultural evolution can change more rapidly than genetic evolution may account for this observable human capacity to be behaviourally sensitive to culture/environment. In the words of economists Nikolaus Robalino and Arthur Robson:

> Preferences were shaped by the joint action of genetic and cultural evolution. We argue that preferences are partly innate, the output of genetic forces, and partly plastic, the output of cultural forces; but that the very plasticity of the culturally determined component of preferences was shaped genetically. (Robalino & Robson, 2013, p. 151)

A preference remains a contested concept, but, from an evolutionary multilevel selection perspective, one must assume a plurality of evolved traits even when some traits seem to be present almost universally, and we can say the same about preferences. Some preferences might work as given or innate while others are malleable and subjected to the framing of the context. It is in this sense I will articulate preferences during Chapters 4, 5, and 6. However, for the purpose of comparison, I will deal with preferences in Chapter 3 in a more traditional way, on the basis of rational choice theory, before moving on to an evolutionary approach.

2.3.2 Fitness

When shifting from a purely rational/public choice institutional analysis to an evolutionary one, it becomes important to highlight the two different "currencies" to measure success that these two theoretical approaches use. While rational/public choice theory uses utility (i.e. preference satisfaction/maximisation) as the main standard of measurement, evolutionary theory applies reproductive fitness to measure evolutionary success. Still, these two different "currencies" can sometimes make it complicated to understand the connection between these two realms. It may be difficult to convert one "currency" into the other. Still, it is possible to interpret each one of them in light of the other. For instance, the satisfaction or maximisation of all preferences of an individual might not lead to the maximisation of fitness. The opposite is equally true, if there are maladaptive preferences (Boyd & Richerson, 2005, Chapter V), then the maximisation of fitness does not mean that one is maximising preferences. An example of this mismatch would be the consumption of heavy drugs. While one might rationally want to enjoy drugs and to pay the price of physical decay (i.e. loss of fitness), one may increase relative fitness if a government prohibits such drugs and successfully enforces the prohibition. Put differently, assuming individuals would be against such prohibition, they might increase their relative fitness "against" their own will.

The standard maximisation of preferences used in rational/public choice approaches relies on the positive notion that individuals try to maximise their preferences, and, more often than not, based on a normative liberal notion that individuals should maximise their preferences (i.e. maximise their utility functions). On the other hand, evolutionary theory is rooted in the positive notion that living individuals exist because their ancestors successfully reproduced throughout the millennia. Yet, the normative side of fitness is more contentious. Clearly, maximising fitness is not something that all individuals consciously choose. Many choose to be childless, pursuing other goals instead, or even choose to act in physically self-destructive manners. Hence, there is a conflict between the satisfaction of preferences of individuals and the maximisation of their fitness. Should institutions correct the former when it collides with the latter?

Referring to western public policy, evolutionary economist Paul Rubin (2007) believes that the maximisation of fitness of individuals and groups should not be normative and that political institutions should maintain liberal neutrality by providing conditions for individuals to satisfy their utility functions, regardless of what they might be, even when they are maladaptive and therefore reduce fitness. Contrarily, following Charles Darwin, political ethologist Frank Salter argues that the maximisation of fitness should be a normative collective goal. On this point, Salter quotes Darwin (1871) on such a normative side of fitness, defending fitness maximisation as a vital element of morality:

> Darwin (…) explicitly rejected reliance on happiness, and thus preferences, as the thing to be maximized. Instead, he argued for a survivalist ethic, in which a good act is defined as one that increases the reproductive fitness of the greater number. In the *Descent of Man*, Darwin states that morality consists of advancing the 'general good', the 'rearing of the greatest number of individuals in full vigour and health, with all their faculties perfect, under conditions to which they are subjected'. (Salter, 2004, p. 521)

Such a morality that includes the maximisation of fitness transforms the satisfaction of preferences into a secondary element of morality, subjected to the evaluation of fitness. Likewise, the prominent biologist Richard Alexander postulates that interests are not always present in conscious preferences. In his own words:

> We need not be concerned with the possible argument that interests are only definable in terms of what people consciously believe are their

> interests or intentions. Biologists continually investigate the life interests of nonhuman organisms while lacking knowledge of this point. (R. Alexander, 1995/1985, pp. 182–183)

In the language of utility and preferences, the fitness interests of individuals are the "ultimate utility" of reproductive fitness (Salter, 2007), which contrasts with "proximate utility", a utility based on the happiness postulates of pleasure, material wealth, etc. Still, these fitness interests are not part of many people's conscious utility function and to have moral institutions that strive towards such a goal would violate the achievement of their "real" expressed preferences (Rubin, 2007). Even considering that preferences are not well defined a priori and can change through political framing (Tversky & Kahneman, 1981), it is possible that some individuals would never voluntarily accept certain restrictions on their stated preferences in the name of a morality that includes the maximisation of fitness. Framing, morality and culture can shape preferences at large scales (Boyd & Richerson, 2005), but as a dialectical argument per se, it is likely that some would always reject such a fitness-oriented morality.

When assessing institutions, I will take no normative position on the maximisation of fitness. Still, when analysing institutions in terms of their preference satisfaction, fitness has an important role. The institutions conducive to the fitness-maximisation of their users are more likely to prevail in time and to shape the preferences of their present and future users. Conversely, institutions that tend towards fitness reduction are more likely to be unsustainable and disappear in due time.

To reanalyse public choice theory's postulates from an evolutionary perspective, it is now important to understand the connection between evolutionary fitness and "self-interest".

2.3.3 Self-Interest

One of the main assumptions in classic public choice theory is that humans are self-interested. This assumption stands within the paradigm of rational choice. However, evolutionary theory explains the evolution of altruism via reciprocity (Trivers, 1971), which is a tit-for-tat process, or via inclusive fitness (Hamilton, 1963), which is the tendency to take care of our own genes in other people's bodies. Both of these evolutionary perspectives seem in line with the postulate of self-interest. In these two situations, the real goal is to maximise one's fitness. But what about multilevel selection, which claims altruism to be real because there is an effective loss of fitness by the individual who helps others (the group)? If altruism is real, then public choice theory could be wrong in claiming that individuals, regardless of being market or political agents, will act in a self-interested manner. Yet, this mostly depends on what self-interest means.

If one considers self-interest from an evolutionary perspective, it may mean the maximisation of fitness, which means maximising survival and reproduction. Here, all acts are self-interested because, regardless of an act being altruistic or egoistic, the ultimate evolutionary goal of fitness maximisation is always present. But if one can act against one's own fitness, it means that one is not purely self-interested. If self-sacrifice exists, then the postulate of self-interest is inaccurate. Thus, it is preferable to talk about altruistic and egoistic acts, at least at the practical level. However, a broader definition of self-interest is not so much about evolution but about psychological predispositions, or, ultimately, it is about a philosophical heuristic approach. It is then possible to see self-interest as being present in every single act, regardless of the act's impact on the fitness of the individual. For example, if a politician voluntarily serves the public interest instead of his own interests or helps another at his own cost, that can be seen as a form of psychological self-interest, because ultimately she/he valued the altruistic act more than an apparent selfish act. In this sense, if one feels good in helping others at one's own cost, the concept of self-interest is valid. Because it seems logical that nobody voluntarily acts against his or her own interest both at a psychological level and at a fitness level at the same time, self-interest remains a broad, sensible concept of analysis. David Sloan Wilson gives an example that demonstrates this multilevel selection reasoning on a colony of ants:

> Foraging above ground is more dangerous than staying below ground so the forager substantially reduces her fitness compared to the other queens in her colony. How can we explain this apparent example of altruistic behavior? (…) The correct answer appears to involve a very strong form of among-group selection. Many colonies are initiated at the same time and the first to raise a generation of workers succeeds at becoming established in competition with the other colonies. If a specialized above-ground forager provides a sufficient competitive edge in among-group competition, the behavior can evolve despite its selective disadvantage within groups (…). Knowing all this, we can imagine the specialized forager reasoning

> about her options as if she were a person who cares only about her absolute fitness: 'If I don't forage, I might die but if I live my colony will prevail against other colonies and I will share their success. Therefore I will forage based only upon my self-interest'. (Wilson, 2004, p. 212)

Even in certain cases like drug addiction or depressions that lead to suicide, one cannot doubt that at least at a psychological level, a person sees a particular act, like committing suicide or taking drugs, as psychologically desirable at a certain point. It might not be rational in the sense that pros and cons are coldly and impartially measured in terms of survival/fitness, but there is clearly some drive that leads to instinctively desired actions. Hence, if self-interest represents "what the individual wants", the postulate of self-interest used by public choice and rational choice theory remains valid and compatible with multilevel selection theory. Still, it is important to understand that not everything that evolves is selfishness and that altruism exists in practice, even if in psychological terms one might see everything as self-interest. Therefore, even though the self-interest postulate is right as a rule of thumb, it can obscure important nuances. Behind the psychological assumption of self-interest, one should always assume that in a given population, because of group and individual forces, both evolutionary altruism and selfishness might be present in individuals.

Having discussed the meaning of self-interest, I now introduce and examine the importance of morality in shaping individual preferences.

2.3.4 *Morality*

Especially when analysing institutions (i.e. markets, democracy), it is complicated to make sense of individual preferences in the social world without understanding the influence of morality. The alternative has often been a rational choice approach to preferences that remains agnostic about what causes them (Becker & Stigler, 1977). What is important to point out from the beginning is that morality is not equivalent to preferences. While it is possible to have moral preferences, morality is in a separate category composed of ideal values that can shape mass preferences through internalisation and systematic collective imposition. While there is no consensus regarding what morality exactly is (Rachels & Rachels, 2012, p. 1), there are general guidelines that allow one to make sense of the concept and to operate with it. At a fundamental level, morality deals with behavioural distinctions that can be categorised as good or bad, acceptable or not acceptable. Beyond this point, ethicists approach the concept of "morality" in two ways: a descriptive and a normative one. The descriptive approach refers to codes of conduct that religions, groups or individuals put forward, while a normative approach refers to a body of principles of conduct that, after defined and established, all rational individuals would put forward. Contrary to the latter approach, the former does not have universalist claims on morality and, as moral philosopher Bernard Grent wrote, it "results in a denial that there is a universal morality, one that applies to all human beings" (Gert, 2012). This denial does not have to represent all people who work within the descriptive approach, but the tendency for this conclusion is pervasive. It is the descriptive approach to morality that I apply in this book. Hence, I postulate no moral theory that all rational individuals would follow. Some philosophers like James Rachels and Stuart Rachels think any morality that rejects this role of universal rationality "encounter serious difficulties" and that most philosophers incorporate this minimum conception of morality in one way or another: "Morality is, at the very least, the effort to guide one's conduct by reason- that is, to do what there are the best reasons for doing- while giving equal weight to the interests of each individual affected by one's decision" (Rachels & Rachels, 2012, p. 13). However, even though morality seems to refer to other-regarding behaviour, it is possible to define it in a way that does not imply universal rationality. Coming from a Neo-Humean tradition, philosopher Simon Blackburn provides a definition of morality that not only is in line with the naturalist approach I apply in this book but also bypasses the emphasis on reason. In his own words: "Morality is the system by which we put pressure, including coercive pressure, on ourselves and others to obey social rules" (Blackburn, 2012).

In this sense, morality is a system that aims at providing group/social cohesion. This descriptive definition says less about the origins of morality than about its social procedure or manifestation. Yet, we know that individuals are more than willing to defend certain values they hold dear and that those values affect their choices/preferences. The connection between morality and preferences derives from our perception of good and evil. Examples of the influence of morality on preferences are easy to find: for instance, the preference for certain types of meat depends on our beliefs, as it is the case with the rejection of pork or beef when one is a devout Muslim or Hindu, respectively. In such cases, because the respect for religious values is high, preferences of flavour become irrelevant when choosing the type of meat that one will have for lunch. Hence, it is possible to conclude that morality strongly shapes and regulates preferences (like flavour). This logic also applies to non-religious forms of morality. For example, one might choose not to eat meat at all due to sacralising the value of protecting the lives of animals. In the same way, the morality present in certain cultural norms also points in this direction. For instance, many in the western world regard eating dogs and cats as immoral or unacceptable, regardless of flavour, but most westerners do not apply the same logic to pork or beef. Finally, because politics relies heavily on moral values, morality can also shape individual preferences in that realm. As an illustration, one might prefer a public system of social security because of giving more importance to the value of equality than to the value of a good private system, which could eventually serve the person better at an individual level.

Examples of how morality can influence individual preferences are plentiful. Still, only by engaging in the social process of morality can we understand individual choices beyond the point of simply acknowledging that individuals have preferences (while remaining agnostic about their origins). To understand the relationship between morality and preferences is especially important when comparing the potential for preference satisfaction in different social institutions.

2.3.4.1 Key Ideas on Morality Within Philosophical Naturalism

In this volume, I theorise on the nature of morality within the tradition of philosophical naturalism. Naturalism in this realm is a methodological approach to theorisation holding that philosophical enquiry should be continuous with the empiricism present in science.

Historically, the naturalist tradition has been present in numerous thinkers in western philosophy. For this approach to morality, three authors are particularly relevant in providing key ideas: Friedrich Nietzsche (who holds that morality is an expression of physiology), David Hume (who holds that morality is an expression of sentiments) and Emile Durkheim (who holds that morality serves the purpose of creating group cohesion/power).

From Nietzsche, it is possible to take the notion that morality is in connection with one's physiology. In this sense, one's body and instincts strongly influence the morality one espouses. For the German thinker, a philosopher embracing a particular morality is only showing "who he is" and espousing the "innermost drives of his nature" (Nietzsche, 1966, p. 14). Therefore "answers to the questions about the value of existence may always be considered first of all as the symptoms of certain bodies" (Nietzsche, 1974, p. 35). Moralities, for Nietzsche, are values that spring from certain physiological mechanisms in detriment of others. For instance, he claims that a "morality of sympathy" is "just another expression of … physiological overexcitability" (Nietzsche, 1954, p. 540) and that *ressentiment* and its moral representation has an "actual physiological cause" (Nietzsche, 1989, p. 127). The will to power drives these moralities and is a "higher than all reason" natural energy that abhors "any kind of disturbance and hindrance which blocks or could block his path to the optimum" (Nietzsche, 2003, p. 81).

These ideas about morality and physiology are in line with the postulates of social psychologist Jonathan Haidt (2012), who shows that liberals and conservatives show different instinctive reactions to the same morally charged events. Furthermore, David Hume (2005, Book III) understood morality in a similar way. He is famous for postulating that reason is nothing but the slave of passions. He is together with Nietzsche in postulating that reason alone cannot be the guide of morality. For the Scottish philosopher, sentiments (what we may call "intuition" or "passions") are the prime mover of morality. These sentiments or passions can be calm, and therefore sometimes mistaken for reason, or they can be strong and visibly expressed by rage, love or fear. Here, morality has its basis on an expression of sentiments that makes one feel pleasure when observing an external trait that one feels is beneficial and displeasure when such external trait is harmful. In this way, individuals have sensory mechanisms that provide information about "good" and "evil", which then becomes moral patterns. In the words of David Hume:

> Morality is nothing in the abstract Nature of Things, but is entirely relative to the Sentiment or mental Taste of each particular Being; in the same Manner as the Distinctions of sweet and bitter, hot and cold, arise from the particular feeling of each Sense or Organ. Moral Perceptions therefore, ought not to be class'd with the Operations of the Understanding, but with the Tastes or Sentiments. (Hume, 1748, pp. 14–15)

Similarly, the feeling of sympathy is a part of individuals, decisively influencing the way one builds or adheres to moral precepts. Hence, when one reflects upon a trait or action likely to benefit others, one feels enjoyment, while when one reflects upon a different trait that hurts others, one feels uneasiness (Hume, 2005, Book III, Part III, Section I, Paragraph Number VII–VIII). This natural sympathy might be in line with what evolutionary biologists regard as altruism (i.e. other-regarding behaviour that has a cost to the individual). Especially if sympathy leads the individual to sacralise a certain value to the point of sacrificing his/her own fitness for the benefit of others.

Another relevant thinker in the naturalist tradition is Emile Durkheim (Baert, 2005, p. 10). In line with the previous philosophers discussed, Durkheim postulated that moral-religious values where created by men themselves to increase their collective power, but, by doing so, men remain captive of their own creations. In his own words:

> In this way, the power of souls increases from all that is attributed to them, so much so that, in the end, man finds himself a captive in this imaginary world, even though he is its creator and model. He becomes the vassal of those spiritual forces that he has made with his own hands and in his own image. (Durkheim, 1995, p. 49)

Durkheim is referring to a religious set of values, but the definition of "religion" for him is open enough to represent any morality that sets the normative landscape of a social group. He defines religion as "a unified system of beliefs and practices relative to sacred things, that is to say, things set apart and forbidden beliefs and practices which unite into one single moral community called a Church, all those who adhere to them" (Durkheim, 1995, p. 44).

Ideologies, or a set of values, can become "sacred" even in the absence of a specific god. For example, liberalism as the cult of the individual, he says, is nothing but a collective worship of a particular group.

> Thus very far from there being the antagonism between the individual and society which is often claimed, moral individualism, the cult of the individual, is in fact the product of society itself. It is society that instituted it and made of man the god whose servant it is. (Durkheim, 2009, p. 29)

Hence, the French thinker sees the sacredness of moral-religious values as having "secular utility". They solve the problem of order in a group, especially large groups. To sacralise the morality of society and its symbols is then a form of worshipping/respecting society. Finally, David

Sloan Wilson translates the meaning of Durkheim's central ideas into the language of evolutionary theory: "In modern evolutionary terms, Durkheim interpreted religion as an adaptation that enables human groups to function as harmonious and coordinated units" (Wilson, 2002, p. 54); and, one should add, for purposes of group evolutionary competition.

The ideas of these authors, which influenced the insights postulated in this book, rely on the study of nature as one universal entity with the same laws and rules. seventeenth-century philosopher Spinoza summed it up in the following way:

> Nature is always the same, and its virtue and power of acting are everywhere the same, i.e. the laws and rules of nature, according to which all things happen, and change from one form to another, are always and everywhere the same. So the way of understanding the nature of anything, of whatever kind, must also be the same, viz. through the universal laws and rules of nature. (Spinoza, 1985, Pref. Part III)

In sum, I regard morality as a system to confer group cohesion and collective power. Through the evolutionary logic of multilevel selection theory, morality is a system that shapes preferences of individuals in groups to generate collective cohesion under evolutionary inter-group competition. Nietzsche and Hume postulated that morality depends on physiology and sentiments, which is in line with the logic of evolved types (i.e. "pluralism of types") as an analytical tool. Hence, different individuals with considerably different drives have the tendency to adhere to different moralities. In Chapters 4, 5, and 6, I will analyse individual preferences and behaviour through these lenses.

References

Alexander, R. (1995/1985). A Biological Interpretation of Moral Systems. In P. Thompson (Ed.), *Issues in Evolutionary Ethics* (pp. 179–202). New York: State University of New York Press.

Alexander, G., Wilcox, T., & Woods, R. (2009). Sex Differences in Infants' Visual Interest in Toys. *Archives of Sexual Behavior, 38*, 427–433.

Ariely, D. (2008). *Predictably Irrational: The Hidden Forces That Shape Our Decisions.* New York: HarperCollins.

Arrow, K. J. (1951). *Social Choice and Individual Values.* London: Chapman & Hall.

Baert, P. (2005). *Philosophy of the Social Sciences: Towards Pragmatism*. Cambridge: Polity Press.

Barkow, J. H., Cosmides, L., & Tooby, J. (1992). *The Adapted Mind: Evolutionary Psychology and the Generation of Culture*. New York: Oxford University Press.

Barnea, A., Cronqvist, H., & Siegel, S. (2010). Nature or Nurture: What Determines Investor Behavior? *Journal of Financial Economics, 98*, 583–604.

Becker, G., & Stigler, G. (1977). De Gustibus Non Est Disputandum. *American Economic Association, 67*(2), 76–90.

Blackburn, S. (2012). Do Evolution and Morality Talk Much? David Sloan Wilson & Simon Blackburn Discuss. *Neuron Culture*. Retrieved from http://www.wired.com/2012/06/how-is-evolution-related-to-morality-david-wilson-simon-blackburn-discuss/.

Boyd, R., & Richerson, P. (2005). *Not by Genes Alone: How Culture Transformed Human Evolution*. Chicago: The University of Chicago Press.

Buchanan, J. M. (1979). *What Should Economists Do?* Indianapolis: Liberty Press.

Buchanan, J. M., & Tullock, G. (1999). *The Calculus of Consent: Logical Foundations of Constitutional Democracy*. Indianapolis: Liberty Fund.

Cesarini, D., Dawes, C., Johannesson, M., Lichtenstein, P., & Wallace, B. (2009). Genetic Variation in Preferences for Giving and Risk Taking. *Quarterly Journal of Economics, 124*, 809–842.

Cesarini, D., Johannesson, M., Lichtenstein, P., Sandewall, P., & Wallace, B. (2010). Genetic Variation in Financial Decision Making. *Journal of Finance, 65*, 1725–1754.

Cochran, G., & Harpending, H. (2009). *The 10,000 Year Explosion: How Civilization Accelerated Human Evolution*. New York: Basic Books.

Cronqvist, H., & Siegel, S. (2013). *The Origins of Savings Behavior*. AFA 2011 Denver Meetings Paper. Retrieved from http://ssrn.com/abstract=1649790.

Darwin, C. (1871). *The Descent of Man and Selection in Relation to Sex*. New York: Appleton.

Dawkins, R. (2006). *The Selfish Gene* (30th anniversary ed.). Oxford; New York: Oxford University Press.

Durkheim, E. (1995). *The Elementary Forms of Religious Life* (K. Fields, Trans.). New York: The Free Press.

Durkheim, E. (2009). *Sociology and Philosophy*. New York: Taylor & Francis.

Elster, J. (1986). *Rational Choice*. Washington Square, NY: New York University Press.

Evans, J. (2002). Logic and Human Reasoning: An Assessment of the Deduction Paradigm. *Psychological Bulletin, 128*(6), 978–996.

Feilden, T., Firth, C., Kanai, R., & Rees, G. (2011). Political Orientations Are Correlated with Brain Structure in Young Adults. *Current Biology, 21*(8), 677–680.

Ferejohn, J. (1991). Rationality and Interpretation: Parliamentary Elections in Early Stuart England. In K. Monroe (Ed.), *Economic Approach to Politics: A Critical Reassessment of the Theory of Rational Action*. New York: Harper Collins.

Fishburn, P. C. (1988). *Nonlinear Preference and Utility Theory*. Baltimore; London: Johns Hopkins.

Gert, B. (2012). The Definition of Morality. *The Stanford Encyclopedia of Philosophy*. Retrieved from http://plato.stanford.edu/archives/fall2012/entries/morality-definition/.

Green, D. P., & Shapiro, I. (1994). *Pathologies of Rational Choice Theory: A Critique of Applications in Political Science*. New Haven; London: Yale University Press.

Haidt, J. (2012). *The Righteous Mind: Why Good People Are Divided by Politics and Religion*. London: Allen Lane.

Hamilton, W. D. (1963). The Evolution of Altruistic Behavior. *American Naturalist, 97*, 354–356.

Hooker, J. (2012). Moral Implications of Rational Choice Theories. In C. Lütge (Ed.), *Handbook of the Philosophical Foundations of Business Ethics*. Berlin: Springer.

Hume, D. (1748). *An Enquiry Concerning Human Understanding*. London: A. Millar.

Hume, D. (2005). *A Treatise of Human Nature*. New York: Barnes & Noble Publishing.

Jones, G. (2008). Are Smarter Groups More Cooperative? Evidence from Prisoner's Dilemma Experiments, 1959–2003. *Journal of Economic Behavior & Organization, 68*, 489–497.

Kahneman, D., Slovic, P., & Tversky, A. (1982). *Judgement Under Uncertainty: Heuristics and Biases*. Cambridge; New York: Cambridge University Press.

Kahneman, D., & Tversky, A. (1983). Extensional Versus Intuitive Reasoning: The Conjunction Fallacy in Probability Judgment. *Psychological Review, 90*(4), 293–315.

Kanazawa, S. (2012). *The Intelligence Paradox*. Hoboken, NJ: Wiley.

Keskitalo, K., Tuorila, H., Spector, T., Cherkas, L., Knaapila, A., Silventoinen, K., & Perola, M. (2007). Same Genetic Components Underlie Different Measures of Sweet Taste Preference. *The American Journal of Clinical Nutrition, 86*(6), 1663–1669.

Lichtenstein, S., & Slovic, P. (2006). *The Construction of Preference*. Cambridge; New York: Cambridge University Press.

McChesney, F. S., & Shughart, W. F. II (1995). *The Causes and Consequences of Antitrust: The Public-Choice Perspective*. Chicago: University of Chicago Press.

Nietzsche, F. (1954). Twilight of the Idols. In W. Kaufmann (Ed.), *The Portable Nietzsche* (pp. 463–565). New York: Viking.

Nietzsche, F. (1966). *Beyond Good and Evil* (W. Kaufmann, Trans.). New York: Vintage.

Nietzsche, F. (1974). *The Gay Science* (W. Kaufmann, Trans.). New York: Vintage.
Nietzsche, F. (1989). *On the Genealogy of Morals & Ecce Homo* (W. Kaufmann, Trans., W. Kaufmann Ed.). New York: Vintage.
Nietzsche, F. (2003). *On the Genealogy of Morals* (K. Ansell-Pearson Ed.). Cambridge: Cambridge University Press.
Okasha, S. (2006). *Evolution and the Levels of Selection*. Oxford: Oxford University Press.
Pinker, S. (2002). *The Blank Slate: The Modern Denial of Human Nature*. New York: Viking.
Plomin, R. (2018). *Blueprint: How DNA Makes Us Who We Are*. Cambridge, MA: MIT Press.
Przeworski, A. (1991). *Democracy and the Market: Political and Economic Reforms in Eastern Europe and Latin America*. Cambridge: Cambridge University Press.
Rachels, J., & Rachels, S. (2012). *The Elements of Moral Philosophy* (7th ed.). New York: McGraw-Hill.
Riker, W. (1990). Political Science and Rational Choice. In J. Alt & K. Shepsle (Eds.), *Perspectives on Positive Political Economy*. Cambridge: Cambridge University Press.
Robalino, N., & Robson, A. (2013). Genes, Culture, and Preferences. *Biological Theory, 8*(2), 151–157.
Rowley, C. K., & Schneider, F. (2008). *Readings in Public Choice and Constitutional Political Economy*. New York; London: Springer.
Rubin, P. (2007). Utility, Fitness, and Immigration: Reply to Salter. *Journal of Bioeconomics, 9*, 53–67.
Salter, F. (2004). Is Ethnic Globalism Adaptive for Americans? *Population and Environment, 25*(5), 501–527.
Salter, F. (2007). Proximate and Ultimate Utilities: A Rejoinder to Rubin. *Journal of Bioeconomics, 9*, 69–74.
Samuelson, P. (1938). A Note on the Pure Theory of Consumers' Behaviour. *Economica, 5*(17), 61–71.
Sen, A. (1986). Behaviour and the Concept of Preference. In J. Elster (Ed.), *Rational Choice*. New York: New York University Press.
Sober, E., & Wilson, D. S. (1998). *Unto Others: The Evolution and Psychology of Unselfish Behavior*. Cambridge, MA: Harvard University Press.
Spinoza, B. (1985). *The Collected Works of Spinoza* (E. Curley, Trans., E. Curley Ed.). Princeton: Princeton University Press.
Sunstein, C. (2006). Preface. In S. Lichtenstein & P. Slovic (Eds.), *The Construction of Preference*. New York: Cambridge University Press.
Trivers, R. L. (1971). The Evolution of Reciprocal Altruism. *Quarterly Review of Biology, 46*, 35–57.

Tullock, G., Seldon, A., & Brady, G. L. (2002). *Government Failure: A Primer in Public Choice*. Washington, DC: Cato Institute.
Turchin, P. (2006). *War and Peace and War: The Rise and Fall of Empires*. New York: Penguin Books.
Tversky, A., & Kahneman, D. (1981). The Framing of Decisions and the Psychology of Choice. *Science, 211*(4481), 453–458.
Wilson, D. S. (2002). *Darwin's Cathedral: Evolution, Religion, and the Nature of Society*. Chicago: The University of Chicago Press.
Wilson, D. S. (2004). The New Fable of the Bees: Multilevel Selection, Adaptive Societies, and the Concepts of Self Interest. *Advances in Austrian Economics, 7*, 201–220.
Wilson, D. S., & Wilson, E. O. (2007). Rethinking the Theoretical Foundation of Sociobiology. *The Quarterly Review of Biology, 82*(4), 327–348. Retrieved from http://www.ncbi.nlm.nih.gov/pubmed/18217526.
Zucker, M. (1945). *The Philosophy of American History*. New York: The Arnold-Howard Publishing Co. inc.

CHAPTER 3

Public Choice Theory: Liberal Democracy's Shortcomings and Their Institutional Market-Enhancing Solutions

3.1 Liberal Democracy and Its Shortcomings

The main reason why I chose liberal democracy as the object of analysis—among many other models of democracy—is that it is currently the most prevalent political system in the western world. Hence, I chose this political system on the basis of relevance.

By liberal democracy, I mean a democracy that fulfils or respects the main principles of liberalism, this being the defence of individual freedom and equality. Liberal democracies usually operate under constitutions that protect individual rights and minorities from the abuse of power of illegitimate autocratic regimes or from the tyranny of the majority. Hence, rule of law, universal suffrage (formal equality), political and civil freedoms and the upholding of human or natural rights are part of the liberal democratic concept.

The tradition of the rational actor within political theory in general and within public choice theory in particular has tried to identify the internal and structural problems of democracy. By identifying these problems, classic public choice theory has developed a reputation of being hostile towards democracy. Still, by working under the general premise of universal preference satisfaction and, like in the strand of Buchanan and Tullock (1999), under the ethical premise of consensus or unanimity politics, one might say from a normative perspective that the nature of classic public choice is fundamentally democratic. A hostility towards despotism and the claim that we should judge governments by

F. N. Faria, *The Evolutionary Limits of Liberalism*, Palgrave Studies in Classical Liberalism, https://doi.org/10.1007/978-3-030-31496-5_3

how well they serve the interests of all citizens show how pro-democratic public choice theory's orientation is (Brennan & Hamlin, 2004, p. 102). Put differently, a desire to improve democratic workings is behind the criticism of the failures of liberal democracies, even if these criticisms imply changing the current institutional framework to achieve the democratic ideal (i.e. acknowledging democratic market alternatives). This motivation is particularly obvious in the field of constitutional political economy, where public choice theorists design constitutional rules of a liberal nature to fix recognised democratic failures and enhance a more "democratic" satisfaction of preferences. The American nature of public choice theory literature means that the American liberal democratic system inspired the discovery of most democratic shortcomings. Next, I depict some of the most important structural "problems" of democracy identified by the tradition of the rational actor.

3.1.1 The Principal–Agent Problem

The principal–agent problem underpins a general challenge of democracy, which is to align the interests of the political representatives with the interests of the citizens. This concept is taken out of economics literature and refers to a modelling framework in which a principal hires an agent to act in the name of the principal's interests. The problem itself refers to the asymmetry of information and to the higher skills or abilities that the agent can use for his/her own interests at the expense of the ones of the principal. This problem is particularly relevant under the assumption of rational egoism, given that such egoistic individuals would or could use their comparative advantage in knowledge and skills to put their interests above everybody else. Common examples are politicians (agents) and voters (principals) or, in the marketplace, managers (agents) and shareholders (principals).

Scholars usually present solutions for these problems in terms of a contractual design that creates incentives, through gains and punishments, for the agent to act according to the principal's interests (e.g. bonus attached to performance, wages depending on performance, periodical voting periods for the reassessment of politicians). Still, because these contracts are far from perfect, even under the best contracts, the agent holds an advantage he/she can use for his/her own benefit. In the words of Brennan and Hamlin: "such cures are rarely perfect, and the agent normally receives an 'informational rent' even under the best feasible contract" (Brennan & Hamlin, 2004, p. 100).

Public choice theory's traditional approach addresses the principal–agent problem by comparing the problem in politics to the same problem in the market. But is this problematic phenomenon more acute in markets or in politics? Mark Pennington (2011a) claims political institutions suffer from this problem in a much more harmful way than markets because of political institutions hardly having exit options—like exiting from the welfare state—and because of the concentration of power that increases the distance between principals and agents. Pennington's position is one that pervades most public choice literature, which sees the capacity to align democratic governments with the interests of the citizens as limited. Many public choice theorists are therefore more hospitable to decentralised competitive market institutions. An example of the promotion of competition as a solution to the principal–agent problem is Anthony Downs (1957) median voter model. In this model, politicians ideologically move to the position of the median voter to get as many votes as possible while in competition with others, becoming more aligned with the average voter (Brennan & Hamlin, 2004, p. 102). This is just one example of how competitive measures supposedly mitigate the principal–agent problem in politics. So, the most common option in public choice literature is to let market institutions operate when they show that they comparatively suffer less from this problem.

While the principle–agent problem is a general and not only a democratic shortcoming, it relates to most other "democracy problems" identified by the rational/public choice literature. One of the main foundational premises of public choice theory is that it is not enough to identify a problem in an institution, be it market or democratic/political, it is equally important to understand if the alternative is better. The "obligatory" comparison began as a critique of the market failure literature that often postulated government solutions to market failures. The opposite is also true: to identify a political failure does not mean that the market can solve it. In fact, this "obligatory" comparison carries with it a certain degree of imperfection in any institution, but dares nonetheless to identify a comparative superiority.

3.1.2 The Aggregation Problem

The severity of the principal–agent problem increases when there are numerous principals (citizen-voters) whose interests differ widely among themselves, making it complicated for principals to give precise instructions to the agents (political representatives). Put differently, the aggregation of preferences might not produce an accurate representation of the common will. It might even question the very own existence of the concept. With his famous impossibility theorem, Kenneth Arrow (1951) put a strong question mark on the whole concept of "common will". From that point on, aggregative democratic postulates based on this concept had to rethink their grounding. John Dryzek elegantly sums up what Arrow's theorem showed:

> Arrow showed that it is impossible for any mechanism for the aggregation of individual preferences into collective choices to satisfy simultaneously five seemingly innocuous and undemanding criteria. The first criterion is unanimity: any unopposed individual choice should be incorporated in the collective choice. The second is non-dictatorship. The third is transitivity: if the collectivity prefers A to B and B to C then A should be preferred to C. The fourth is unrestricted domain: there is no restriction on the preferences individuals can have across the available alternatives. The fifth is independence of irrelevant alternatives: the collectivity's preference between A and B should not be affected by the introduction of option C. (Dryzek, 2000, pp. 34–35)

What we can infer from Arrow's theorem of impossibility is that it is impossible to produce a voting process (e.g. majority rule) or any other collective form of decision that does not become highly vulnerable to dictatorship or to manipulation of agendas by skilful participants. A good example of this impossibility is the identified problem of cycling, which allows for winning majorities to violate the principle of transitivity. In practice, this means that option A can win against option B, option B can win against option C, and option C can win against option A. Hence, a simple manipulation of the agenda in favour of option A would make sure that a first electoral dispute would take place between B and C so that C is knocked out and then manipulators can introduce option A to win against B. When it becomes possible to manipulate winners and losers, the democratic process becomes a complex process that shifts away from the simple notion of the rule by the people (Dryzek, 2000, p. 35).

Even if no manipulation exists, results appear to be arbitrary and simply the result of random ordering (Shapiro, 2003, p. 11), not the rational representation of a general will.

Based on Arrow's insights, William Riker (1982, p. 241), the founder of the Rochester School of Rational Choice Theory, claimed that there is no such thing as "the will of the people" and that therefore there could not be authentic democracy. For Riker, the existence of a "common will" depends on a mechanism to measure it; and because there seems to be no mechanism to assess it, any notion of a "common will" is mere populism. McKelvey's (1976) proof that small changes in the variation of preferences can completely shift collective choices strengthened this idea. Thus, Riker postulates that the only utility of democracy is to give the voters the opportunity to remove tyrants from power. Yet, as Dryzek (2000, p. 36) notes, Riker's "Arrowian" logic undermines even this notion of "minimal democracy": if there is no mechanism that helps us to identify the "common will", how will we know that the removal of a tyrant from power was the will of the people? Clearly, the postulate of the impossibility theorem conceptually undermines democracy, at least from an abstract and rational perspective. It remains unclear how many of these "Arrowian" problems of aggregation happen in reality.

The "Arrowian" diagnosis of aggregative democracy shows that democracy does not just have the classic problem of the tyranny of the majority, democracy can also be the tyranny of a (manipulative) minority or even the tyranny of arbitrariness under a non-existent popular will. Under these premises, a classical liberal strand of public choice theory with names like Riker, Weingast, Buchanan and Tullock, push for the limitation of collective actions to those strictly necessary, preferring to give priority to individual action (i.e. the market) (Shapiro, 1996, pp. 30–42).

To be sure, not every political theorist thinks Arrow's insights mean the end of majoritarian democracy. Some studies show that the possibility of voting cycles is not problematic because they rarely happen (Mackie, 2003), even when preferences are heterogeneous (Tangian, 2000). Political theorist Ian Shapiro (2003, p. 16) provides some arguments against the strength of the "Arrowian demolition": first, he claims that the possibility of cycles can actually be helpful because it gives the losers of elections incentives to continue fighting for their causes within the democratic system. He asserts that the rareness of cycles prevents government policies from being constantly reversed, even though the prevention of policy reversal might not necessarily be something positive. Second, he claims that hamstringing government to give priority to individual action, rather than to a collective, gives benefits and power to a particular set of collective arrangements (i.e. constitutional). He then argues that these collective arrangements aiming at containing democracy's irrationality are also susceptive to irrational action or design. Ultimately, he claims that there are no good reasons to think Arrow's conditions for rationality are desirable.

Also, for Brennan and Hamlin (2004, pp. 105–106), one should not consider Arrow's impossibility as a conclusion about democracy but as a starting point for normative analysis. For example, they claim that instead of accepting dictatorship, one should talk about degrees of dictatorial power and that we should design institutions to minimise dictatorship. In their approach, it is not because we lack precise ways to measure the public interest that we should stop pursuing it from a moral and hence institutional perspective. They think we should regard Arrow's problem as one of an ethical nature and not so much as one of a political nature. Still, especially in the rational choice theory analysis of politics, there is a large consensus that the "is" influences the "ought", and therefore Arrow's theorem mostly means that individual choices should have priority over collective ones. This is especially visible among the more classical liberal faction of public choice theorists.

3.1.3 Rational Ignorance

In blunt terms, the rational ignorance model attributes the failures of democracy to the "stupidity" of voters/citizens, but this analytical approach to the ignorance factor focuses on the problem of information asymmetry. Since Anthony Downs' postulates in his *An Economic Theory of Democracy* (1957) that the concept of rational ignorance became central to the explanations of democracy from a public choice perspective, even though Gordon Tullock (1967a, p. 102) coined the term itself only in 1967. Rational ignorance refers to a situation where the costs of getting more information to make better decisions outweigh the benefits that those decisions might bring. In this case, it is rational to be ignorant and refrain from attaining more information. According to standard microeconomics, we expect individuals to acquire information until expected marginal benefits match the expected marginal costs (Stigler, 1961). The way this logic relates to democracy is relatively intuitive:

unlike the marketplace where the consumer pays the costs of buying the wrong product because of ignorance, in a democracy, the voter does not directly pay the cost of bad decisions. The voter has practically no chance of changing the result or of deciding the winner in a major election. Hence, to cast a well-informed vote ignores that the payoffs of the vote (i.e. actually making a difference in an election) do not outweigh the costs of getting information (time, research, etc.). In theory, this leads to widespread rational ignorance, because no incentives are in place that motivate voters to become well informed about policies, politicians, party programs, etc.

The immediate implication of rational ignorance in the analysis of democracy is that one can attribute most government failures to this problematic epistemic phenomenon where political actors are much better informed than voters (i.e. information asymmetry). The doors are then open to the abuse of power by the well-informed people (bureaucrats, interest groups, politicians) at the expense of the poorly informed individuals (the general voter). In the words of Bryan Caplan:

> Why can the special interest groups turn legislatures against majority interests? Voters' rational ignorance: many fail to realize that tobacco farmers get subsidies, and few know where their representative stands. Why can politicians defy public opinion? Voter's rational ignorance: few pay attention to politicians' position on unpopular programs like foreign aid, and fewer remember at the next election. Why are inefficient policies like the minimum wage popular? Voter's rational ignorance: few bother to learn enough economics to understand the policies drawbacks. (...) While the voters sleep, special interests fine-tube their lobbying strategy. Just as voters know little because it doesn't pay, interest groups know a lot because – for them – it does: hence the mantra of 'concentrated benefits, dispersed costs'. (Caplan, 2006, p. 97)

The logic of concentrated benefits and dispersed costs means that, because of voters' ignorance, well-informed interests groups can concentrate the benefits of a particular policy on themselves and disperse the costs of that same policy on the unaware citizens. An example of this logic would be an orange tariff that costs the consumer just a few pennies, but that represents millions of dollars for the orange producers that supported such a tariff.

Empirical data on the political knowledge of the public is usually consistent with the postulates of rational ignorance. Comprehensive works show that political knowledge is scarce, many times limited to simple things like the name of the president and little more (Delli Carpini & Keeter, 1996). Still, not everyone thinks rational ignorance is the end of a prosperous democracy. For instance, the theory known as "the miracle of aggregation" (Wittman, 1995) claims that voters' ignorance is not problematic because if the 90% of uninformed voters in society vote randomly they will split votes 50% each, leaving the 10% of informed voters to decide the outcome of the election. The economics of crime (Becker, 1968) suggests another solution for democracy in the face of widespread political ignorance. The prescribed solution is simple: the existence of a well-informed public is unnecessary, what is necessary is to over-punish every politician or agent who abuses the public office. Even minor infractions would have to be over-punished by removing the "criminals" from their jobs, overly fining them, demonising them or jailing them. In addition, even the logic of the "concentrated benefits, diffused costs" that comes from voters' ignorance may not be so problematic. To overcome such a problem, an omnibus repeal may be a solution (Wittman, 1995). This repeal consists of bundling numerous abuses against the taxpayer in one bill and eliminating them. By creating a bundle, the problem becomes visible enough to the public, who can then fight the abuses. Of course, these solutions are alleged antidotes against the harm caused by voters' rational ignorance, but the feasibility of such solutions is far from given. Therefore, one cannot easily dismiss widespread ignorance as an intrinsic problem of democracy. Still, its impact on government is also a matter of contention. While it is common to hear that government's inefficient growth happens because of rational ignorance and of the asymmetry of information between voters and political agents, there are reasons to think rational ignorance would make uninformed rational individuals expect less from the government instead of more. But the opposite seems to be true, the government seems to grow indefinitely in its scope of action and interference (Caplan, 2004a, p. 470).

3.1.4 Rational Irrationality

Economist Bryan Caplan is unconvinced that rational ignorance has the explanatory power that standard public choice attributed to it. His concept of rational irrationality is a criticism of the incompleteness of rational ignorance. Caplan is sceptical about the idea that voters' ignorance explains, for example, inefficient government growth. For him, it is rational irrationality that accounts for this expansion of government.

Rational irrationality entails that people have systematic biases instead of simply making random mistakes. Hence, when the cost of engaging in these systematic feel good biases is low, humans choose to act on them (i.e. a form of expressive behaviour). What this behaviour means to democracy is that individuals vote for bad policies because of the low cost of voting. While in the market the individual cannot stray too much from the search for truth if he or she does not want to buy a bad product, in democracy, it is possible to vote for inefficient, but feel-good policies, without immediately suffering the consequences or without establishing a direct relationship between the choice made in the ballot box and the detrimental effects of those policies. If individuals have systematic biases and not random ones, if they keep making the same mistakes over and over again, then this is the definition of irrationality, not of rational ignorance.

Caplan's concept deals with people's strong sense of morality that blinds them to empirical evidence. As he puts it: "They look at new evidence and empirical tests more as a threat than an opportunity to learn" (Caplan, 2004b, p. 470). A communist might not want to see the failures of communism, a libertarian might never recognise certain market deficiencies, a social democrat might not want to see the problems with the welfare state, etc. Basic economics of information suggests that the ignorant will rationally be humble to prevent mistakes; still, in politics, the opposite is true: ignorance is usually attached to intolerance and strong beliefs about the benefits of certain policies. Caplan illustrates this point with an example of economic protectionism:

> Consider, for instance, the common argument that voter ignorance of international economics leads to protectionist policies. This story has been shot down on the grounds that purely random errors resulting from lack of information should cancel out. If voters are ignorant about international trade, leading some to overestimate the benefits of protectionism and others to underestimate them, there is no reason to expect the equilibrium platform to be biased in a protectionist direction. In contrast, if voters are rationally irrational, they could systematically tend to overestimate the benefits of protectionism, driven perhaps by xenophobia. (Caplan, 2004b, pp. 471–472)

The same reasoning can apply to other policies like drug decriminalisation, price controls or any other policy where strong emotions neglect empirical reality. Hence, rational irrationality offers us an extra explanation to why democratic government failure takes place: not only individuals are rationally ignorant, they also have systematic biases that make them ask for inefficient policies. Without surprise, and according to Caplan (2004b, p. 472), numerous inefficient policies are extremely popular (e.g. protectionism, drug regulation…). So the phenomenon of interest groups engaging in concentrating benefits and dispersing costs does not happen only because of rational ignorance but also because voters systematically ask for policies conducive to such a phenomenon.

In sum, rational ignorance highlights how the "tyranny" of the informed minorities is a more prevalent democratic failure than the standard tyranny of the majority. Yet, rational irrationality seems to claim that there is also a "tyranny of the masses" in which voters exert the "tyranny" or "harm" on themselves.

3.1.5 Rent-Seeking and the Logic of Collective Action

Another classic failure of democracy within public choice literature is the phenomenon of rent-seeking. This phenomenon refers to the capture of the political process by well-organised interest groups that attain their favourite policies at the cost of the ordinary voter, mostly through lobbying. Gordon Tullock (1967b) developed the concept, but Anne Krueger (1974) coined it. Tullock himself defines rent-seeking as "the use of resources for the purpose of obtaining rents for people where the rents themselves come from some activity that has negative social value. For example, if the U.S. automobile industry invests resources in persuading the government to impose a tariff on Korean cars, citizens of the United States are worse off" (Tullock, Seldon, & Brady, 2002, p. 43). Hence, to get their preferred policies, interest groups engage in rent-seeking, which entails illegal or legal activities that aim at achieving special privileges such as monopoly status, quantitative restrictions on imports, bribes or protective tariffs. But rent-seeking does not have to apply only to obvious economic actors like corporations, it also applies to interest groups of a more "social" nature such as identity groups, gay, pro/anti-abortion or green activists, just to name a few.

As Gordon Tullock explains it, before his development of this concept, the former orthodoxy on interest groups thought monopoly profits were only a redistribution of wealth from the consumers to the monopolists, but no meaningful deadweight loss in production happened (Tullock et al., 2002, p. 44). Consumers could resent this redistribution, but many economists believed that, from the point of view of the whole society, no loss took place. If it was only a problem of redistribution, the government could fix the problem with fair redistribution (e.g. taxation), so no major issue existed. Still, what rent-seeking changed in this line of reasoning was that this privilege seeking implied huge investments in lobbying, generating vast deadweight losses in the whole society. The general process works in the following way: when facing competition from foreign companies, a firm can either invest in gains of competitive efficiency to compete better, to produce higher quality products with lower prices, or it can invest money, time and resources lobbying the government to get protective tariffs against foreign competitors. The overall result of the latter process is less production, less innovation, higher prices and more scarcity, which shows that rent-seeking is not simply wealth redistribution, but a detrimental phenomenon for a large part of society.

Another classic idea in public choice theory explains the prevalence of the rent-seeking phenomenon: Mancur Olson's logic of collective action, which relates to the capture of government policies by interest groups. According to Olson (1971), interest groups are difficult to organise. Because groups have common benefits but also common burdens, they suffer from free rider problems. In particular, rational egoists contribute nothing and expect to enjoy the public good that other contributors built. Hence, because of such problems, it is very difficult to mobilise groups. Yet, these free rider problems do not affect all groups equally. Some groups, like professional groups or trade unions, successfully coerce supply for their benefit, while other groups solve their collective action problems (i.e. suppressing free riders) because they are homogenous and small. However, large and heterogeneous groups suffer from free riding and cannot mobilise themselves to defend their interests. The most common examples of such unsuccessful groups are consumers and taxpayers (Rowley & Schneider, 2008, p. 14). Hence, successful interest groups will create diversions that are opaque and often hidden from the public, preferring to get favourable regulations instead of lump-sum transfers (Olson, 1982). Still, Chicago School's economist Gary Becker (1983) challenged Olson's logic. Becker assumed that groups could organise and reorganise at minimal cost while suppressing free riding at minimal costs. His general conclusion was that if interest groups were damaging the public welfare (i.e. generating deadweight costs to society), other groups that were more efficient in not damaging the general welfare would replace the damaging groups. Still, public choice evidence seems to refute such claims (Ekelund & Tollison, 2001). Without surprise, Mancur Olson's logic of collective action is still today a framework of reference.

In theory, rent-seeking can generate tremendous losses in productivity. The basic idea is that political power generates rents available for distribution, rents that will be the object of action by interest groups trying to get them. These groups will then have the incentive to invest in rent-seeking until the point where the opportunity cost equals the benefits of the rent. It is even possible that sometimes the opportunity cost is even greater than the rent because it is preferable to gain the rent by paying a higher price than to lose it completely after so much investment in lobbying. Still, as Brennan and Hamlin point out, this process seems to imply that political agents have discretionary power to distribute those rents. But, in reality, institutional mechanisms constrain political agents; maybe the most important of these mechanisms is the democratic process (i.e. the will and interests of the voters). Once again, this becomes a principal–agent problem, and the severity of such a problem will depend on the institutions and the agents' capacities to align the interests of the principals with the ones of the agents (Brennan & Hamlin, 2004, p. 118).

It is possible to assume that at least some investment in lobbying represents transfers and thus benefits someone (e.g. campaign workers). Also, under some situations, promoting competition for the best government services can add quality to such services. Hence, the normative evaluations of rent-seeking depend on its results. By the same token, considering that self-interested groups will aim at concentrating the benefits of rents on themselves and dispersing the costs on voters, one can infer that a rational politician depending on elections will not want to impose too many costs on too many individuals. This conclusion, of course, assumes that rational voters vote for instrumental reasons. If so, they would vote against such politicians, especially if the costs were too high to hide, even under rational ignorance. But, like Brennan and Hamlin (2004, pp. 119–120) claim, if voting is essentially an expressive behaviour that owes more to voting for moral reasons than for instrumental reasons, interest groups can dress their instrumental interests in moral rhetoric that politicians can use to convince the voters.

Overall, even though the process is not exactly clear, public choice theorists widely believe that rent-seeking is a fundamental problem of democracy. Such a problem turns the rule of the people into the rule of the well-organised minorities and their interest groups. Once again, under liberal democracy, the tyranny of the majority seems to be less prevalent than the tyranny of the minorities.

3.2 The Autocratic Market Solution

After depicting the main democratic shortcomings found in public choice literature, it becomes important to understand the main alternative to democracy in the real world: autocracy. This is especially relevant in relation to the market. Assuming that the market has the potential to be more efficient in maximising preferences than democracies regarding choice (i.e. that market failures are pale compared to democratic government failures) (Pennington, 2011b; Tullock et al., 2002), could autocracy be a suitable framework for the market? Surely, there must be implications for choosing such a framework, especially in relation to democracy. Under a market autocracy, there is the potential to prevent many of the failures attributed to democracy by public choice theorists. Still, the workings of an autocratic political system require analysis, given that the mechanisms that allow autocrats to prevent certain democratic failures (e.g. rent-seeking, rational irrationality) might generate failures of another sort, in particular in relation to the market.

I will next analyse autocracy from a rational/public choice perspective. In particular, I assess what rational/public choice theory has to say on the suitability of a market-enhancing autocracy as an alternative to the shortcomings of liberal democracy in respect of preference satisfaction.

3.2.1 *The Market: Autocracies vs Democracies*

Whether autocracies or democracies are the best political framework for the generation of wealth in the market is a question analysts often pose. Every time autocratic regimes show a high degree of economic growth and development, liberal democrats may fear that autocracy is, after all, a better framework for the market. Some scholars see the examples of high economic development in places like Singapore or China as evidence that autocracy is better suited to economic growth. This conclusion is what Amartya Sen (1993) called "The Lee thesis", a label given after Singapore's "enlightened" autocrat Lee Kwan Yew. The work of empirical researchers like Robert Barro (1996a, 1996b) emphasises the advantages of autocracies over democracies in that the former are better able to stop redistributive pressures and are better suited to curtail the wasteful activities of rent-seeking, while democracy is intrinsically vulnerable to those problems. Confirming this logic, Mancur Olson, in his famous book *The Rise and Decline of Nations* (1982), postulated that the older a democracy gets, the more distributional coalitions it will generate. Ultimately, the weight of rent-seekers, economic monopolies and general economic deadweight become so prevalent that it negatively affects economic growth. This result severely frustrates the aim of preference satisfaction. Namely, lower economic growth prevents more products, services and wealth from being available, therefore limiting the capacity for individuals to discover and satisfy their preferences.

There is a general assumption by economists that more growth equals better conditions of life and more choice, and that therefore a higher growth means a higher satisfaction of preferences. F. A. Hayek's definition of the market as a discovery process can explain this general assumption. Even though he does not operate under the standard assumptions of rationality (i.e. rational choice theory), his market vision has been underpinning economic thought about preferences. For von Hayek (1945), because everybody faces a knowledge problem, even in relation to understanding what one wants or needs, the market is the best place to discover our preferences. It is then a general assumption that more wealth, more products and services (i.e. options) will help to maximise the satisfaction of preferences. Hence, it is important to analyse the theoretical postulates within rational/public choice in relation to the topics of economic control, rent-seeking, redistribution and economic growth in autocracies versus democracies. These are topics that decisively influence the capacity of autocracies to maximise the satisfaction of preferences by enhancing the market. Does rational/public choice theory offer any conclusive insight on the hypothesis of a market-enhancing autocracy being a suitable alternative to the shortcomings of liberal democracy?

3.2.1.1 The Main Models of Autocracy in Rational/Public Choice Theory

3.2.1.1.1 The Stationary Bandit

The "stationary bandit" is a model of autocracy and political organisation that tries to explain the prevalence and workings of dictatorship. This theoretical framework developed by Mancur Olson (1993) rejects the idea that rational self-interest/egoism will operate mostly without coercion. Hence, Olson does not make this assumption. For Olson, a rational egoist will use whatever means to get to his/her goal, violence and theft included.

To explain the birth of autocracy, Olson, like many academics, conceptualises a state of nature where individuals pursue their self-interest and clash against each other, which leads to conflict, domination and exploitation. In this state of nature, Olson (1971) claims roving bandits will move around searching for whatever they can opportunistically plunder from the populations. Large populations cannot solve the problem of collective action and cannot form a voluntary social contract because each individual will, unmonitored, have the incentives to cheat. Hence, collective protection for the populations will not arise easily. This leads to the formation of small groups of thieves (i.e. warlords) that can solve their collective action problems because of being small and therefore properly monitored. Such thieves can then plunder any wealth they find. Property rights and incentives to produce for the long run are thus almost non-existent in the presence of these roving bandits. Yet, these roving bandits also have incentives to become stationary bandits. If they monopolise theft in a specific jurisdiction, they would give the population incentives to produce more (i.e. it would be possible for citizens to stay with what they produced after paying taxes) so the bandits could "plunder" even more wealth. The stationary bandit would then provide security against other roving bandits in exchange for steady plundering in the form of taxes. This, according to Olson, is a much better situation than to live under roving bandits where no property rights or production can flourish. So is Olson's account of the nature of autocracy. It is also why, Olson claims, autocratic rulers tend to claim that they rule with the voluntary consent of the people, even though in reality such consent does not exist. Olson thinks it is in the self-interest of the ruler to provide public goods to society because the autocrat has an encompassing interest in these goods. In this sense, public goods will help improve productivity and therefore the autocrat can extract more wealth than he or she would without those public goods.

3.2.1.1.2 Repression vs Loyalty

Ronald Wintrobe (1998) developed a systematic and analytical account of dictatorships in the rational/public choice tradition that tries to correct what he saw as the main problem with Olson's logic: too much emphasis on the autocrat's motive of wealth maximisation and a lack of emphasis in the competition for power. Wintrobe notes that the main difference between democracies and autocracies is that autocracies can use the tool of repression to stay in power. More broadly, he claims that autocrats use two instruments to maintain power: loyalty and repression. The use of these two variables determines the type of autocrat in question. But before presenting the four types of dictators in Wintrobe's taxonomy, it is necessary to introduce his notion of the "Dictator's Dilemma"; a dilemma that, depending on the way it is managed, eventually gives rise to a specific type of autocrat. In a nutshell, the dilemma that every autocrat deals with is the difficulty to know the right amount of necessary repression to remain in power. A dictator, by using repression, removes the apparent conflict from society and makes his political seat safer, at least in the short run, but repression has the downside of erasing the signals that allowed him to know who was conspiring against him or to know what the population thinks of his policies. This creates a signalling problem between the autocrat and his subjects (Wintrobe, 2004, pp. 82–83).

Because of this signalling problem, the autocrat lives under permanent suspicion of betrayal. The lack of an enforcement mechanism aggravates the problem. According to Wintrobe, the dictator could solve his lack of support by buying off those significant others opposed to him, but the lack of an enforcement mechanism guaranteeing that both parties will keep the agreements means that such agreements become difficult to attain or are inherently unstable. Still, Wintrobe (2004, p. 77) claims that the typical dictatorship works on that basis: buying off opponents for support, which makes an autocratic regime a much more fertile field for "pork barrel politics" than democracies.

Given that the main tools of autocrats are loyalty and repression, the way they will combine such variables will determine the type of autocrat they are. Wintrobe (2004, p. 78) created a taxonomy of autocratic regimes according to the nature of the autocrats, that is, by assessing if they invest more or less in repression and more or less in the attainment of popular loyalty. These four types are tinpots (they use low repression and low loyalty), the tyrants (high repression and low loyalty), totalitarians (high repression and high loyalty) and timocrats (low repression and high loyalty). The first two types seek personal consumption and wealth maximisation while the totalitarian is interested in maximising power over society to apply a given social vision. The timocrat is the only altruistic/benevolent one.

Still, in a straightforward rational/public choice fashion, Wintrobe (1998, p. 95) claims it is very doubtful that such a timocrat ever existed, attributing such a notion more to wishful thinking than to actual reality. Overall, these types of regimes end up representing different combinations of repression and loyalty, thereby defining the behavioural type of the autocrat. For example, for Wintrobe, supposing that there is an increase in economic growth, an increase of the autocrat's popularity will follow. Thus, one can predict that the behavioural response of tinpots and timocrats to this rise of popularity will be to lower the levels of repression while totalitarians and tyrants will raise such levels. This is because the first two have specific goals: respectively, personal consumption and benevolence, while the second two mainly want to maximise power over society. Finally, it is important to add that the use of repression by an autocrat does not mean he is not popular. Actually, as Wintrobe (2004, pp. 77–78) shows, more repression can increase his popularity either by providing stability or by creating a single popular mindset.

3.2.1.2 Economic Control, Rent-Seeking and Redistribution

Even though Mancur Olson was critical of democracies, he did not present autocracy as an improvement over democracy. On the contrary, he hints that, in theory, democratic majorities have a larger encompassing interest in letting the market produce more than an autocrat would; this is because the autocrat would try to maximise his wealth extraction. In his own words:

> The more encompassing an interest – the larger the share of the national income it receives taking all sources together – the less the social losses for its redistributions to itself. Conversely, the narrower the interest, the less it will take account of the social costs of redistributions to itself. (Olson, 1993, p. 571)

The problem, according to Olson, is that real democracies do not work for the interest of the majorities, but for the interest of well-organised interest groups that capture power and rents over time. He offers an example:

> A typical lobby in the US (…) represents less than 1% of the income-earning capacity of the country. It follows from the reciprocal rule that such

> a group has an incentive to stop arranging further redistributions to its clients only when the social costs of the redistribution become at least a hundred times as great as the amount they win in redistributional struggle. (Olson, 1993, p. 571)

Hence, he concludes that it is incorrect to claim that democracies will be less redistributive than autocracies

Ronald Wintrobe's theory on this point reaches a different conclusion: that autocracies are more prone to redistribution than democracies. But, to understand why, it is necessary to understand the background theories of rent-seeking in democracy. Since Anthony Downs' (1957) work, many scholars assumed that, in democracies, producer groups dominate over consumer groups. This is because the former are usually small, with powerful incentives, well organised and can solve collective action problems. The latter are too big to give high returns to each member of the group and to prevent free riding, so these groups will not mobilise. Hence, most rational/public choice theorists assumed "producer domination" in democracies, from Mancur Olson (1982) to George Stigler (1971) to Gary Becker (1983), among many others. Yet, as Stephen Haggard (1990) claims, the advantage of autocracy is that the ruler can repress potential rent-seekers, hence, even in democracies, political systems should insulate some economic policies from democratic voting or participation. Still, Wintrobe counters by asserting that the rational autocrat always needs to buy off support and that, like in democracies, the producer groups, being small and well-organised, are the ones better placed to offer support in exchange for tariffs or subsidies, unlike the consumer or environmental groups. Therefore, Wintrobe claims, "this implies that producers typically have more power under dictatorship than democracy" (Wintrobe, 2004, p. 85). Still, he adds that this stronger power of producers in dictatorships might explain the good economic performance of dictatorships at low levels of repression because producers especially benefit from economic growth. But he also adds that this strong growth might not be a Pareto improvement because it might come at the cost of repressed groups or at the cost of important elements like the consumers or the environment. Ultimately, if repression becomes too high, information problems arise and growth will probably diminish (Wintrobe, 2004, p. 85).

According to the standard rent-seeking model, rent-seeking competition for privileges is wasteful. Because democracy cannot exclude anybody from this competition while autocracies can, wasteful rent-seeking activity is bigger in democracies. Still, Wintrobe claims that this is far from evident. In a democracy, if the rent-seekers could directly trade with each other (e.g. bribe a politician), the other rent-seekers would not waste resources bidding, so the waste would almost disappear. This corrupt practice would eliminate waste, but the existence of corruption would not necessarily guarantee the interests of the public. Yet, if there is no corruption and politicians just accept the offers that serve the public, waste would also diminish; but, because the rent-seeking model rules out this possibility due to discarding the existence of public-minded politicians, the only result left is waste. Still, in an autocracy, the autocrat does not have many constraints on rent distribution and will use rents to buy off support. Hence, even under the possibility that the autocrat can shut down waste, Wintrobe claims the main conclusion to take under this assumption of politicians who are not public-minded is that democracies are less corrupt than autocracies.

A related question that affects the working of the market is one of redistribution. It should be relatively obvious that when comparing democracy to autocracy, the character of the autocracy should determine the answer: a more "left wing" dictatorship should be more redistributive than liberal democracies, which have a plurality of social visions in competition and some safeguards in terms of individual property rights. Still, if an autocracy uses authoritarianism to keep capitalism working without disturbances (i.e. so called "right wing capitalist authoritarianism"), it becomes controversial to claim that these autocracies are more hurtful of property rights and more redistributive than democracies. Nonetheless, a problem arises: one is comparing redistribution in democracies and autocracies to what standard? This standard can only be the free distribution of income in the free market. By claiming that, empirically, there is no such thing as a free market, Wintrobe points out that even right-wing capitalist authoritarianism is potentially more redistributive than democracies. He describes "the fallacy of free market" as "the common assumption in this literature that markets operate costlessly so that to have free markets, it is only necessary for government to get out of the way" (Wintrobe, 1998, p. 160). This ignores the central role of power in assigning property rights, shaping how the competitive market will take place. Examples of dictatorships like Chile under Pinochet or South Korea under the generals show how these regimes redistributed wealth, not by transferring money from A to B, but by altering rights in the workplace. By raising the cost of job loss to workers, by outlawing the right of collective bargaining, by generating relative low wages even under-skilled workers, these regimes transfer rights from the workers to the employers. This transfer benefits mostly large firms and the military and might boost economic growth, although generating higher material inequalities. His analysis of the question of redistribution and the "free market" suggests, in his own words, "that the economic success of capitalist-authoritarian governments is not difficult to explain. It is not because they do not redistribute income, but because they do redistribute the capacity to earn income – in particular, by adopting measures which transfer rights over the control of labor from labor to capital" (Wintrobe, 1998, p. 161).

3.2.1.3 Trade: More or Less Growth?

Economists have empirically researched the impact of the type of political regime, whether democratic or autocratic, on economic growth, even though the answers are not always entirely conclusive. The famous and controversial empirical work of Robert Barro (1996a, 1996b) shows that when one holds constant certain growth-oriented variables, like free markets, rule of law, small government consumption and high human capital, the effect of democracy on growth is weakly negative. In fact, he concluded that democracy increases growth when the levels of political freedom are low but decreases growth when there are moderate or high levels of political freedom. There is also the finding that economic growth tends to increase democratisation but high democratisation does not necessarily lead to the stabilisation of the rule of law, especially given the slight negative impact democracy has on growth. Democracy then becomes a consumption good: rich countries can afford to consume a little democracy, but if high democratic levels make a country substantially lose growth, individuals may question the goodness of the democratic rule of law. Hence, the conclusion is that autocracies, with their alleged higher capacity to shut down the interests of rent-seekers, can efficiently promote growth. This growth becomes the main social driver, underpinning the rule of law or democracy.

The same type of empirical work by Przeworski et al. (1993, 2000) is inconclusive about whether democracy is better suited for markets and economic growth than autocracies. Not being able to answer the question completely, they still remark something of considerable importance: that there is something else apart from the political regime that makes a difference. From an evolutionary perspective, this book hints at different behavioural types and moralities. But in their own words:

> Our own hunch is that politics does matter, but "regimes" do not capture the relevant differences. Postwar economic miracles include countries that had parliaments, parties, unions, and competitive elections, as well as countries ran by military dictatorships. In turn, while Latin American democracies suffered economic disasters during the 1980s, the world is replete with authoritarian regimes that are dismal failures from the economic point of view. Hence, it does not seem to be democracy or authoritarianism per se that makes the difference but something else. (Limongi & Przeworski, 1993, p. 65)

Accordingly, they discover no substantial differences between the rates of growth of these two regimes in question, even though they do not see politics as irrelevant. For example, they reveal that changes which cause unrest, whether changes in political office or strikes, affect the growth of dictatorships more than they affect the growth of democracies (Przeworski, 2000).

In another study, Edward Glaeser et al. (2004) "answer" to two important points made by Przeworski et al. (1993) and Robert Barro (1996a). One is that the missing variable mentioned by Przeworski, which might explain economic growth, is human capital; Glaeser et al. find that human capital is a stronger source of growth than institutions. The other point is that economic growth usually precedes democracy, like Barro claims. Specifically, the paper reveals that poor countries get out of poverty through good policies often pursued by dictators and that only afterwards do these countries reform their political institutions.

In yet another comprehensive study of 130 countries for 1962–2000 that aims at understanding the impact of the political regime on growth and markets, Toke Aidt and Martin Gassebner (2010) find that autocracies import substantially less than democracies, which shows that the former are considerably more protectionist than the latter. However, as Wintrobe (1998, p. 338) points out, to average out economic comparisons between democracies and autocracies in a simple formula misses the diversity of autocratic regimes. He recommends those who think such a simple formula exists to compare totally different regimes like the economies of apartheid South Africa, Nazi Germany, Papa Doc Duvalier's Haiti, Pinochet's Chile, the former Soviet Union or, should we add, Lee

Kwan Yew's Singapore. This autocratic diversity is the reason Wintrobe developed different analytical frameworks for each behavioural type of autocrat. Even though liberal democracies can also be considerably different from one another, it seems logical that dictatorships, by their very nature, can be much more diverse. The main reason is that, while democracies seem to suffer from chronic inaction in the face of important problems that require consensual unpopular actions, which is difficult to happen, an autocrat has a much higher margin of action to solve difficult problems, whether it is an increase of taxes, war, an increase in hard laws to impose order, etc. The autocrat can even choose what part of the population will bear the cost and use enough repression to stop their protests, regardless of doing it for personal aims or for the greater good of the population. In sum, while in a liberal democracy liberal pluralism is the standard, autocracies can come in very different ideological or institutional shapes, thus reflecting the autocrat's preferences.

Yet, although higher economic growth and greater wealth seem to lead to a demand for greater democratisation, the estimated size of this effect is not very significant, especially in non-European countries. Londregan and Poole (1996) showed that in non-European countries it is not so clear that one does not have to wait a long time before seeing some democratisation taking place under strong economic growth.

The general effects of openness to trade on autocracies are also doubtful. Depending on the type of dictator, the autocrat might use the higher tax revenues and possibly popularity that come with economic growth to strengthen power and repression. Conversely, the autocrat might use growth to ease repression, leading to some degree of democratisation. Wintrobe gives examples of totalitarian regimes like the ones of Hitler or Stalin, where each time the economy improved they used the extra resources to increase repression and consolidate power. He also gives China as an example of non-democratic opening, despite years of economic growth caused by "free market communist". Wintrobe (2004, pp. 85–86) asserts that trade and economic openness lead to widespread contact with the rest of the world, thus weakening the dependence of regions and individuals to central authoritarian governments. But it is also true that this openness between civilisations can lead to mistrust and conflicts. It is important to remember that World War I took place at the last peak of openness of the international system.

In conclusion, it remains difficult to understand the effects of political institutions on markets and growth. Given that both democracy and autocracy will have problems representing the preferences of the people, it is tempting to let the market mechanism take the main role in such an aim. In this chapter, I tried to understand the workings of autocracies and how they perform as a framework for the market. It is not conclusive that, in this regard and according to rational choice theorists, autocracies are better or worse than liberal democracies. But the fact that classic public choice does not assume that political agents can be altruistic produces the general impression that a market autocracy is not the ideal system to satisfy preferences because of the potential for autocratic egoistic exploitation. Therefore, these public choice theorists see the identified democratic problems as challenges to overcome within liberalism, within a specific form of liberal democracy. They aim at reforming liberal democracy by transforming it into a political framework for market liberalism. I will now describe such a solution.

3.3 The Liberal Market Solution: Constitutional Political Economy

The main market institutional solution found in public choice literature is James Buchanan's contractarianism. His social contract is a way to solve the shortcomings of current liberal democracy by transforming politics into a market where voluntary exchange is the norm, therefore redefining the concept of liberal democracy.

3.3.1 The Contractarian Approach

The need to limit the freedom of the individual to escape anarchy seems to be an unavoidable topic in political philosophy. In the previous sub-chapter, autocracy was regarded as a possible way to limit such an anarchic and boundless freedom. Here, I will conceptualise such limits as a way to maximise individual freedom and equality. Thus, I postulate these limits from a liberal perspective. While autocracy restricts the freedom of individuals to achieve aims that are not necessarily the maximisation of liberty and equality, the constitutional political approach aims at safeguarding the sovereignty of the individual by normatively postulating a political/moral framework chosen by individuals themselves (i.e. they choose the limits of liberty).

I will now provide the solutions to the shortcomings of current liberal democracies that public choice theorists found within the tradition of the rational actor, contractarianism, democracy and liberalism. This means that the subject of study will be constitutional political economy, a field of study directly connected to the work of James Buchanan, especially in its normative approach, and broadly connected to public choice theory. Through this lens, it is possible to understand how the market can become a central component of a "true" and functional liberal democracy. I will put a special emphasis on how market solutions can supposedly enhance universal individual preference satisfaction, therefore correcting the problems found in current liberal democracies.

The shortcomings of democracy identified by public choice theorists are the reason James Buchanan considers the liberal democracy of the United States to be a "constitutional anarchy" (Buchanan, 2000b, p. 19), and one can say the same about current western liberal democracies. These majoritarian democracies reveal a total disregard for the preferences of sovereign individuals. In such political systems, the will of rent-seekers, self-interested politicians, judges, legislators or faceless bureaucrats determines the resulting policies, with these actors imposing their preferences on the disempowered public. Even though these democracies are "liberal constitutional democracies", they simply transfer the anarchy of power from the non-constitutional realm to the constitutional one, frustrating the liberal aims of individual liberty and equality. As a result, these democracies are degenerations of what true liberal democracies can be. In reality, from Buchanan's (2000a, 2000b) constitutional contractarian perspective, they are non-liberal and nondemocratic given that they do not aim at having universal constitutional content or respect the individual as the only one capable of expressing value for himself or herself. Thus, respecting individual consent is the only way to have a true liberal democracy.

3.3.1.1 The Moral/Social Contract

Before analysing the liberal market solution coming from constitutional political economy, it is important to reveal the normative (moral) underpinnings behind this contractarian approach. This approach, which James Buchanan developed, is often the basis for the normative logic of constitutional political economy. The methodology is identical to classic public choice theory (e.g. methodological individualism, rational choice theory, etc.), which is why constitutional political economy is a public choice sub-field. Still, there are some moral precepts that shape the normative side of this theoretical framework.

For James Buchanan, the individual is the sole source of value and so he rejects any notion of a collective good that might come out of external sources of evaluation. Thus, his defence of liberal democracy aims at building a political system that can truly maximise the satisfaction of individual preferences, both in the private and in the public sphere. For him, it is only possible to satisfy this aim under a moral/political theory of contractarianism. He believes that individuals in a community should directly choose the rules they will live by. In the words of Buchanan and Brennan: "The contractarian derives all value from individual participants in the community and rejects externally defined sources of value, including natural rights" (Brennan & Buchanan, 2000b, p. 25).

Yet, from Buchanan's traditional point of view, if we base democracy on individual sovereignty and self-rule, then we must acknowledge that only liberal contractarianism can achieve such a democratic ideal. In the same way, because of individual sovereignty, Buchanan's vision postulates that there is no reason to have different evaluative standards in the market and in political realms (Meadowcroft, 2013, pp. 60–63). This means that one should respect the preferences of the individuals both in the private-economic and in the public-political spheres. In this sense, we must found democracy on Wicksellian principles of consent. As Knut Wicksell (1896) postulated, any collective action will have costs, and autonomous individuals should in principle judge those costs and unanimously agree on the costs of such an action in order for the action to materialise. Hence, we should base collective actions on unanimous consent if they are to respect the will of the individuals. Buchanan and Congleton then regard current "liberal" democracies as a form of "constitutional majoritarianism", which is, in their own words:

> the conception of democratic politics that we propose to use to be descriptive of the most widely held modern attitude in Western politics. So long as the voting franchise is universal, elections are periodic, majority or plurality rules determine electoral winners, and legislative bodies operate with internal majority rules, there are no limits on the range and scope for political action. (...) so long as political actions are determined by majoritarian coalitions, there are no grounds for complaint or concern on behalf of those persons or groups that may be differentially exploited. There is, indeed, no constitutionally protected sphere of activity into which politics

> cannot potentially enter. In essence, majoritarian agreement is the ultimate source of value. (Buchanan & Congleton, 2006, p. 19)

Put differently, their vision is one that sees the label of democracy being used to justify profoundly undemocratic regimes (Meadowcroft, 2013, pp. 60–63).

As a solution, they claim it is possible to reach the ideal of liberal democracy through the moral/social contract in the liberal contractarian tradition. This is a contract where all the individuals of a given political community come together to define the rules of their society, establishing how authority should act. According to Buchanan's tradition, there is no such concept as the common good or social welfare that one can define independently (Brennan & Buchanan, 2000b, p. 27). Hence, in the words of Brennan and Buchanan: "consistency requires that all persons be treated as moral equivalents, as individuals equally capable of expressing evaluations among relevant options" (Brennan & Buchanan, 2000b, p. 26). They thus present the moral/social contract as the liberal democratic solution:

> Individuals will be led, by their own evaluation of alternative prospects, to establish by unanimous agreement a collectivity, or polity, charged with the performance of specific functions, including, first, the provision of the services of the protective or minimal state and, second, the possible provision of genuinely collective consumption services. (Brennan & Buchanan, 2000b, p. 26)

This contract tries to solve the problem of anarchy, where all individuals have the freedom to do anything they desire, including predation, murdering, stealing, etc. In such a context, in the Hobbesian state of nature of all against all (Hobbes, 1975), there would supposedly be a race to the bottom, with evermore resources devoted to protection instead of production. This social contract is then a multilateral agreement among individuals that requires unanimous consent by the participants, thus supplying Pareto improvements (i.e. no person is worse off and at least one person is better off).

Buchanan (2000b, pp. 50–55) believes that no individual would use the veto option because the price of staying outside the contract would be too high. Not only the dissident would become an outcast in political society, he or she would also not enjoy the government protection of life and property, thus not being able to engage in a fruitful exchange with the members of society.

Buchanan and Brennan conceptualise the contract, and the political sphere in general, as a system of exchange between free individuals. As in the market, individuals will depart from unequal positions in terms of their material possessions but are equal in terms of participation and consent. To find these meta-rules for society, they will trade their preferences and the game will eventually stop at equilibrium. The equilibrium will maximise the value of the elements involved in the collective bargain. Still, in terms of the final outcome, which one cannot predict beforehand, Buchanan and Brennan say the following:

> What can we say about the outcomes so attained? We can say that given the initial endowments and the existing rules of the trading game, the outcome is whatever maximizes value. But note that the source of value lies exclusively within the preferences of the persons who trade. There is no external source of evaluation. (Brennan & Buchanan, 2000b, p. 28)

They conceptualise politics as an exchange ("politics as exchange"), and exchange, they claim (Brennan & Buchanan, 2000b, p. 30), is only possible if parties have a previous agreement on how to define property rights (i.e. to define who owns what). Even the rights of persons are only legitimate when agreed among individuals as part of a polity.

Finally, Buchanan and Brennan recognise that unanimity and consent are too high requirements to ask for in our daily disputes. Still, according to their vision, this difficulty does not undermine the logic of the moral contract, because there is a conceptual separation between meta-rules and rules within those meta-rules. They believe that people can agree on the meta-rules (i.e. general principles) under consent and unanimity, while rules under the meta-rules can work under principles of something less than unanimity. Here is one of their examples to show how someone can agree on a general rule and still be against it when it becomes particularised:

> As an example, consider the position of a dairy farmer confronting choices at the two levels. He might strongly oppose a specific reduction in milk price supports, since such action will almost surely reduce his net wealth. At the same time, however, he might support a generalized rule that would eliminate political interference with any and all prices for services

> or goods. The effect of such a rule change or institutional reform on his own net wealth is less determinate in the latter case than in the former. (Brennan & Buchanan, 2000b, p. 34)

Individuals could then agree on the meta-rules of the contract under a "veil of uncertainty", which derives its notion from the more famous "veil of ignorance" social contract mechanism by political philosopher John Rawls (1971). Unlike Rawls's veil of ignorance, where individuals are non-corporeal and know nothing about their actual conditions when defining the rules of the contract, the veil of uncertainty makes fully embodied individuals more likely to agree on general rules when choosing the rules and institutions for society. Put differently, the uncertainty of the future (i.e. fear of anarchy) would lead individuals to such an agreement. As an illustration, at the constitutional level, individuals would not elect a dictator, even though any of them could become one. This is because of the uncertainty behind such a decision. The costs of accepting such an option (of a dictator) would surely outweigh the probable and expected benefits (i.e. it would be unlikely that the average individual signer of the contract would reach such a dictatorial position) (Brennan & Buchanan, 2000b, p. 35).

3.3.1.2 The Market as Complementary and Crucial for the Democratic Ideal

Because these public choice theorists acknowledge that it is hard to agree on specific allocational decisions beforehand, they hint that the contract would have general premises that people could regard as the minimum for a state (i.e. protection of life and property plus the production of some public goods). Individuals might or might not leave all subsequent decisions to private market decisions. But, under the principle of unanimity, which easily blocks collectivist decisions, such an option is likely to be a strong one at the constitutional stage.

Because classic public choice regards politics as a form of exchange for the purpose of satisfying preferences, the sharp conceptual division between politics and markets becomes blurred. Liberal democracy in this constitutional-contractarian perspective is a way for individuals to realise mutual gains, with politics and the market working as a continuum for such a democratic aim. In Viktor Vanberg's words:

> there is neither a 'market as such' nor a 'democracy as such'. Both, markets and democracies exist only as arenas for social cooperation that are framed by specific "rules of the game" and their working properties will be critically dependent on the nature of these (constitutional) rules. (Vanberg, 2013, p. 21)

Hence, liberalism and democracy merge into the same concept of individual sovereignty, achieving a theoretical integration of the two. James Buchanan himself explains why the sharp distinction between politics and markets is misleading from a democratic-individualistic perspective:

> If we adhere strictly to the individualistic benchmark, there can be no fundamental distinction between economics and politics, or more generally between economy and polity. The state, as any other collective organization, is created by individuals, and the state acts on behalf of individuals. Politics, in this individualistic framework, becomes a complex exchange process, in which individuals seek to accomplish purposes collectively that they cannot accomplish noncollectively or privately in an tolerably efficient manner. (Buchanan, 2001, p. 62)

This democratic-individualistic methodology is clear when Buchanan (2000b, pp. 5–11) describes himself as a democrat, an individualist, a constitutionalist and a contractarian, blending these concepts into a unitary approach in which the term democratic "is merely a variant of the definitional norm of individualism" (Buchanan, 2000b, p. 4).

If one defines the respect for individual sovereignty and for the satisfaction of preferences as democratic, then the market becomes a gateway of democracy that might occupy a larger piece of the social spectrum than political action. Thus, markets have the potential to "replace" most political decisions, provided that all elements choose this replacement when choosing the meta-rules of the social contract. Buchanan's scholarly tradition is one that tries to show how it would be rational for individuals to choose mostly market/private solutions to satisfy the democratic-individualist principle.

But how would poor people accept a contract where wealth transfers require the consent of wealthy people? One solution he proposes is a renegotiation of property rights to convince the poor people who are reluctant to accept such a contract under extremely inegalitarian wealth positions. Buchanan suggests that the rich man who may want a restriction on the state's powers to redistribute wealth, may "potentially agree on a once-and-for-all or quasi-permanent transfer of wealth to the poor man, a transfer made in exchange for the latter's agreement to a genuinely new constitution that will overly limit governmentally directed fiscal transfers" (Buchanan, 2000b, p. 225).

Buchanan, once again, believes that uncertainty can lead to such an agreement. Namely, the uncertainty felt by the rich who fear future punitive taxation or expropriation and the uncertainty felt by the poor who fear a non-constitutional revolution made by the rich to protect their high wealth. If all individuals renegotiated property rights, there would exist a potential common understanding that could lead to such a moral contractarian agreement (Buchanan, 2000b, pp. 225–226). After this renegotiation of property, which would level the field in terms of wealth and property, individuals could then freely pursue their own goals, even if that meant future material inequality, because the precepts of democratic liberal individualism were being satisfied.

Moreover, for Buchanan, this constitutional revolution could not only result from rational self-interest but also from an ethical "revolution"; because, as he points out, in any large collective agreement "exists little or no incentive for any single player to participate actively in any serious evaluation of the rules" and the "fully rational players will refrain from participating in the choice among regimes" (Buchanan, 1999a, p. 370). Therefore, the full participation of all individuals might "require the presence of some ethical precept that transcends rational interest for the individual" (Buchanan, 1999a, p. 371). According to Viktor Vanberg, this is not a call to shift the rational choice methodology, this is rather a recognition that individuals unwilling to invest in the construction of the social contract fail to achieve the mutual gains that the contract aims at. An ethical revolution would mean to create something like a "civil religion", where individuals incentivise each other to adhere to the ethical obligation of dialoguing in the constitutional enterprise. It thus becomes vital to emphasise the point that it is in everybody's self-interest to participate. In other words, people should actively cultivate democratic citizenship.

3.3.1.3 Constitutional Political Economy: On Behaviour

It is also important to understand what kind of version of homo economicus is recommended for the logic of constitutional political economy. For this purpose, it is possible to identify at least two versions:

a narrow (or thick) version, described by G. Brennan and J. Buchanan as "the selfish brute who devotes himself single-mindedly to maximizing the present value of his measurable wealth" (Brennan & Buchanan, 2000a, p. 19); and a more open (or thin) version which considers that homo economicus can have many propensities, from extreme altruism to hedonism, and that all those behavioural tendencies can be part of rational self-interest.

For the specific task of constitutional political economy, James Buchanan recommends the narrow version (Kirchgassner, 2014). This is because of a normative prescription about what a legitimate government should be. He prescribes that such an institutional government should aim at preventing abuses of power by any individual in charge. To achieve this ideal it is better to consider that individuals will not act altruistically, but to assume instead that they are prone to act as self-interested individuals who hope to maximise wealth and status. As Buchanan puts it:

> When selecting among alternative constitutional constraints, however, the individual is required to make some predictions about the behaviour of others than him. And, in such a setting there is a powerful argument that suggests the appropriateness of something akin to the Homo economicus (narrow version) postulate for behaviour. (Buchanan, 2008, p. 290)

With such a prescription, J. Buchanan and G. Brennan stand in a long tradition of liberal political philosophy that assumes individuals to be knaves even though admitting that they are probably more complex than that. In the words of John Stuart Mill:

> The very principle of constitutional government requires it to be assumed that political power will be abused to promote the particular purposes of the holder; not because it is always so, because such is the natural tendency of things to guard against which is the special use of free institutions. (Mill, 1861, pp. 217f.)

David Hume makes a similar point: "It is, therefore, a just political maxim, that every man must be supposed a knave: though at the same time, it appears somewhat strange, that a maxim should be true in politics, which is false in fact" (Hume, 1963, pp. 40–42).

Like David Hume, James Buchanan (2000a, p. 121) also does not believe that the narrow version of homo economicus accurately represents human individuals, both in markets and in politics. For him, if such a model was accurate, voters would not vote and those who would vote would be ignorant; bureaucrats would always use their powers to their own advantage, among other empirically unlikely scenarios. But his endorsement of such a model for constitutional political economy is methodologically and morally normative, not scientific in the sense of accurately reflecting real universal behaviour. To have a method that offers better chances of achieving "true" liberal democracy is a priority over having an accurate model of behaviour.

3.3.1.4 Two Concepts of Liberal Democracy

Under the liberal solution presented in this chapter, there is a clash between two concepts of liberal democracy. As I previously noted, what western people often regard as a constitutional liberal democracy (e.g. the democracy of the United States), James Buchanan's contractarian position sees as "constitutional anarchy". Put differently, his constitutional political economy tradition considers that the failures of these alleged liberal democracies rely on them not upholding the sovereignty of the individual, therefore losing their liberal democratic ideals. This becomes clear when public choice theorists show that majoritarian decision-making rules (Buchanan & Tullock, 1999) or the will of politicians and minority groups (i.e. rent-seekers) impose tremendous coercive costs on individuals, therefore denying the liberal democratic ideal of self-rule (Tullock et al., 2002).

There seem to be two versions of the same concept of "liberal democracy", one that is loose (e.g. United States's liberal democracy) and another that is tight (e.g. Buchanan's liberal democracy). The first version, which is the reference of this book, tries to fulfil general notions of liberalism and democracy (i.e. constitutionalism, institutionalised human rights to protect minorities from majority voting, universalist voting, majoritarian decision-making rules); but this version is not contractarian, hence, it does not conceptualise nor crystallise politics as the accurate representation of the will of sovereign individuals, still having something of an elitist constitutional conception. The second version, which is the basis of Buchanan's liberal democracy, accepts nothing less than a social contract in which all individuals agree on the constitutional meta-rules that will govern them, even if, on the sub-constitutional level, unanimity decision-making rules disappear. This tight, and, one might say, irreducible vision of liberal democracy tries to attain the liberal democratic enlightenment aim of creating autonomous individuals who choose their own rules and also choose how to live privately and in the community. Such a vision has the aim of creating individuals with no undemocratic obstacles to fulfil individual preferences.

In terms of preference satisfaction, when assessing the potential for markets to be an alternative to current liberal democratic politics, it is important to distinguish the answers for the two types of liberal democracy aforementioned—loose and tight. Given the identified problems of "loose" liberal democracies, it becomes clear that, according to most public choice scholars studied in these chapters (Buchanan, 1975; Pennington, 2011b; Tullock et al., 2002), markets might solve many of these pathologies of democracies. On the other hand, from the constitutional political economy perspective of James Buchanan, markets are an intrinsic part of liberal democracy. Markets and political voting/choice procedures are a simple continuum that defines the liberal democratic paradigm, the prevalence of each context (market vs politics) being decided by individuals in the social contract. In this tradition, even though rational individuals have advantages in choosing to give a larger role to economic markets and private decision in society, the selection of social rules is ultimately political. For Buchanan, true liberal democracy is a market; it works as the politics of exchange. In such a market, individuals have the incentives to let most choices take place in the economic marketplace because of the high decision and external costs of collective decisions (Buchanan & Tullock, 1999). Ultimately, this liberal market solution is the redefinition and reformation of liberal democracy, transforming it into a "market".

3.3.2 *Political Problems with Market Solutions*

To understand how markets can offer a more democratic solution than to assign most decisions to the "democratic" political process, one has to go through the analysis made by constitutional political economy. James Buchanan naturally leads the normative approach. If Buchanan, on the one hand, proposes no specific set of rules that individuals should choose at the meta-level, on the other hand, he spent most of his career analysing the best solutions that people could choose at that level. Thus, he studied the problems of current western "liberal democracies", which he found neither democratic nor liberal, and in many, if not most cases, he tried to show the superiority of markets in satisfying individual preferences. This superiority, one can infer, would lead to rational individuals choosing market solutions when discussing the social contract under unanimity rules. Because to respect the sovereignty of the individual is here the true liberal democratic ethics, individuals would prefer to make most decisions in the marketplace because of the high costs of collective decision-making (Buchanan & Tullock, 1999) that such respect brings. In short, what the market can do efficiently should be done in that realm. We now turn to the analysis of choices made in the market and made in politics, which will help us understand how, from a constitutional political economy point of view, individuals have several advantages in choosing market solutions over government solutions; and to understand how, under Buchanan's contractarianism, the market is ultimately a vital component of democracy.

3.3.2.1 Individual Choices in Democratic Politics Versus the Market

Before analysing how market solutions might be preferable to a political system heavily based on a political voting process, it is important to understand the main differences inherent to individual choices in both contexts. James Buchanan (1999b) suggested six main distinctions between individual choice in voting (pure democracy) and in the marketplace (through the price system).

The first distinction between the two is the "degree of certainty": while in the market the individual chooser is the choosing entity, in voting the individual chooses for a bigger entity, which is the collective. Thus, the chooser in the market can predict with almost absolute certainty the result of his choice; but, in voting, the individual chooser can never predict with certainty the choices that others will make, which brings a higher level of uncertainty to the process compared to market choices.

The second distinction is the "degree of social participation": the chooser in the marketplace assumes that all social variables not related to his choice are external and that an individual market choice will not change major collective trends or institutions. Yet, in the voting booth, the individual consciously recognises that he or she is participating in the determination of a final collective choice, which might make the individual's "values" influence his or her ordering of preferences, while "tastes" might be more important in the market.

The third distinction is the "degree of responsibility". Market choices concentrate responsibility on the individual. There can be no abstention.

Conversely, in the voting process, it becomes difficult to understand why an individual voted in a certain way. It could be because of public interest values, miscalculations or because of narrow self-interest in preferring a collective social outcome that will most benefit him or her. Buchanan illustrates this point by noting that this distinction was the reason economist Ludwig von Mises (1951, p. 21) thought that individuals are less corruptible in the market.

The fourth distinction is "the nature of alternatives": while in the market alternative choices conflict only in the sense that the law of diminishing returns is in place (i.e. to buy more of one product one has to buy less from another product), choices in voting tend to be mutually exclusive (i.e. to choose one political candidate means to reject another). Choosing in democratic politics can be problematic because of the nature of bundling; that is, to vote for one candidate usually means to choose the whole program of policies he represents and to give away many highly regarded policies that are part of the program of another candidate that the voter had to forsake. With market choices, the problem of bundling seems to be less acute as it is possible to combine several options within the limits of a budget.

The fifth distinction is the "degree of coercion": even though one can make the analogy of "one dollar vote", dollars, or any other unit of currency, are distributed unevenly, which creates unbalances in purchasing power in the market (i.e. some have more purchasing power than others). Yet, each "dollar vote" always prevails and money units are, in the formal sense, an equalising force that puts nobody in a losing or winning minority. Conversely, in the voting realm, any voter can lose against a majority voting and so the losing voter must abide by laws that go against his or her expressed preference. While the social group one belongs to influences earning and expenditure patterns, there is an important distinction between this indirect coercive force and the direct and unavoidable coercion of collective action decisions.

Finally, the sixth distinction is the "power relations": market choices operate under conditions of monetary inequality via the "one-dollar-one-vote analogy", while voting often takes place under conditions of formal equality. Still, market choices also occur under a condition of formal equality in the sense of allowing equal formal freedom; namely when such a freedom is defined as the absence of coercion, while unfreedom is a state where one is prevented from using one's capacities to achieve one's goals.

In conclusion, James Buchanan points out that the greater degree of certainty and responsibility of choices in markets reveals enhanced individual rationality. And if one prefers rationality, then one should prefer the market. Still, just because the market seems to enhance individual rationality, it does not mean that market choices will tend to generate stronger social rationality. He also emphasises that markets reveal a higher degree of freedom, but voting choice confers individuals a greater sense of participation in some notion of the "public interest". Yet, he postulates that voting can only produce "rational" social choices if men can agree on the ultimate goals, and for that, they will need to agree on what genuine morality is. In the end, the choice between market decisions or voting decisions will depend on the ordering of moral values held by individuals of a given polity. In the words of James Buchanan:

> If consistency in individual behavior and individual freedom are highly regarded relative to other values, the market will tend to be favored. If, on the other hand, the somewhat vague, even though meaningful, concept of "social welfare" is the overriding consideration, voting choice may be preferred. (Buchanan, 1999b, p. 87)

The preference of one decision mechanism, such as the market, over the other, such as voting, will also be influenced by the extent to which individuals see their self-interest better represented: collectively or individually. If it is individually, the market offers a better way to satisfy preferences, but if it is collectively, Buchanan recommends that:

> the electorate should select the ballot box over the market place in those areas where individually determined market acts tend to produce results which are in conflict either with those which a large group of voters estimate to be their own or the social welfare and where the conflict is significant enough to warrant the sacrifice both of the individual freedom and the individual rationality involved. (Buchanan, 1999b, p. 87)

Still, at the meta-constitutional level, the selection of rules must be political. It is at the sub-constitutional level that choices between markets or voting are important for decision-making. Accordingly, it becomes necessary to understand when market solutions can be superior to political ones, like voting. We now turn to the analysis of the shortcomings of the political voting process and of the advantages of market solutions under the constitutionalist contractarianism framework of constitutional political economy.

3.3.2.2 Preferences: Understanding the Market Advantages Over Majoritarian Democracies

As aforementioned, the public choice theorists in question claim that current western liberal democracies like that of the United States are constitutional anarchies because these democratic systems do not respect the sovereignty of individuals, often relying on majoritarian voting rules. Hence, these political systems are also majoritarian democracies. This nature of democracies leads to situations where the political system is out of touch with the preferences of individuals. Still, scholars often thought that these majoritarian democracies actually represent the will of the voters. The reasoning behind this idea is that by voting for a political program and afterwards for another (i.e. a rival with a better program), a competitive invisible hand would make politicians offer programs more and more aligned with the preferences of the median voter. Even today many in the West think of majoritarian democracies as democratic (i.e. ruled by the people). Yet, even under the best scenario, one can merely say these democracies represent the preferences of majorities. But majority voting is only one way to make decisions that one might call democratic, qualified majority voting is another. As I showed in the first chapter, scholars have been acknowledging majority decision as a decision rule that can lead to intransitive collective choices at least since de Condorcet (1785). This means that when a collective is choosing between 3 alternatives (A, B and C), even if the majority of voters prefer A to B and B to C, it is possible they still choose C over A, which would normatively transform such choice into irrationality. Scholars also see this issue as the problem of cycling.

An important point made by Buchanan and Tullock (1999, p. 122) was that, even if we hold the preferences of individuals constant, a change in the collective decision-making rule will produce different outcomes. Worse still, different rules of this kind will give power to coalitions of different people. They have shown that, under majority rules, coalitions that try to control the outcomes are necessarily smaller than the coalitions needed under qualified majority voting, making the latter preferable because of having less exploitative potential.

Market solutions can avoid many tensions that arise because of the natural imposition of coercive policies on the voting losers by the voting winners. It is therefore important to understand when market solutions can be superior in maximising individual liberty. In the work of James Buchanan, it is possible to find specific points where this market superiority in choosing seems relatively clear (Meadowcroft, 2013, pp. 65–96).

3.3.2.2.1 Bundling

The first point is the problem of bundling in the voting process, which is that in the market it is possible to think marginally (i.e. to add or remove marginal units according to our preferences) while politics has an exclusive nature (Buchanan, 1999c, p. 56). As a market consumer, it is possible to purchase more or less food or clothes according to preferences and this process gives price signals to producers for them to increase or diminish the production of those goods. In politics, it is not possible to produce many services or goods in marginal units adjusted to every individual preference. Bridges or highways are either built or not, to go to war means that the nation will go or not, regardless of differences of preferences among voters. Because of this exclusive nature of political decisions, from a normative perspective, individuals should restrict such decisions to the minimum as much as possible. Thus, people should restrict political decisions to what markets cannot produce equally well or cannot produce at all. That individuals often have to choose between bundles of policies, such as political programs from different candidates, only makes the problem of political voting decisions more acute.

3.3.2.2.2 The Negligible Impact of the Single Vote

Another point that negatively impacts political voting decisions in terms of satisfying individual preferences is the negligible influence that a single vote has in contemporary practices. This happens because most national polities have thousands or millions of voters, which transforms the single vote into something statistically meaningless. Hence, G. Brennan and J. Buchanan (2000b, p. 85) postulate that there is a fundamental difference between choosing in public or in private scenarios in the sense that an individual understands that to change/inform his preferences may be irrelevant in the public case. This leads to people being rationally ignorant because there are no incentives for them to get information about politics. After all, a single individual vote will hardly change any large election outcome. As Vanberg and Buchanan put it: "the prospects of an individual's improving the outcome by casting a single better informed vote do not provide significant incentives for a voter to incur the costs of becoming better informed, even if these costs are quite small" (Buchanan & Vanberg, 2001, p. 132). The lack of incentives for voters to acquire good information leads to elections becoming a "choice in dark", where politicians rule on behalf of an uninformed majority. With this in mind, it is possible to understand that decisions in the political and economic contexts differ and might be analogous to "the difference between a choice among experts themselves and a choice among their products" (Buchanan & Vanberg, 2001, p. 137). Here, the advantages of choice in the market are clear: it is more likely that individuals would satisfy their preferences by choosing a car produced by experts than they would by choosing experts to produce cars (Buchanan & Vanberg, 2001, p. 138). Non-experts, because of their ignorance, would have difficulties in identifying the correct experts, in the same way as ignorant voters have problems identifying the candidates that will enact policies in line with their preferences. The problem of rational irrationality is similar (Caplan, 2004b). One can observe rational irrationality when voters vote for their ideal world because of the low cost of voting. Even though voters are ignorant, they still have strong moral opinions on what the government should do, resulting in voters voting for policies that will hurt them in the medium-long run, not satisfying their preferences (e.g. voting for economic policies that will damage economic growth). Once again, this problem is "solved" by letting individuals choose in the market, because when an individual chooses a bad product in the market (e.g. bad car, bad TV) the consequences are immediate and he or she internalises the costs and benefits of such a choice. Choosing in the market "forces" people to be more responsible in their calculations if they are to satisfy their preferences.

3.3.2.2.3 Dependence on the Votes of Others

As I described before, the uncertainty in the voting process is much higher than in the market because, in the former, people depend on the votes of others, while in the latter, they choose exactly what they need according to their budgets (i.e. by assessing costs and benefits). Furthermore, Buchanan and Tullock (1999, pp. 37–38) argue that in the voting context individuals try to guess the choices of others, which many times leads them to vote for least-bad alternatives, which in turn also leads to intransitive preferences and cycling. For example, individuals might prefer A to B and B to C, but they may vote for C against A when they believe that C might have a better chance of defeating the least-desirable option D.

3.3.2.2.4 The Temporal Dimension of Choices

The temporal dimension of choices in the market and of choices in collective voting is also distinct. When one is making a private choice, one knows that, ceteris paribus, a decision to save for the future will be successful and will cause an increase in wealth. Still, in public choices, the same hardly happens. For example, one might vote against building a road because, even though it might be advantageous, one believes that the government should build it in more economically favourable times. But to save for the future in a public setting is more complicated because even if one votes against building the road to save money, the government might spend the same money on other public expenditure projects that one prefers less than the road. Hence, it becomes rational to choose to build the road immediately to prevent the same money from being spent in other less preferred projects (Brennan & Buchanan, 2000b, p. 86). Overall, the time horizon in private choices is longer than in public choices, which allows for better planning and for a more efficient satisfaction of preferences.

3.3.2.2.5 Priced Choices Versus Uncosted Choices

Yet another sharp difference between choices in these two realms is that choices in the market have prices, but in the political realm, they are generally *uncosted*. This becomes obvious when one realises that it is a contemporary practice to treat the costs and benefits of public policies separately. For example, individuals often vote on public expenditure (i.e. public projects) separately from fiscal policies; yet, the same individuals vote on fiscal issues (i.e. to levy more or less taxation) also separately from the public projects that make up public expenditure (Buchanan, 1999d, pp. 90–92). This division transforms political choices into a blind and opaque process that separates policy outcomes from the individual chooser. A choice in the market, where everything comes with a price, allows for costs and benefits to represent the preferences of the chooser. Moreover, this blind and opaque system of public voting facilitates the creation of public debt. James Buchanan (1999d, p. 102) explains that because public projects are *uncosted*, individuals are more willing to support them than if taxpayers knew that they would have to pay the correspondent increase in taxes. For example, an individual that supports space programs could change his mind if he knew that he would pay the respective price in taxes, but if there is the option of financing it with public debt, then the burden will fall on the next generation. If an individual believes that such a program will bring long-term benefits and he will not have to pay for it, it is too tempting to vote in favour. On the other hand, one might think that this direction of voting proves that there is a strong correlation between individual preferences and policy outcomes, but such an assertion is misguided. John Meadowcroft explains why that is the case, it is misguided:

> because individual preferences properly understood reflect people's evaluation of the relative costs and benefits of different courses of action, rather than an infinite wish list of goods and services that would be consumed if such consumption were costless. By offering seemingly costless consumption the political process in fact creates a disparity between what people would choose if they were fully cognizant of the relevant costs and benefits and the choices people make in the political realm. (Meadowcroft, 2013, pp. 77–78)

Such choices in an unreal realm of costless consumption can lead to unsustainable public policies with debt "explosions" and problematic generational burdens, which will be beyond the preferences of most individuals.

3.3.2.2.6 The Intensity of Preferences

The intensity of preferences is another feature that separates the choices in these two contexts. Buchanan and Tullock (1999, p. 134) scrutinised this point to find that the voting process produces the inherent failure of not taking the intensity of preferences into account. This is clear in the "one vote – one person" system of universal voting, where a vote counts exactly the same regardless of the intensity of preferences about different issues. Conversely, when choosing in economic markets, the multiple monetary units (dollars, euros) that the individual possesses make up multiple "votes" that one utilises to acquire highly valued goods, even if those goods are not appreciated by others (i.e. even if one is on a small minority) (Buchanan, 1999b, pp. 82–88). In elections, issues that are very important for a certain minority of individuals can get trumped by voting majorities that are not even very interested in the fate of that particular issue. Hence, Buchanan and Tullock (1999, p. 134) note that the popular idea that people have a duty to vote harms the capacity of current democratic polities to satisfy preferences. Still, in the current majoritarian democracies, it seems to be almost impossible to overcome this problem. Market solutions show a considerable advantage in this regard.

3.3.2.2.7 Coercion, Exploitation and the Governmental Over-Supply of Goods

Because of the absence of marginal thinking, dependence on the decisions of others and a lack of an exit option, majoritarian voting politics will be inherently coercive; unlike the market, which relies on voluntary actions. It is also possible to identify a "majoritarian equilibrium" where the majorities impose their will on the minorities, the latter being effectively ruled by the former. Such an imposition of will defeats the liberal democratic logic of self-rule. Because there is no exit option, individuals have incentives to demand public goods that benefit themselves before other individuals demand other goods that are less valuable. This "majoritarian anarchy" resembles the tragedy of the commons, where individuals have to exploit open resources for personal benefit in the short run before others do the same, which leads to the depletion of the common good (Hardin, 1968). Hence, James Buchanan (1999d, pp. 71–87) postulates that governments will tend towards an over-supply of public goods. Over-supply happens because individuals will have incentives to correct all the public goods that are being under-supplied while being less motivated to correct the ones that are being excessively supplied. As a result, because government spending dramatically increases in relation to the private sector, state institutions force individuals to pay taxes for several goods and services that do not interest them, hence increasing dissatisfaction and widening the gap between individual preferences and policy outcomes.

The majority rule does not even necessarily work for the benefit of poor individuals because majorities will also decide the redistribution of wealth and, as Brennan and Buchanan put it, "the poorest cannot be expected to be in the decisive majority any more often than anyone else" (Brennan & Buchanan, 2000b, p. 142). Still, when one expands the models to include the logic of representation in liberal democracies, which are not direct, Buchanan and Tullock show that "in the real world, as the number of voters and constituencies increases, the minimum-sized coalition required for dominance under simple majority voting approaches ¼ of all voters as a limit, so that, for example, if there are 39,601 voters arranged in 199 constituencies of 199 voters each, only 10,000 voters would be required to secure passage of any given policy proposal- only 100 more than one-quarter of all the voters" (Buchanan & Tullock, 1999, p. 220). In other words, an organised minority of voters can have coalitions to dominate the disorganised majority.

If in a direct majoritarian democracy the majority dominates, in a representative majoritarian democracy it is the well-organised minorities that take the dominating and exploitative position; something that Mancur Olson's (1971) logic of collective action identified.

3.3.2.2.8 Rent-Seeking

It is because of this "weakness" of representative majoritarian democracies that rent-seeking becomes so prevalent. James Buchanan defines rent in the following way: "So long as owners of resources prefer more to less they are likely to be engaged in rent-seeking, which is simply another word for profit seeking" (Buchanan, 1999e, p. 103). Hence the distinction between rent-seeking in the market and in politics: while in the market profit/rent-seeking leads to competition for better and more products that can satisfy preferences according to supply and demand and to the free entry of competitors, in politics rent-seeking can have detrimental effects by granting privileges to some at the cost of the general population. Additionally, the costs of trying to achieve such privileges will deviate resources from companies that could use these resources to improve products and satisfy consumer preferences but instead waste capital with lobbying to get government rents. Moreover, as the ones outside of the winning coalition of rent-seekers try to become a winning coalition by replacing the former winners, a process of "majority cycle" starts (i.e. a cyclical production of new majority coalitions that aim at rent-seeking). Because the new winners fear that others may replace them, their activity is more connected to the extraction of wealth (e.g. through monopoly privileges) than connected to the creation of wealth. As a result, rent-seeking leads to a relative impoverishment of society (Brennan & Buchanan, 2000b, pp. 131–135). Ultimately, Buchanan (1999e, p. 108) claims markets have the ultimate and decisive advantage of having free entry, which creates true competition for wealth creation, while that is not the case in politics. As a result, the larger the government (i.e. the more resources it allocates), the more opportunities there will be for rent-seeking. The protective state, created to protect individual rights, becomes a physical force that regularly infringes those rights (e.g. property, liberty, etc.) (Brennan & Buchanan, 2000b, p. 31). Because current liberal democracies tend to combine representative and majoritarian elements of voting, a combination of minority and majority rule also arises as a consequence, reinforcing Buchanan's idea that such polities represent a form of constitutionalised anarchy.

3.3.2.2.9 The Worst Tend to Get on Top

A final reason for the market to be less exploitative and possibly more in line with individual preferences than majoritarian liberal democracies is the nature of the individuals that usually get to power. According to G. Brennan and James Buchanan, F. A. von Hayek's (1944, Chapter 10) claim that in centralised polities the worst tend to get on top is essentially correct. Conceptualising power in economic terms, they postulate that it is likely that the highest bidders for political power will be the most ruthless and power-driven individuals. In their own words: "positions of political power will tend to attract those persons who place higher values on the possession of such power. These persons will tend to be the highest bidders in the allocation of political offices" (Brennan & Buchanan, 2000b, p. 72). Importantly, they claim that people who aim for the common good or who strive for altruistic motives will not be motivated enough to go through the hardship of fighting for power. The rational-egoists, on the other hand, will be the ones sufficiently motivated to do whatever it takes for personal gain (Brennan & Buchanan, 2000b, pp. 72–73). If that is so, then the benefits of political power will be the largest for those whose preferences are not so much in line with the general public, which leads Brennan and Buchanan (2000b, p. 73) to the conclusion that individuals whose interests conflict with the ones of ordinary individuals will tend to populate political systems. Thus, also because of this reason, these public choice theorists claim polities ought to be "knaves" proof and citizens should leave most decisions to private institutions like the market.

References

Aidt, T., & Gassebner, M. (2010). Do Autocratic States Trade Less? *World Bank Economic Review, 24*(1), 38–76.

Arrow, K. J. (1951). *Social Choice and Individual Values.* London: Chapman & Hall.

Barro, R. J. (1996a). Democracy and Growth. *Journal of Economic Growth, 1*, 1–27.

Barro, R. J. (1996b). *Getting it Right: Markets and Choices in a Free Society.* Cambridge, MA: MIT Press.

Becker, G. (1968). Crime and Punishment: An Economic Approach. *Journal of Political Economy, 76*, 169–217.

Becker, G. (1983). A Theory of Competition Among Pressure Groups for Political Influence. *Quarterly Journal of Economics, 98*, 371–400.

Brennan, G., & Buchanan, J. M. (2000a). *The Power to Tax: Analytical Foundations of a Fiscal Constitution*. Indianapolis: Liberty Fund.

Brennan, G., & Buchanan, J. M. (2000b). *The Reason of Rules: Constitutional Political Economy*. Indianapolis, IN: Liberty Fund.

Brennan, G., & Hamlin, A. P. (2004). *Democratic Devices and Desires*. Cambridge, UK: Cambridge University Press.

Buchanan, J. M. (1975). *The Limits of Liberty: Between Anarchy and Leviathan*. Chicago; London: University of Chicago Press.

Buchanan, J. M. (1999a). The Ethics of Constitutional Order. In *The Logical Foundations of Constitutional Liberty* (Vol. 1, pp. 368–373). Indianapolis: Liberty Fund.

Buchanan, J. M. (1999b). Individual Choice in Voting and the Market. In *The Logical Foundations of Constitutional Liberty* (Vol. 1, pp. 75–89). Indianapolis: Liberty Fund.

Buchanan, J. M. (1999c). Politics Without Romance: A Sketch of Positive Public Choice Theory and Its Normative Implications. In *The Logical Foundations of Constitutional Liberty* (Vol. 1, pp. 45–60). Indianapolis: Liberty Fund.

Buchanan, J. M. (1999d). *Public Finance in Democratic Process: Fiscal Institutions and Individual Choice*. Indianapolis: Liberty Fund.

Buchanan, J. M. (1999e). Rent Seeking and Profit Seeking. In *The Logical Foundations of Constitutional Liberty* (Vol. 1, pp. 103–119). Indianapolis: Liberty Fund.

Buchanan, J. M. (2000a). The Achievement and Limits of Public Choice in Diagnosing Government Failure and in Offering Bases for Constructive Reform. In *Politics as Public Choice* (Vol. 13, pp. 112–126). Indianapolis: Liberty Fund.

Buchanan, J. M. (2000b). *The Limits of Liberty: Between Anarchy and Leviathan*. Indianapolis: Liberty Fund.

Buchanan, J. M. (2001). Contractarian Political Economy and Constitutional Interpretation. In *Choice, Contract and Constitutions* (Vol. 16, pp. 60–67). Indianapolis: Liberty Fund.

Buchanan, J. M. (2008). Constitutional Political Economy. In C. K. Rowley & F. Schneider (Eds.), *Readings in Public Choice and Constitutional Political Economy* (pp. 281–295). New York: Springer.

Buchanan, J. M., & Congleton, R. D. (2006). *Politics by Principle, Not Interest: Towards Nondiscriminatory Democracy* (1st digitally printed pbk. ed.). Cambridge; New York: Cambridge University Press.

Buchanan, J. M., & Tullock, G. (1999). *The Calculus of Consent: Logical Foundations of Constitutional Democracy*. Indianapolis: Liberty Fund.

Buchanan, J. M., & Vanberg, V. (2001). Constitutional Choice, Rational Ignorance and the Limits of Reason. In *Choice, Contract, and Constitutions* (pp. 127–148). Indianapolis, IN: Liberty Fund.

Caplan, B. (2004a). Rational ignorance. In C. K. Rowley & F. Schneider (Eds.), *The Encyclopedia of Public Choice* (Vol. 2, pp. 468–470). New York: Kluwer Academic Publishers.

Caplan, B. (2004b). Rational Irrationality. In C. K. Rowley & F. Schneider (Eds.), *The Encyclopedia of Public Choice* (Vol. 2, pp. 470–472). New York: Kluwer Academic Publishers.

Caplan, B. (2006). *The Myth of the Rational Voter: Why Democracies Choose Bad Policies*. Princeton: Princeton University Press.

de Condorcet, M. (1785). *Essay on the Application of Analysis to the Probability of Majority Decisions*. Paris: De L'Imprimerie Royale.

Delli Carpini, M. X., & Keeter, S. (1996). *What Americans Know About Politics and Why It Matters*. New Haven, CT: Yale University Press.

Downs, A. (1957). *An Economic Theory of Democracy*. New York: Harper & Row.

Dryzek, J. S. (2000). *Deliberative Democracy and Beyond: Liberals, Critics, Contestations*. Oxford: Oxford University Press.

Ekelund, R., & Tollison, R. (2001). The Interest-Group Theory of Government. In W. F. Shughart & L. Razzolini (Eds.), *The Elgar Companion to Public Choice* (pp. 357–378). Cheltenham, UK: Edward Elgar Publishing.

Glaeser, E., Porta, R., Lopez-De-Silanes, F., & Shleifer, A. (2004). Do Institutions Cause Growth? *Journal of Economic Growth, 9*, 271–303.

Haggard, S. (1990). *Pathways from the Periphery: The Politics of Growth in the Newly Industrializing Countries*. New York: Cornell University Press.

Hardin, G. (1968). The Tragedy of the Commons. *Science, 162*(3859), 1243–1248.

Hobbes, T. (1975). *Leviathan*. London: Dent.

Hume, D. (1963). Of the Independency of Parliament. In *Essays: Moral, Political and Literary* (pp. 40–47). Oxford: Oxford University Press.

Kirchgassner, G. (2014). The Role of Homo Oeconomicus in the Political Economy of James Buchanan. *Constitutional Political Economy, 25*(1), 2–17.

Krueger, A. (1974). The Political Economy of the Rent-Seeking Society. *American Economic Review, 64*, 291–303.

Limongi, F., & Przeworski, A. (1993). Political Regimes and Economic Growth. *The Journal of Economic Perspectives, 7*(3), 51–69.

Londregan, J., & Poole, K. (1996). Does High Income Produce Democracy? *World Politics, 49*, 1–30.

Mackie, G. (2003). *Democracy Defended*. Cambridge, UK; New York: Cambridge University Press.

McKelvey, R. (1976). Intransitivities in Multidimensional Voting Models and Some Implications for Agenda Control. *Journal of Economic Theory, 12*, 472–482.

Meadowcroft, J. (2013). *James M. Buchanan* (Vol. 17). New York; London: Bloomsbury Academic.

Mill, J. S. (1861). *Considerations on Representative Government.* London: Parker, Son and Bourn.

Olson, M. (1971). *The Logic of Collective Action: Public Goods and the Theory of Groups.* Cambridge, MA: Harvard University Press.

Olson, M. (1982). *The Rise and Decline of Nations: Economic Growth, Stagflation, and Social Rigidities.* New Haven: Yale University Press.

Olson, M. (1993). Dictatorship, Democracy and Development. *The American Political Science Review, 87*(3), 567–576.

Pennington, M. (2011a). *Principal-Agent Theory and the Welfare State.* Retrieved from Cato.org website: http://www.cato.org/policy-report/septemberoctober-2011/principal-agent-theory-welfare-state.

Pennington, M. (2011b). *Robust Political Economy: Classical Liberalism and the Future of Public Policy.* Cheltenham: Edward Elgar.

Przeworski, A. (2000). *Democracy and Development: Political Institutions and Material Well-Being in the World, 1950–1990.* Cambridge: Cambridge University Press.

Rawls, J. (1971). *A Theory of Justice* (Original ed.). Cambridge, MA; London: Belknap Press of Harvard University Press.

Riker, W. (1982). *Liberalism Against Populism: A Confrontation Between the Theory of Democracy and the Theory of Social Choice.* Oxford: Freeman.

Rowley, C. K., & Schneider, F. (2008). *Readings in Public Choice and Constitutional Political Economy.* New York; London: Springer.

Sen, A. (1993, October 1). *Political Rights and Economic Needs.* Paper presented at the The John M. Olin Lecture in Law and Economics, University of Toronto Law School.

Shapiro, I. (1996). *Democracy's Place.* Ithaca, NY: Cornell University Press.

Shapiro, I. (2003). *The State of Democratic Theory.* Princeton, NJ: Princeton University Press.

Stigler, G. (1961). The Economics of Information. *Journal of Political Economy, 69,* 213–225.

Stigler, G. (1971). The Theory of Economic Regulation. *Bell Journal of Economics and Management Science, 2*(1), 3–21.

Tangian, A. (2000). Unlikelihood of Condorcet's Paradox in a Large Society. *Social Choice and Welfare, 17,* 337–365.

Tullock, G. (1967a). *Toward a Mathematics of Politics.* Ann Arbor: University of Michigan Press.

Tullock, G. (1967b). The Welfare Costs of Tariffs, Monopolies, and Theft. *Western Economic Journal, 5*(3), 224–232.

Tullock, G., Seldon, A., & Brady, G. L. (2002). *Government Failure: A Primer in Public Choice.* Washington, DC: Cato Institute.

Vanberg, V. (2013). *James Buchanan's Contractarianism and Modern Liberalism.* Freiburger Diskussionspapiere zur Ordnungokonomik. Department of Economic Policy and Constitutional Economic Theory. University of Freiburg. Retrieved from http://www.econstor.eu/handle/10419/88108.

von Hayek, F. A. (1944). *The Road to Serfdom.* London: Routledge.

von Hayek, F. A. (1945). The Use of Knowledge in Society. *The American Economic Review, 35*(4), 519–530.

von Mises, L. (1951). *Socialism.* New Haven: Yale University Press.

Wicksell, K. (1896). *Finanztheoretische Untersuchungen nebst Darstellung und Kritik des Steuerwesens Schwedens.* Jena: s.n.

Wintrobe, R. (1998). *The Political Economy of Dictatorship.* Cambridge, UK; New York, NY: Cambridge University Press.

Wintrobe, R. (2004). Dictatorship. In C. K. Rowley & F. Schneider (Eds.), *The Encyclopedia of Public Choice* (Vol. 1, pp. 77–91). New York: Kluwer Academic Publishers.

Wittman, D. A. (1995). *The Myth of Democratic Failure: Why Political Institutions Are Efficient.* Chicago: University of Chicago Press.

CHAPTER 4

The Evolutionary Framework: Multilevel Selection, Morality and Preferences

4.1 Utilising Multilevel Selection

Multilevel selection is a model originally developed in the biological sciences, but it is no less relevant for the social sciences. It is important to recall that multilevel selection asserts that altruism evolves because altruistic behaviour benefits a group of individuals when such a group competes against other groups. Still, if individuals are easy to identify, groups are not so, especially because of their ever-changing nature and sometimes unclear limits. Hence, it is important to translate these multilevel selection insights into social terms to identify how such insights apply to the social realm and its institutions.

4.1.1 Multilevel Selection and the Logic of Groups in the Social Realm

When applying the logic of group selection to real case examples, James Buchanan (2000) chose a basketball team to explain this logic in real terms. Buchanan claims that individuals show explicit love and altruism towards their relatives because they truly love them. Yet, he claims that even when such genuine altruism does not exist, an individual can show altruistic behaviours. The individual can help the members of his or her group to achieve their interests because that also helps him or her to achieve personal goals. In his own words:

F. N. Faria, *The Evolutionary Limits of Liberalism*, Palgrave Studies in Classical Liberalism, https://doi.org/10.1007/978-3-030-31496-5_4

> The individual may place no value on the well being of any particular other members of the group, but at the same time, she may exhibit behaviour that furthers the interests of others because group success, as such, is valued alongside and separately from individual success. (Buchanan, 2000, p. 1)

In a basketball game, it is possible to observe which team players are more altruistic and which players are more selfish. The altruistic ones try to play collectively and will do everything to make the team win (e.g. to pass the ball to a player in a better position of scoring instead of trying to score themselves). Conversely, the egoists will try to get as many points for themselves as they can, regardless of the team result. As Buchanan puts it:

> The person who voluntarily contributes to the production of a commonly shared and individually valued good over and beyond the amount dictated to be strictly rational is analogous to the altruist. The person who behaves in accordance with the norms of rational choice, with measurable wealth specifically defined as an argument in the utility function, remains the free rider. (Buchanan, 2000, p. 2)

Hence, a team that has more altruistic players providing public goods (i.e. which can play collectively) is the one that increases the chances of winning over a team suffering from an abundance of free riders. Following the logic of multilevel selection theory, in order for a group to outcompete other groups, it must suppress the within-group selection, strengthening the collective and punishing free riders, so that between-group selection forces can favour such a group. Still, altruism is by default always selected against within groups, so there is a stability problem with any mechanism that attempts to suppress egoistic behaviour. Here, teams have the incentive to hire players that show a natural tendency to provide public goods (i.e. sacrifice for the team). They also have the incentive to punish free rider behaviours through enforced rules that force players to play in favour of the team. Because the costs of enforcing rules increase with the number of egoists, teams search for naturally altruistic individuals.

That the multilevel selection logic of group competition is as important as individual competition, claims Buchanan, "must be recognized in any explanatory model" and "can be useful beyond the natural science limits" (Buchanan, 2000, p. 6).

Hence, in the social realm, it is important to understand what potential groups can exist and how they interact with each other, generating group forces and group competition alongside individual competition.

4.1.2 *Theories of Groups and Politics Under Multilevel Selection and Rational/Public Choice*

The most obvious tangible group in politics is probably the state. Competition between states has been a common force throughout history, either through warfare or through cultural and economic hegemony. If group selection in humans requires cultural norms to make groups/tribes/societies cohesive through the punishment of free riders, the state, as the ultimate monopolist of "legitimate" violence and creator of laws, seems to be the most important group unit. Nonetheless, within states, one can identify numerous group units that affect and can determine the very own existence of a particular state. For example, a state might or might not correspond to a nation. A nation is a group that relies on a natural feeling of belonging. It is constituted by individuals with certain traits that see themselves as members of that institutional group (i.e. the nation). As aforementioned, association by traits is more important than a simple territorial concentration, as, for example, the Jewish diaspora can be seen as a nation in the same way as the Basque country is (i.e. stateless nation). A state does not always correspond to a nation (e.g. Spain, Yugoslavia, USSR), but many times it does. Unsurprisingly, following the logic of multilevel selection, states that contain multiple nations or/and ethnic affiliations inside their jurisdiction often suffer from violent between-group conflicts (Vanhanen, 1999). Still, even within states and nations, many other group affiliations can develop, namely: class, caste, socio-economic corporatist interests, ideological interests, family, among many others.

In the tradition of public choice theory, Mancur Olson presented an explanation for this observable tendency for humans to create groups and affiliations to serve their interests. His book *The Rise and Decline of Nations* (1982) explains the economic decline of nations with the formation of several groups that, during stable periods, capture rents from the government, concentrating benefits on themselves while dispersing costs on the unorganised majority. He therefore identifies the formation and growth of these groups, or distributional coalitions, as the main feature of any stable country with defined boundaries. In other words, any country that has not suffered severe social disruptions tends to "naturally" generate these groups (classes, castes, professional guilds, etc.). As these groups protect themselves from competition to extract rents, lower economic inefficiency is the result, which ultimately leads nations to reduced economic growth. Relying on many empirical cases taken from the whole globe, Olson's work provides examples of countries that experienced rapid growth because of the war-caused destruction of their established traditional coalitions; examples such as Germany and Japan after World War II.

Olson (1971) does not use the logic of multilevel selection to explain the tendency for group forces to operate in society. Instead, he uses the logic of collective action, which depends on rational choice assumptions. Still, what is relevant in this case is his acknowledgment of how group forces are natural, constant and empirically observable throughout the world. Yet, by basing his assumptions on rational choice theory, Olson's theory of collective action is substantially different from the logic of multilevel selection, especially in explaining group formation. He argues that large groups will always suffer from the effect of self-interested free riders that will contribute nothing to the group but still reap the benefits. As in a public good scenario, each self-interested and rational individual has incentives to contribute nothing to the public good and to reap the benefits of what others invested. These incentives ultimately make the provision of public goods very difficult to achieve. Hence, because it is easier to monitor and prevent free riding in smaller groups, small groups will tend to prevail while large groups cannot mobilise and defend their common interests. Put differently, the larger a group is, the higher the costs of monitoring cheaters and the more the benefits will have to be distributed by more people, diminishing the gains for each group member. Thus, group members will not provide the public goods required for the existence of the group if the costs of punishing free riding outweigh the benefits. In theory, the bigger the group is, the harder it will be to solve this collective action problem and big groups will not achieve their common goals; only small groups will do so efficiently (Olson, 1971).

While the question of group size is surely relevant in a multilevel selection logic, this logic emphasises group competition vs individual competition. Hence, the observed social outcomes will depend on group competition; and these group forces will determine if groups successfully suppress within-group (i.e. individual) competition, allowing group forces to prevail over individual forces. Therefore, a group of altruists will have much lower costs of punishing free riders than a group of mostly egoistic individuals. This challenges Olson's logic of collective action in the sense that a large group of altruists can mobilise collective action more efficiently than a small group of egoists. If large altruistic groups are better at mobilising is, of course, a question of empirical assessment. It is possible that, in many situations, groups work just like rational choice economists theorise. Still, it is also possible to observe real cases of individuals providing public goods, which are non-excludable and non-rival, without the need to punish free riders extensively. Peter Turchin gives one example related to war:

> There is, however, one area where the rational choice theory fails utterly-in explaining why people cooperate. Take volunteering for the army when your country is attacked. The cost—the risk of injury or death—is substantial. The benefit—preventing the defeat that might entail paying war reparations, being evicted from your home, enslaved, or even killed—is also substantial. However, the cost of enlisting you bear directly, whereas the benefit is shared equally among everybody (what economists call the public good). Your participation, or not, in the army of millions is not going to make any appreciable difference to the outcome of the war. By failing to join the army, you will reap all the benefits of victory without bearing any of the costs. According to the rational choice theory, this is precisely what a rational agent should do. Of course, if everybody behaves in this rational manner, nobody will volunteer, and the invaders will win. If nobody volunteers, however, you have even more reason not to enlist—a one-person army is certainly going to be defeated. In other words, whatever others do, it is in your interest not to enlist (to "defect"). In a society of rational agents, everybody will defect, with the end result that collective action will always fail. The economist Mancur Olson called this logical deduction the "collective-action problem". (Turchin, 2006, p. 93)

Of course, one could argue that people go to war because others force them to, but this would simply be a second-order collective action problem: governments could send enforcement squads to the cities to shoot all the ones that do not volunteer. Here, the rational citizen that does not want to die would volunteer. But one must ask who would take part in these enforcement squads. Rational egoists would probably not participate in these squads because the costs might be too high, such as being killed by masses of rioters that reject being drafted. Also, the benefits of resisting invaders are dispersed among everybody, so the same logic that applies to enlisting in the army also applies to enlisting in the enforcement squads (Turchin, 2006, p. 93). This second-order collection action problem seems to have no solution if only rational egoists populated the world.

One could apply a similar logic to other situations, like taxation, where if nobody wanted to pay voluntarily, it would be impossible to solve the second-order collective-action problem and therefore taxation would be impossible. This is not to say that all taxation is voluntary, but that part of this process of financial contribution to the government of one's group is indeed voluntary. Hence, it is possible to explain eusociality and the evolution of altruism with group forces that operate within the framework of multilevel selection. Individual sacrifice in favour of one's group is empirically observable in situations where the egoistic/self-interested and rational decision of all individuals would be to cheat and to free ride.

Both multilevel selection and Olson's logic of collective action explain the natural formation of groups in the social realm, but they differ in their assumptions and theoretical explanation. From the evolutionary perspective of multilevel selection one should adhere to behavioural pluralism in every group of individuals. Along with within and between-group forces, cooperation will then depend on the level of altruists, egoists and cooperators in each group. Elinor Ostrom came to a similar conclusion after acknowledging public goods games data that show different behavioural propensities by individuals: "I believe that one is forced by these well-substantiated facts to adopt a more eclectic (and classical) view of human behaviour" (Ostrom, 2000, p. 141).

Ostrom uses a slightly different categorisation than Peter Turchin. While Turchin divided individuals into Knaves (egoists), Moralists (conditional cooperators) and Saints (unconditional cooperators), Ostrom uses 3 types of norm-using players: conditional cooperators, willing punishers and rational egoists. She explains that conditional cooperators are the ones that "are willing to initiate cooperative action when they estimate others will reciprocate and to repeat these actions as long as a sufficient proportion of the others involved reciprocate" (Ostrom, 2000, p. 142). Still, these conditional cooperators vary in their level of tolerance for free riders, so some will cooperate and contribute more than others to collective causes. Moreover, conditional cooperators seem to be a substantial proportion of the population, since most one-shot experiments show initial cooperations rates between 40 and 60% (Ostrom, 2000, p. 142). The willing punisher is a type of player that "is willing, if given an opportunity, to punish presumed free riders through verbal rebukes or to use costly material payoffs when available" (Ostrom, 2000, p. 142). Many times, a willing punisher is also a willing rewarder, rewarding those who contributed the most to the common cause. In addition, a conditional cooperator can also be a willing punisher. As Ostrom puts it: "Together, conditional cooperators and willing punishers create a more robust opening for collective action and a mechanism for helping it grow" (Ostrom, 2000, p. 142). The question of knowing exactly why these punishers exist and engage in costly second-order altruism is one of considerable importance in evolutionary theory. Nonetheless, public goods games that allowed for a mechanism of punishment of free riders ended with a considerable level of punishment at the cost of the punisher, which contradicts the assumption that all individuals are rational egoists and that they would not be willing to contribute to a cause with dispersed benefits. Punishment, as aforementioned, enhances collective action in relation to the absence of it. Finally, the last type of player is the rational egoist that behaves like standard rational choice theory predicts: unless a group is very small, rational self-interested individuals will not act to achieve common goals, at least not without coercion or some similar mechanism.

4.1.3 The Evolution of Cooperation: Inclusive Fitness, Multilevel Selection and Rational Choice

Elinor Ostrom suggests that the reason we find more conditional cooperators than other types of individuals can be found in evolutionary theories: "Those of our ancestors who solved these problems most effectively, and learned how to recognize who was deceitful and who was a trustworthy reciprocator, had a selective advantage over those who did not" (Ostrom, 2000, p. 143). Thus, evolutionary theories can provide useful explanations to the key question that Ostrom poses: "How could these norm-using types of players (conditional reciprocators and willing punishers) have emerged and survived in a world of rational egoists?" (Ostrom, 2000, p. 143).

Multilevel selection theory is an evolutionary approach that might be useful to answer such a question, explaining the dynamic of group competition and how that competition affects social norms. It is also helpful to explain how social norms and free riding punishment enhances adaptability and survival rates; or in the language of multilevel selection: individual egoists evolutionarily beat altruists within groups, but more cohesive, cooperative and altruistic groups evolutionarily beat more egoistic groups. This process enhances the perpetuation rates of the individuals inside altruistic groups in relation to less altruistic groups.

In the social realm, groups differ according to the different types of individuals that constitute them. Still, different types of interests are likely to imply different forms of cooperation. Even though the ultimate evolutionary interests of individuals rely on reproductive success, proximate interests can vary considerably. These proximate interests can be crystallised in the various and distinctive ways people cooperate. Also, proximate interests can be maladaptive when the context changes and old evolutionary preferences/capacities that remain no longer serve ultimate interests. Surely, ultimate interests, such as maximising reproductive fitness, appear to be obvious in the way people cooperate with kin and family. Yet, proximate interests are probably more difficult to assess: these differ substantially in the way people cooperate at work, in the way they cooperate for collective defence, in how they work in the marketplace or in how they deal with family members. It is reasonable to assume that individuals interested in cooperating in one field (e.g. at work) might not be interested in cooperating in another field (e.g. reproduction or common defence), or individuals might cooperate with different intensities and commitments.

Inclusive fitness theory offers a good rule of thumb. Inclusive fitness claims altruism can evolve if individuals are more altruistic towards the ones that carry a higher percentage of their altruistic genes (Hamilton, 1975). Scientists have empirically verified this predictive power in the last decades in various fields, like sex allocation, policing, conflict resolution, cooperation, altruism, kin discrimination, cannibalism, eusociality, sibling conflict, etc. Even though inclusive fitness is not the only evolutionary model, it has already proven to be very successful and productive in explaining social behaviour (Abbot et al., 2011). Even when Martin Nowak, Corina Tarnita and E. O. Wilson (2010) generated a scientific controversy by arguing, against a scientific consensus, that inclusive fitness theory is not a precise evolutionary model, they conceded that it can be a heuristic (Nowak, Tarnita, & Wilson, 2011). This heuristic, of course, can be useful for social scientists studying human affairs without directly applying biological mathematical models. In addition, proponents of multilevel selection models like David Sloan Wilson or Herbert Gintis (2012) postulate that inclusive fitness theory is also part of multilevel selection theory, being just another perspective on the study of the evolution of altruism that ultimately should lead to the same predictions. David Queller (2012), a proponent of inclusive fitness theory, claims the same. In the words of David Sloan Wilson:

> Multilevel selection theory accounts for gene frequency change in the total population by creating the categories 'within-group selection' and 'between-group selection'. The inclusive fitness theory method creates the categories 'genes identical by descent' vs. 'genes that represent a random draw from the gene pool'. Neither is wrong and they deserve to coexist if they are useful for different purposes. (Wilson, 2012)

If the strength of cooperation can vary according to the type of activity/goal and to the traits/relatedness of individuals in groups, it is possible to talk about intensities of cooperation and, accordingly, about different kinds of collective interests. In Hamilton's (1975) revised theory of inclusive fitness, relatedness means a statistical measure of the number of similar genes individuals share with each other, which may influence their degree of altruism. A concept that is, in his own words, "more general than (simple) kin selection" (Hamilton, 1975, pp. 140–141). Hence, the fact that a gene can increase its evolutionary success by promoting the perpetuation of those individuals who carry it influences the intensities and direction of cooperation. Yet, unlike inclusive fitness, multilevel selection does not focus on genetic relatedness only and any trait can, in theory, define a group. This trait can be of a genetic/behavioural nature and also of a cultural kind. Because inclusive fitness has a strong empirical validation (Abbot et al., 2011), as Frank Salter puts it: "the most likely and hence common type of group selection has probably operated between extended kin groups, or, more accurately, between groups separated by a significant genetic distance" (Salter, 2003, p. 47). It is not surprising that genetic similarity can play an important part since, according to neo-darwinist theory, genetic propagation is an ultimate interest. This, of course, from a multilevel selection perspective, does not invalidate other types of group selection operating on class, family, guild or caste or, generality speaking, cultural groups.

Using his classic, rational choice-based, logic of collective action, Mancur Olson (1982) explained the existence of guilds by describing them as rent-seekers. These rent-seekers protect their business by legally capturing the government in order to prevent economic competition, concentrating the benefits on the in-group users and dispersing the costs on everyone else (i.e. on the unorganised majority). He suggests that it is possible to explain the existence of castes, namely the Indian ones, in the same way. The castes' purpose, he claims, is to monopolise resources, and rules like endogamy and out-group discrimination are in place to keep power and to prevent the group from getting too big. Becoming a large group disperses benefits too much and hence diminishes the benefits for each group member. Keeping the group at a small level is also important to lower the costs of monitoring free riding.

Along with the rational choice model of collective action espoused by Olson, the same example of the caste system can be explained both by multilevel selection theory and by inclusive fitness theory in distinct ways that do not clash. The two evolutionary models merely see the same phenomenon from a different accounting perspective. Multilevel selection would explain the logic of castes by emphasising group competing forces that maximise the fitness of the group vis-à-vis other groups. It can also explain the endogamous laws that Olson mentions in terms of suppression of free riders, laws that prevent egoists from undermining the strength and cohesion of the group when competing against other collectives (i.e. suppression of within-group competition to favour between-group competition). The caste itself relies on a specific amount of traits that bind the group. On the other hand, inclusive fitness theory would set an explanation based on an evolved preference to protect others that are genetically related; which can explain the rules for endogenous mating and also the ostensive in-group (caste) preference in behavioural terms. In this case, the logic would be: the more concentration of their own genes in a group the more cooperation one could expect.

These three visions of collective action and human behaviour (rational choice, multilevel selection and inclusive fitness) are different accounting perspectives of the same phenomenon, which is the tendency for humans to set groups and cooperate with them and against them. Such perspectives are not incompatible with each other, apart from what Elinor Ostrom called: Olson's "zero contribution thesis" (Ostrom, 2000, p. 137). Here, all individuals try to free ride and contribute nothing to any public good unless the group is quite small, working with face to face accountable members, or unless there is coercion to force them to cooperate towards common interests. Still, this "zero contribution thesis" is contradicted by real-world evidence (Ostrom, 2000, p. 137). Hence, to have a "logic of collective action" based on rational choice, one must relax the meaning of rational self-interest and include a more pluralistic set of behaviours.

4.2 Morality as a Group Phenomenon

My understanding of morality and of its impact on preferences derives from the logic of multilevel selection. I therefore conceptualise morality as a group phenomenon that tries to suppress free riding within groups in competition with other groups. Next, I discuss the social controls and punishment mechanisms that groups utilise to keep moral conformity, while equally analysing how morality/culture can be adaptive or maladaptive.

4.2.1 Morals Within Multilevel Selection: Group Cohesion Under Inter-group Competition

In relation to the origins of morality, prominent primatologist Frans de Waal (2006, Part I) criticised the conception he coined "the veneer theory". This theory characterises morality as a cultural overlay, as a thin veneer that hides a true selfish and brutish nature. Discordantly, Waal (2014) shows that other animals, in particular primates, also reveal instinctive unselfish and cooperative behaviour without having what we might call "a morality" in the human sense of the word (i.e. which implies conscience through reason). His finding enlightens what Hume, Nietzsche and others have already conceptualised: that morality is a product of human innate psychological mechanisms. In particular, Waal demonstrates that animals show purpose and ideal states of social organisation to which they strive for. These ideal states might be physical structures like nests and webs or behavioural standards of social relationships. In his own words, animals "frequently correct deviations from this ideal by reconciling after conflict, protesting against unequal divisions and breaking up fights amongst others. They behave normatively in the sense of correcting, or trying to correct deviations from an ideal state" (de Waal, 2014, p. 64). They act in group-oriented ways, or at least in ways that aim at preserving harmony within their social network. Yet, differences in relation to human morality remain: it becomes difficult to know if primates experience shame or feel any sense of obligation to be good, as they do not seem to extend their concerns to spheres beyond theirs (de Waal, 2014, p. 64). There may be considerable differences in the mechanisms through which groups produce morality, but the observation of primates shows that for a cooperative behaviour to arise, reasoned morality is not a necessary condition.

However, human groups can and do use morality in ways which are not simply instinctive but that also involve reasonable, intelligible and often verbalised understanding. It is not just a brute instinct with no normative abstract theorisation. Morality in human groups can therefore be shaped and come to existence via several means. Social psychologist Jonathan Haidt offers a descriptive and functional account of moral systems:

> Moral systems are interlocking sets of values, virtues, norms, practices, identities, institutions, technologies, and evolved psychological mechanisms that work together to suppress or regulate self-interest and make cooperative societies possible. (Haidt & Kesebir, 2010, p. 800)

Although evolved social norms and prevalent ideologies/values make up common forms of morality, religion is a special source of moral guidance. According to the expert on religion Ara Norenzayan, growing evidence suggests that supernatural monitoring and related practices increase the level of prosociality towards strangers in imagined moral/religious communities. Still, he adds that the origins of morality do not relate to religious cognition, as Waal hinted by observing the prosociality of naturally unreligious primates. Thus, "religious prosociality is (…) best explained as a cultural process, where supernatural beings, over time and in some places, became more omniscient, more omnipotent, and more moralizing. In doing so, these gods spread by galvanizing large-scale cooperation at an unprecedented scale" (Norenzayan, 2014, p. 244). This cultural process can have a religious nature. Yet, it can also assume secular forms of moral systems because humans possess innate moral instincts that are often directed towards family, friends and allies, but can also extend to strangers under the "right" conditions (Norenzayan, 2014, pp. 243–244). Accordingly, it is possible to witness examples of majority atheist societies (e.g. Northern Europe) that are cooperative and relatively peaceful (Zuckerman, 2008). Norenzayan attributes the existence of such moral, yet non-religious societies to cultural evolution. That is, the same cultural process that gave rise to prosocial religions with big gods also gave rise to recent secular institutional mechanisms that promote large-scale cooperation. Hence, "these social monitoring and norm-enforcement mechanism, coupled with an innately given repertoire of moral emotions (…) have fashioned a new social phenomenon (…): cooperative moral communities without belief in big gods" (Norenzayan, 2014, p. 244). This, of course, does not determine that morality without gods can be more adaptive or even as adaptive as moralities with gods, it merely shows that there is a natural morality beyond religion.

The notion of culture, which is the immaterial property of social groups, contains all these elements that derive from morality (social norms, institutions, etc.), regardless of the latter being of a secular or religious nature. Culture can be something larger than morality but morality is certainly underpinning culture. For instance, the use of a language in a particular group is part of culture and not necessarily a moral feature, but the choice, duty or obligation to speak such a language entails notions of good or bad, appropriate or inappropriate. Robert Boyd and Peter Richerson give a general definition of culture based on information:

> Culture is information capable of affecting individuals' behaviour that they acquire from other members of their species through teaching, imitation, and other forms of social transmission. By information we mean any kind of mental state, conscious or not, that is acquired or modified by social learning and affects behavior. (Boyd & Richerson, 2005, p. 5)

Culture encompasses ideas, beliefs, skills, knowledge, that is, any immaterial process that affects behaviour. In this sense, culture is larger than morality, but morality is part of culture. Morality is the part of a culture that regulates what skills are "permissible", what ideas should be materialised and even what beliefs individuals should allow if they are to respect a given group culture. Also, it is important to refer that single individuals can produce and rethink morality, but such new ideas will only become morality when one intends to apply them to groups (i.e. to more than one individual in interaction with others). Ultimately, morality aims at group cohesion while immorality is an infringement on such cohesion.

If one traces evolutionary theory back to Charles Darwin, one can note that he considered tribe (group) selection to be essential in understanding the process of natural selection. On this he wrote clearly:

> There can be no doubt that a tribe including many members who, from possessing in a high degree the spirit of patriotism, fidelity, obedience, courage, and sympathy, were always ready to aid one another, and to sacrifice themselves for the common good would be victorious over most other tribes; and this would be natural selection. (Darwin, 1871, p. 166)

Here, Darwin identifies the role of morality in transforming groups into adaptive units of selection, at least to a degree. From the logic of multilevel selection, it is possible to understand that there is a prevalent tension between the interests of the individual and the ones of the group. Therefore, the point where a group works as a perfect unit of selection is difficult to achieve. Still, as David Sloan Wilson points out, groups can evolve into adaptive units (i.e. units of selection) under the right special conditions. He postulates that "in human groups it is often religion that provides the special conditions" (Wilson, 2002, p. 6). As we have seen, morality does not need religious supranatural gods to create those special conditions as long as the mechanisms are strong enough to punish free riders, i.e. anti-group elements, and to enforce group moral norms.

Multilevel selection theory postulates that natural selection occurs at different levels: gene, individual organism and groups. For selection to occur at the group level instead of the individual level, group forces (competition between groups) must be stronger than individual forces (competition within groups) (Wilson, Sheldon, & O'Gorman, 2008). Groups that suppress anti-group free riders who act for their own benefit outcompete other groups that cannot overcome such a collective action problem. Hence, cohesive groups are better prepared to maximise fitness than groups plagued by egoistic free riding. Moreover, in relation to the actual processes of selection, even though warfare and tribal conflicts have been notoriously prevalent throughout human evolution (Keeley, 1996) and are likely to be a strong source of selection, they are not the only selection processes. Other forms of selection can come from differential birth rates, migration in large numbers, conquest or dominant assimilation. Ultimately, by influencing these outcomes, morality becomes entwined with the fitness-based success of groups.

4.2.2 Morality: Social Controls and Adaptation

Social control is a fundamental part of maintaining the moral standards of a collective. Such a control takes place via the punishing of anti-group/free rider elements. It then appears that highly functional and competitive groups could exist simply on the basis of social control, without the need to have true self-sacrificing, group-oriented individuals. Perhaps even a society of pure rational egoists would act functionally because of the fear of being punished for deviation. But this begs the question of who would engage in the dangerous tasks of enforcing rules and morals. Only self-sacrificing pro-group altruistic individuals would pay the costs of engaging in such tasks because to cause others to provide a public good is also a public good. This is what economists call a second-order public good (Heckathorn, 1990, 1993). Natural altruism, or some degree of it, is necessary to solve these collective action problems, to create social control mechanisms and to enforce moral norms. Still, not all members of a group must be natural altruists for the group to function on a uniform moral basis. Some might be simply "overt altruists" (Wilson, 2002, p. 19) who are good at avoiding punishment for deviation and therefore conform to the prevailing social norms, even if their acts of altruism within conformity are not, strictly speaking, voluntary. In these cases, perhaps the fear of punishment is stronger than existing free riding/self-serving tendencies. For David Sloan Wilson and philosopher Elliott Sober (1998, Chapter IV), social control "can be regarded as a form of low cost altruism that evolves to promote behaviours that would qualify as high-cost altruism if they were performed voluntarily" (Wilson, 2002, p. 19). Yet, it is likely that a moral framework will give more advantages (prestige, higher reputation, etc.) to individuals who voluntarily show high virtue in fulfilling morals than to those who simply do not infringe rules. Hence, any moral framework will select individuals who are naturally fit to thrive under that framework and will also select against those individuals who are not, often through removal, incarceration or ostracisation.

Morality serves the function of transforming human groups into adaptive units or units of selection (Wilson, 2002, p. 20). Anthropologist Chris Boehm developed the idea that human groups are moral communities by recalling a consensual point within the field of anthropology: humans evolved in small hunter-gatherer societies that were considerably egalitarian. Evidence shows that, within the community, hunter-gatherers shared meat, water and general resources, regardless of the community having hunters that were better than others. This is also true for families. Immediate families of good hunters would get no more resources than the rest of the group, even though the groups themselves would probably make up an extended family of genetic relatedness (Hill, Hurtado, & Kaplan, 1984; Kaplan & Hill, 1985a, 1985b). Boehm (1999) identified this moral egalitarianism as a form of "reverse dominance", where numerous tribe members band together to force the most dominant, stronger, with better skills, alpha male elements to share the product of their accomplishments and to prevent being dominated by these "stronger" individuals. In the language of multilevel selection: the "weaker" elements band together to suppress individual advantages at the cost of the group (i.e. within-group selection), thus attempting to create a more cohesive group (i.e. between-group selection). Of course, societies can have hierarchies, inequality and higher authority to operate functionally when these societies grow to high numbers and face-to-face organisation is no longer viable, but this was not the case with small hunter-gatherer groups. Boehm claims that human groups are naturally hierarchical, but he adds that "egalitarianism is in effect a bizarre type of political hierarchy: the weak combine forces to actively dominate the strong" (Boehm, 1999, p. 3) (…) and also adds that "egalitarianism involves a very special type of hierarchy, a curious type that is based on antihierarchical feelings" (Boehm, 1999, p. 4). This is a similar notion to the moral phenomenon that Friedrich Nietzsche (2003b) dubbed "slave morality", in which the "weak" generate and institutionalise an egalitarian morality to prevent the "strong" from being dominant. Still, some domination within groups in the form of hierarchy can be adaptive if it increases the adaptability of large groups. Therefore, the domination of certain individuals within groups can be a matter of "within group" selection, but it can also be a question of "between-group" selection. Each case must be analysed separately. David Sloan Wilson sums up this point in the following way:

> It is (…) an open question whether extreme status differences and other seeming inequalities in large-scale societies represent domination pure and simple or rather design features that enable the society to function at a large scale, especially in competition with other societies. There can be little doubt that size itself can be a group-level adaptation. Larger societies tend to replace smaller societies unless their larger size is offset by problems of coordination and internal conflicts of interest. (Wilson, 2002, p. 36)

The idea of human groups as moral communities can shed light on the nature of moral patterns. This idea can explain why ideologies, myths/social norms and religion are so prevalent in human societies. Boehm goes as far as claiming that "ideologies are at the core of this analysis" because, in the case of "reverse dominance", to "equalize a political society it is necessary for the rank and file to form a moral community, develop an egalitarian ethos and deliberately take charge" (Boehm, 1999, p. 12). The same could be said of any non-egalitarian hierarchical ideology that aims to maximise group welfare. Hence, communities and governments require a specific morality to function in harmony. This moral requirement equally explains why governments (e.g. ancient regime...) have traditionally relied on the clergy for social-moral guidance. It appears that religion is effective for social control: not only individuals monitor each other for deviant behaviours, but individuals also monitor themselves because of having respect towards an omnipresent god. Hence, religion has the incredible potential to coordinate and harmonise large societies even when the capacity for enforcement and monitoring of rules is weak, as it was the case in earlier pre-bureaucratic and pre-technological times.

Morality as a standard framework that underpins social control requires innate tendencies for individuals to cooperate and punish lack of cooperation. Scholars have often observed and tested these tendencies. Most relevantly, Herbert Gintis showed evidence of "strong reciprocity" by identifying strong reciprocators, that is, individuals who are "predisposed to cooperate with others and punish non-cooperators, even when this behaviour cannot be justified in terms of extended kinship or reciprocal altruism" (Gintis, 2000, p. 169). Experimental and behavioural economists Ernst Fehr and Simon Gächter also find that "there is indeed a wide-spread willingness of the cooperators to punish the free-riders"; their experimental results "indicate that this holds true even if punishment is costly and does not provide any material benefits for the punisher"; they equally find that "free-riders are punished the more heavily the more they deviate from the cooperation levels of the cooperators" (Fehr & Gächter, 2000, p. 980). They conclude that potential free riders have the option of avoiding punishment by increasing their levels of cooperation and that punishment can indeed reduce free riding (Fehr & Gächter, 2000, p. 980). Others have come to similar points regarding the innate features that underpin moral systems. Evolutionary psychologists Lena Cosmides and John Tooby's (1992) work suggests that evolution has equipped humans with a set of computational mechanisms whose function is to detect cheaters. Boyd and Richerson (1985) and E. O. Wilson (1998) have stressed the capacity for conformity while Boehm (1996) has studied the capacity for group unity/cohesion in emergency situations.

4.2.2.1 The "Darwin Machines"

The field of evolutionary psychology has explained behavioural traits on the basis of evolved mental modules that helped humans to survive in pre-historical ages and that were naturally selected (i.e. rejecting the idea that the mind is a general-purpose organ) (Buss, 1999; Cosmides & Tooby, 2001). This raises the question of how one can make sense of this apparent contradiction: if moral frameworks require innate psychological mechanisms, how come morality evolves much faster by cultural evolution than by genetic evolution? David Sloan Wilson (2002, p. 30) considers that although these specific cognitive modules are important, humans have also evolved the capacity to learn, create, develop and to generate culture (and morality) as an open-ended process. He compares the natural capacity to generate culture and moralities to another evolved mechanism: the immune system. "The immune system is an open-ended process of blind variation and selective retention". Hence, evolution creates mechanisms "that are themselves evolutionary and therefore capable of providing new solutions to new problems". In a functioning immune system, "antibodies that match antigens reproduce more, not by chance, but because the immune system has been constructed that way" (Wilson, 2002, pp. 30–31) by natural selection. This process where an evolved mechanism contains evolution within its structure is a "Darwin machine" (Plotkin, 1994). The mind is then better understood if one focuses both on its highly specialised features and on its open-ended capacities. Both the natural tendencies for specific behaviours (e.g. innate preferences) and the capacity to generate new moralities and cultural elements interact and feed on each other.

This view allows for an understanding of the evolution of culture and for why humans developed the capacity to generate new moralities more rapidly than genetic evolution would allow. The most likely reason for the higher relative speed of cultural evolution is the need that our ancestors had to adapt quickly to many environments, which were widely different in time and space, and also to adapt to very unstable climatic conditions, especially during the early stages as a species (Boyd & Richerson, 2000). To merely have specialised cognitive mechanisms seems insufficient to deal with such unstable environments. With these "Darwin machines", humans could come up with workable solutions to new problems that had never arisen in their evolutionary past. Trial and error and an evolved capacity for abstract reasoning are means through which individuals find new solutions (i.e. ideas). Some new ideas fail and perish while successful ones spread through a population. In sum, within certain limits defined by innate tendencies, behaviour can change through cultural and moral evolution without the need for genetic evolution. In terms of group competition, groups that spread the "right" ideas will be more adaptive than groups that do not.

Given this understanding, I can now shed light on the relationship between moral-cultural evolution and genetic evolution; a theoretical framework named "gene-culture coevolution" (Boyd & Richerson, 2008), but also known as "dual inheritance theory".

4.2.3 Gene-Culture Coevolution

The main authorities on the logic of gene-culture coevolution are Robert Boyd and Peter Richerson. Their approach is not only central to understand the role of evolutionary culture/morality in biological evolution but also important to understand the impact of such a process on human preferences. As aforementioned, culture in this context stands for information, which essentially means mental states acquired or modified by social interactions that affect behaviour (Boyd & Richerson, 2005, p. 5). Morality is therefore a part of culture, comprising moral regulatory mechanisms.

Gene-culture coevolution is the acknowledgement that genes and culture interact with one another by creating mutual pressures that, by shaping behaviour, generate the outcomes of biological natural selection (i.e. maximising or reducing fitness). Boyd and Richerson briefly summarise it:

> Evidence suggests that we have an evolved psychology that shapes what we learn and how we think, and that this in turn influences the kind of beliefs and attitudes that spread and persist (…). At the same time, culture and cultural change cannot be understood solely in terms of innate psychology. Culture affects the success and survival of individuals and groups; as a result, some cultural variants spread and others diminish, leading to evolutionary processes that are every bit as real and important as those that shape genetic variation. These culturally evolved environments then affect which genes are favored by natural selection. Over the evolutionary long haul, culture has shaped our innate psychology as much as the other way around. (Boyd & Richerson, 2005, p. 4)

In other words, cultures/moralities become frameworks that choose genes coding for psychological behavioural tendencies that are likely to stay, expand and thrive in a population. For example, if a given social morality forces members of a group to be tribe/group-oriented instead of individualistic or nepotistic, these latter types will diminish in that population. Such types will diminish more or less according to the severity of the punishment for an infringement of moral social rules (death, incarceration, expulsion, job loss, etc.). Conversely, those with the qualities required by the moral and cultural framework would increase in numbers and power. Whatever the successful moral and cultural framework may be, this process evolves by cultural group selection, where groups with more fitness maximising social norms outcompete and outgrow other groups with less beneficial social norms. In the language of multilevel selection, even though cultural group selection can also be seen as a form of biological selection at the group level, it is a process that operates at a faster pace and groups can incorporate the social norms of more successful groups before being selected out of existence. Yet, cultural and moral differentiation between groups increases the possibility of selection at the biological group level to take place, especially due to the observed tendency for conformity (Boyd & Richerson, 1985). In particular, conformity allows for groups to function more cohesively but it may also make it more difficult to change maladaptive social norms at a larger scale. Notwithstanding, considerable changes can occur in relatively short periods of time because of cultural and political revolutions (French Revolution 1789; Iranian Revolution 1979, etc.).

4.2.3.1 Morality/Culture Can Be Adaptive or Maladaptive

If humans evolved the capacity to generate and conform to culture and morality because it was a way to change and adapt behaviour in rapidly changing environments, then culture can generate adaptive behaviour while specialised genetic cognitive modules alone could not (Boyd & Richerson, 2005, p. 7). However, by being open to novel ideas that can be useful in changing environments, our minds also become vulnerable to the evolution of pathological cultural maladaptations that reduce individual and group fitness.

It is worth remembering that fitness is a relative concept. It is not important how well an organism reproduces and survives, what is important is that it reproduces and survives better than alternative types of organisms (Wilson, 2002, p. 38). As known, groups may suppress individuals who maximise fitness at the cost of the group, for instance, by preventing a male from taking most females or from killing the infants of other males, only to assure that fitness competition takes place between distinct groups. Competition for fitness maximisation shifts from the individual level to the group level.

Culture and morality can be adaptive or maladaptive, but this is not an assertion that individuals accept all ideas equally. Boyd and Richerson remind us that "individuals with different psychologies will acquire different beliefs and values that will lead to different fitness outcomes" (...) (Boyd & Richerson, 2005, p. 8) and the same is valid for groups, especially if there is a high degree of genetic relatedness. Yet, culture can override even some of our instincts. For example, even though many herbs taste bitter to humans, which can be a sign that such herbs are unhealthy, some of them have medicinal value and therefore we learn to eat them even though our body does not ask for them. Through taste signals, the body even gives signs of not wanting these herbs (Boyd & Richerson, 2005, p. 11). Economist and political theorist F. A. Hayek made this point to claim that even though most people naturally feel that society should work as a small extended family or tribe, civilization (i.e. the great society) demands people to override those desires. What he meant by this is that the natural instincts that humans evolved from living in small egalitarian tribes had to be overridden in order for the great society of the market order to exist. For him, the repression of these egalitarian instincts is the basis of civilization (von Hayek, 1979, p. 174). He believed that the shift from the instinctive morality of the small tribe to the great society morality was a matter of cultural group selection in the sense that the latter morality would be more adaptive than the former. In his own words, to abandon the small tribe egalitarian instincts "was the price we had to pay for being able to raise a larger number of children" (von Hayek, 1979, p. 168). Still, it is doubtful that all or most evolved instincts have no adaptive value and that therefore individuals should "repress" or override these instincts with an opposing morality. It seems that, in some cases, instinctive practices can be beneficial, such as a natural empathy for children. This process of keeping adaptive instincts while repressing some that are not can be a delicate process indeed.

Culture can be adaptive because it allows for shifts in behaviour under situations of uncertainty and environmental change, sometimes overriding aversive stimuli. Imitation and learning are key aspects of this group process; accordingly:

> Culture is adaptive because the behaviour of other individuals is a rich source of information about which behaviours are adaptive and which are not. We all know that plagiarism is often easier than the hard work of writing something by ourselves; imitating the behaviour of others can be adaptive for the same reason. (Boyd & Richerson, 2005, p. 12)

Put differently, imitating the behaviour of successful individuals within a group lowers the costs of trial and error. This is especially relevant for the not so creative, not so tempered or not so smart. The imitative and cumulative aspect of cultural evolution allows for successful innovations to remain in the population, which is more efficient than if individuals would all try to learn better strategies by themselves while disregarding the knowledge and behaviour of others. Therefore, "when lots of imitation is mixed with a little bit of individual learning, populations can adapt in ways that outreach the abilities of any individual genius" (Boyd & Richerson, 2005, p. 13). Such a process leads to two common characteristics: conformity to the behaviour of the majority and a psychological state that makes people more likely to imitate successful/prestigious individuals. People tend to apply prestige bias when acquiring new behavioural ideas, favouring the ideas of high-status opinion makers (Rogers, 1983). The lower classes are especially prone to imitate the local high-status individuals because the socially distant elites are usually in different realities that are difficult to emulate (Labov, 2001).

4.2.3.2 How Can Morality/Culture Be Maladaptive?

Given such tendencies, how can culture and morality be maladaptive? If natural selection produced a psychology that leads humans to imitate the most prestigious and successful, this must mean that in the Pleistocene foraging societies this psychology led to a higher reproductive success (Borgerhoff-Mulder, 1988a, 1988b; Irons, 1979). It also logically means that there was a high correlation between prestige, success, health, some degree of wealth and large families. Yet, Boyd and Richerson argue that the western world, in this case, USA and Europe, is living a paradigmatic example of how culture can be maladaptive. Even though the people of these areas are living in an age of unprecedented high wealth and safety, unlike their ancestors, they are not using such conditions to maximise their fitness. This becomes clear when acknowledging the current low birth rates of Americans and especially of Europeans, which are below replacement rates (World-Bank, 2013).

When asking for the reasons why modern middle classes have such a low fertility, Boyd and Richerson (2005, Chapter V) offer the following explanations: affluent and influential people are extremely busy and they have more hobbies and possibilities than ever to spend their wealth on (e.g. travelling, shopping, political activities, etc.). Raising children takes time, so they restrain their fertility instead of using all their possibilities to maximise it. To achieve positions of influence one has to dedicate time to one's professional career, having little time left to raise children. This means that the traits required to be a successful professional and the traits required to have large families are different. Hence, because successful individuals, like teachers, professors, bosses, politicians, businessmen, tend towards childlessness and marriage postponement, the culture they "propagate" is a culture where the focus of prestige is in the achievement of professional and material individual success. Gradually, these values of putting one's career ahead of reproduction spread through the population via the imitation of these successful individuals. Because high-status people have the largest share of influence in the production of culture and morality, values and beliefs that led to their success are hailed and propagated. Modernity is then characterised by the evolution of selfish cultural variants. Conversely, in the pre-modern agrarian society, as Boyd and Richerson note,

> the family is the most significant social institution for the majority of the population, the primary unit of production, consumption and socialization (...); very often a strong familial ethic encourages reproduction in order to increase the power of one's lineage or clan. Childless couples are pitied. A large and prosperous family is the greatest achievement to which ordinary men and women can aspire. (Boyd & Richerson, 2005, p. 170)

The modern culture of individualism particularly affects women, given that in traditional societies they derive most of their social status and self-respect from having children and raising them, and not necessarily from having careers. Unsurprisingly, one of the main correlates of the start of the current demographic trend towards low fertility is women's access to education (Billy, Kasarda, & West, 1986).

Evidence shows a disjunction between economic development and the beginning of the decline in fertility rates, which emphasises the effect of cultural and moral change. For instance, France started to have lower fertility rates around 1830 while Britain and Germany only had them around

50 or more years later. This happened even though France had a much slower economic/industrial modernisation, but experienced an earlier and more radical social modernisation than the other two countries (Coale & Watkins, 1986). Finally, one can see the importance of culture and morality in the tremendous difference between western low fertility peoples and subcultural and religious groups who live in the same area, like the Anabaptists (Amish and the Hutterites). Even though these groups have mortality rates in line with western industrial countries, their birth rates rival the pre-modern ones. As a result, groups like the Amish can increase their numbers from 5000 in 1900 to around 140,000 in 1992 and more recently, every twenty years, their population has been doubling (Bowman & Kraybill, 2001; Hostetler, 1993; Kraybill & Olshan, 1994; Peter, 1987).

The particular case of the Amish illustrates how a case of cultural group selection can operate (Harpending & Cochran, 2015). Starting with around 200 elements in the eighteenth century and with almost no converts taken in, the Amish expanded from 200 (eighteenth century) to 280,000 (in 2013) despite having considerable defection rates of individuals that leave their group and their strict pre-modern lifestyle. The defection was actually higher in the distant past (18–24%) than it was in recent years (10–15%). With a very high average birth rate (6 children per woman), the Amish strict culture/morality selects for individuals with a capacity for high fertility and for increased "amishness". In the words of Harpending and Cochran, increased amishness is

> an increase in the degree to which Amish find their lifestyle congenial, since those who like it least, leave. We have called this kind of differential emigration 'boiling off'. Obviously, if some of the soup boils off, what is left is more concentrated. (Harpending & Cochran, 2015, p. 58)

Hence, Amish culture/morality operates as a filter of selection, selecting the individuals with the most appropriate traits to thrive in that culture. When evaluating the relative fast demographic growth of this group, this culture seems to reveal adaptive capacities. The case of the Amish also reveals how cultural group selection interacts with genetic group selection and how culture can be adaptive or maladaptive.

4.2.3.3 "Learning" to Adapt

The final point worth enlightening in gene-culture coevolution theory is the generation of morality and culture; namely, their evolutionary development and the creation of novelty and adaptation. As we have seen, conformity and imitation can be adaptive because of allowing individuals to act like the socially successful others and because of cutting the personal costs of learning new ways to adapt to changing environments. Yet these behaviours can also be maladaptive. The fact is that imitators are "parasites who free ride on the learning of others (…) they contribute nothing to the capacity of the population to adapt to the local environment" (Boyd & Richerson, 2005, p. 99). Thus, a population will only increase its average fitness if it has a considerable number of individuals who are capable and willing to learn how to adapt, who produce cultural and moral information, who bear the costs of learning and who increase their own fitness. Populations deprived of these individuals cannot adapt to changing environments, given that a culture or morality that worked in the past might not work in the present.

Natural selection cannot prevent maladaptive cultural traits from entering a population. The reason is that adaptations by definition involve trade-offs. Even though the predisposed psychology of today is prepared to generate moralities and cultural variants that most likely lead to adaptive outcomes, it does not mean that it will. It is impossible for evolution to make these psychological mechanisms very specific without causing the incapacity to adapt to new environments and challenges through culture and morality. Therefore, because this trade-off exists, cultural maladaptations continue to infiltrate in populations. Perhaps it would be better for young individuals to learn from the parents only while ignoring possible cultural maladaptations that run through society, but this trade-off means that they would also miss out on the available adaptive information that society could provide. Still, as Boyd and Richerson point out, this plasticity is not a reason to claim that most observed traits have no adaptive function. As they put it:

> Much of the variation we see in nature likely is adaptive (…) functional studies demonstrate that organisms are well designed and a vast body of evidence from every part of biology illustrates that all kinds of traits can be understood by asking how these parts function to promote reproductive success. (Boyd & Richerson, 2005, p. 102)

Ultimately, it suffices to reiterate that morality/culture is a vital part of genetic evolution and that it represents a social framework for individual selection within groups competing with out-groups.

4.2.4 Moral Types

The evolved plurality of instinctive predispositions and innate capacities, i.e. the "pluralism of types", influences the morality one is likely to adhere to or to generate. Because of clustering and overlapping traits, an analytical framework of moral types becomes relevant to come to any conclusions. According to philosopher Brian Leiter, this "Doctrine of Types" is an approach that F. Nietzsche famously embraced, understanding that "each person has a fixed psycho-physical constitution, which defines him as a particular type of person" (Leiter, 2007, p. 7). These psycho-physical facts can be defined as "type-facts" and Nietzsche's important claim is that "each person has certain largely immutable physiological and psychic traits that constitute the 'type' of person he or she is" (Leiter, 2007, p. 7). Critical theorist Theodor Adorno had a similar approach, reflected in his claim that moral "ideologies have for different individuals, different degrees of appeal, a matter that depends upon the individual's needs and the degree to which these needs are being satisfied or frustrated" (Adorno, Frenkel-Brunswik, Levinson, & Sandford, 1950, p. 2). His claim includes both innate personality traits and traits that are situational; that is, "situational" in the sense that they depend on one's current environmental situation (Jost, 2006, p. 654). As aforementioned, the conjunction and interaction of these two types of traits, physiological and situational, determine the evolution of morality.

4.2.4.1 Composing the Moral Types

The exact definition or composition of these moral types of individuals can vary from author to author. Still, growing evidence from experimental economics, neuropolitics, among other fields, is helping the endeavour of defining "moral types". As I mentioned previously, Peter Turchin and Elinor Ostrom took similar behavioural "types" from the results of experimental public good games. Turchin (2006, pp. 98–99) created three behavioural types: the "knaves" (rational egoists/free riders), the—"saints"—unconditional cooperators (who will always contribute to the common pool regardless of the contribution of others) and the—"moralists"—conditional cooperators (those willing to contribute to the common pool but who will only do it if they can punish opportunistic free riding behaviour). Ostrom (2000, p. 142) exchanges the "saints" by the "willing punishers" and comes up with three types: Conditional cooperators, rational egoists and willing punishers. The first two are similar types to Turchin's model, but the willing punishers are those who volunteer to punish free riders in order to keep cooperation within a group.

Other academics (Haidt, 2012; Jost, 2006) present these types as being situated along a continuous line based on the familiar political dichotomy "liberal-conservative" (or left vs right wing). Following David Hume's assertion that morality is rooted in sentiments or passions, social psychologist Jonathan Haidt identifies five moral foundations that are innate (i.e. organised in advance of experience) and unevenly distributed in individuals. These evolved five moral foundations are Care/harm, Fairness/cheating, Loyalty/betrayal, Authority/subversion and Sanctity/degradation. The Care/harm foundation is the predisposition to protect children or the ones vulnerable to danger; it is the foundation that makes us oppose cruelty, especially towards the helpless and innocent. The Fairness/cheating foundation is the evolved adaptive trait that allows individuals to benefit from group cooperation without being exploited by free riders; it gives us the tendency to interact with reciprocating individuals and avoid or punish cheaters. The Loyalty/betrayal foundation is necessary to form and maintain coalitions; it makes us reward good team players and shun, expel or even kill those who betray the group. The Authority/subversion foundation evolved because groups with individuals that understood the need for hierarchical relationships would outperform dysfunctional groups where most elements were attempting to have the same positions; it makes us sensitive to status, rank and behaviour according to social position. At last, the Sanctity/degradation foundation is the tendency to sacralise purity and to invest objects with an untouchable value; pure environments help to bind groups, fight alien pathogens or parasites and prevent degradation of group properties (Haidt, 2012, pp. 153–154).

The innate foundations identified by Haidt (2012, p. 154) are unevenly present in individuals. Empirical studies on this topic show that "the left (liberal) relies primarily on the Care and Fairness foundations, whereas the right (conservative) uses all five". Specifically, Haidt et al. (2009) found that the more conservative (right) a person was, the more all five foundations were present; while the more liberal (left) a person was, the more Care and Fairness were present but the less the other three foundations were there. Some studies even found that a very conservative person values Loyalty, Authority and Sanctity slightly more than Care and Fairness (Haidt, 2012, pp. 160–161). This evidence seems to show that conservative-minded people have characteristics that are group or tribe oriented (i.e. they value religious postulates, purity, group order, punishment of norms deviators, self-sacrifice, hierarchy, authority, etc.); while liberal-minded people tend to be individualistic; mostly focusing on Care and Fairness, usually of an egalitarian sort, in line with John Stuart Mill's (1859) harm principle, where the only limit on individual action is the prevention of harm to others. Additionally, Haidt suggests a sixth foundation called "Liberty/oppression", which is the natural tendency to rebel and join forces against abusive authority. A distrust of abusive authority is present in both liberals and conservatives, with the main difference that liberals tend to focus on universal humanity and underdogs while conservatives focus on defending their group against supranational entities or against forced/coercive wealth or status redistribution (Haidt, 2012, p. 175).

Social psychologists John Jost and David Amodio (2006, 2012) gathered evidence for the innateness of moral foundations. Most saliently, neuroscientist Ryota Kanai and his team performed MRI scans on 90 British students and found that the greater the level of self-reported conservatism the larger the right amygdala of the brain was (Kanai et al., 2011). This part of the brain relates to the capacity to perceive and identify threats, and also relates to feelings of disgust. Yet, the more liberal students showed a relatively larger anterior cingulate cortex, which is a part of the brain associated with conflict monitoring and with dealing with conflicting information. These results suggest that the difference between moral/political "types" is due to pre-wired evolved traits. Because of a higher perception of possible threats coming from drastic changes, conservatives are more likely to embrace Haidt's six foundations, while liberals, more open to managing novel information and paying less attention to threats, focus mainly on the basics (e.g. Care and Fairness).

Political scientists (2005, 2011) have studied the association between genes and various moral and political behaviours assessing both gene association and twin studies, all pointing towards a considerable degree of genetic influence on social attitudes. For instance, Olson, Vernon, Harris, and Jang (2001) studied 194 monozygotic and 141 same-sex dizygotic twin pairs and found that there are powerful heritability effects for attitudes concerning education, abortion, death penalty, religion, etc. As Jost and Amodio conclude: "Many studies involving quite diverse samples and methods suggest that political and religious views reflect a reasonably strong genetic basis" (Amodio & Jost, 2012,

p. 61). However, they quickly add that, together with dispositional factors, environmental and situational factors are also of importance in defining moral attitudes. Experimental evidence reveals that priming individuals with images of death, like of dead bodies or funerals, makes liberals, moderates and conservatives endorse more conservative opinions on a vast array of public policies, from same-sex marriage to stem cell research, and hence show support for conservative leaders (Fitszimons, Jost, & Kay, 2004). Indeed, approval rates for President Bush increased every time his government would raise the terror alert levels between 2001 and 2004, which is a good example of the capacity of individuals to become more "groupish" in times of out-group menaces (Willer, 2004). There are also examples of "conservative" shifts in people that were not initially conservative: John Jost reveals that "survivors in New York City were asked 18 months after 9/11 whether they had grown more liberal, more conservative or stayed the same since the terrorist attacks (...)" and "results revealed that 38% of the sample overall reported that they had become more conservative which was three times as many people (13%) who reported that they had grown more liberal" (Jost, 2006, p. 663). These results suggest that although conservatives have a comparatively deepened sense of threat and disgust, such a sense is not absent in more liberal-minded people and can be activated in certain situations, even if requiring stronger stimulus.

4.2.4.2 Liberals and Conservatives?

These two moral types are not without controversy. Not only do they seem to reflect western post-French Revolution political categories, they may also present difficulties when carefully analysed. When defining the core dimensions that separate liberalism and conservatism, John Jost (along with D. Amodio) identifies two decisive points: "a) advocating versus resisting social change (as opposed to tradition) and b) rejecting versus accepting inequality" (Amodio & Jost, 2012, p. 56). There is extensive evidence showing that liberals are more open to experience, that they reveal cognitive complexity and that they display a higher tolerance of uncertainty. The same evidence shows that conservatives present higher death anxiety, fear of threat and loss, intolerance of ambiguity and a personal need for order and authority (Glaser, Jost, Kruglanski, & Sulloway, 2003a, 2003b). Hence, judging this evidence by Jost's two core dimensions of these two types, one naturally concludes that, unlike liberals, conservatives accept inequality because of a comparatively higher fear of change and potential chaos. Such an idea is strengthened by Block and Block (2006) who showed that three-year-old children who were rated by their teachers as indecisive, vulnerable, fearful, rigid and inhibited became more politically conservative when they grew up. Conversely, these teachers rated those who would become adult liberals as resilient, energetic and emotionally expressive when they were three years old.

According to this evidence, it is difficult to explain why history is not a flat line of liberal regimes but instead largely constituted by the opposite (kingdoms, theocracies, castes, chiefdoms, autocracies, etc.). After all, it is difficult to imagine that such introverted, vulnerable and fearful individuals could take power and rule in so many societies. Certainly, many regimes and states arose by force or conquest. These individuals (e.g. D. Afonso Henriques of Portugal; Alexander the Great of Macedon) who conquered lands or states by force could not be very fearful of change. They were imposing change. They could not be too fearful of death. They often risked their lives. Hence, by Jost's criterion, these conquerors would not be conservatives. But their aristocratic ethos, the sense of military honour and loyalty, sometimes spiritual devotion, the representation of a specific group identity and hierarchical authority made sure they were not egalitarian and hardly liberals. On the contrary, following Haidt's six moral foundations, the latter characteristics describe conservatives better.

4.2.4.3 Moral Types: Complex yet Necessary

Jost's minimal definition for the distinction of the two types, liberals versus conservatives, is at least incomplete. Haidt's moral types reveal a complexity that is better suited to social analysis because it does not rely so much on the insufficient pro-change/anti-change and equality-inequality foundations. Nonetheless, Haidt's dichotomy "liberal versus conservatism" can be read from another dichotomic point of view: group-phobia versus group-philia types. Group-phobia would characterise individuals that operate against the interests of a given group because of rational egoist reasons or because they do not identify with their current collective. Group-philia represents the classic self-sacrificing group-oriented individual who will strive for the prosperity of the in-group. This can be read in the liberal (individualistic) versus conservative (tribal) dichotomy. Yet, a closer look might reveal incompatibilities. As Christopher Boehm (1999) postulated, all evolved practical political systems are hierarchical. Egalitarian tribal morality is a form of "reverse domination" or egalitarian domination. Such egalitarianism is usually regarded as non-conservative and yet it is perfectly possible to find moral types whose ideologies are egalitarian but who are at the same time very pro-group competition (e.g. Kim Jong-Il communist regime from North Korea). In other words, it is possible that some individuals might think that more egalitarian societies are better prepared for group competition than societies with structural inequalities of ranks or wealth. Once again, this fits badly under the label "conservatism". Moreover, some of these pro-group individuals are revolutionaries; which also fits badly under the term "conservatism" as a doctrine averse to change. Yet, as Haidt (2012, p. 313) pointed out, liberalism, like any system of values, also "binds and blinds" individuals to their moral group. This leads us to think that liberalism/individualism, regardless of its universal ethos, is a group strategy or a group phenomenon, as Durkheim postulated. But by operating mostly with the moral foundations of Care and Fairness, liberal groups have more difficulties in terms of group competition, self-definition, collective union, uniformity of behaviour and cohesion. All these features require more than the two moral foundations of Care and Fairness. Still, it is a group strategy, a form of hierarchical reverse domination, complicating a potential reading of the dichotomy "liberal versus conservatism" as a form of group-phobia versus group-philia.

Individuals can also be seen as anti-group because of trying to generate or impose a new moral framework through the disruption of the prevailing norms of their own group. It is not always clear that this is so. To complicate the question further, it is possible that the intention to reform the current group norms comes from pro-group reasons. For instance, when the generator of a new morality believes that the group will be better off with a new set of morals. Despite the complexity at hand, the construction of behaviourally pluralist moral types is a fundamental basis for the analysis of social institutions and preferences.

4.2.4.4 On Innate Drives

The success of institutions depends heavily on the types that shape and operate in institutional venues. Certainly, to diagnose such types is a difficult task given the interaction of innate drives and cultural/moral social artefacts. Yet, even under these difficulties, the "plurality", i.e. the analysis according to types, has the advantage of removing the conceptual misleading assumption of behavioural uniformity of self-interest/

rational-egoism, which is so prevalent in public choice analysis. In addition, a moral/behavioural type may always be an unfinished and somehow fluid object of study. Individual preferences are the product of innate drives and moral framing. This exogenous framing may not change all preferences, but very often it transforms them. Yet, when one refrains from wanting something because of moral reasons, sometimes even diabolising such a desire, one is equally following drives, simply different and possibly conflicting ones. Friedrich Nietzsche enlightens this important point when he writes:

> that one desires to combat the vehemence of a drive at all… does not stand within our own power; nor does the choice of any particular method; nor does the success or failure of this method. What is clearly the case is that in this entire procedure our intellect is only the blind instrument of another drive which is a rival of the drive whose vehemence is tormenting us… While 'we' believe we are complaining about the vehemence of a drive, at bottom it is one drive complaining about another; that is to say: for us to become aware that we are suffering from the vehemence of a drive presupposes the existence of another equally vehement or even more vehement drive, and that a struggle is in prospect in which our intellect is going to have to take sides. (O'Hara, 1999, pp. 22–23)

However, some drives are stronger than others, thus forming strong behavioural trends. The diversity of trends is what allows for a pluralistic account of behavioural types when analysing social institutions. It is a difficult, but worthy path.

4.3 Shifting Collective Preferences

Given the importance that morality has on shaping the preferences of individuals in groups, it is of importance to analyse the process of moral and political framing. Next, I will focus on how preferences can be shaped and shifted, while equally focusing on the limits of such a process.

4.3.1 Nietzschean Reformers of Humean Morality

Perhaps no other notorious philosopher focused so much on moral reformation or moral shift as Friedrich Nietzsche. He famously developed the concept of "revaluation of all values" (Nietzsche, 2003a). As a moral reformer, he argued that the notion of virtue which derives from the egalitarian, Christian, and life-denying slave-revolt must be revaluated, changed and overcome in order to create a life-affirming master morality. For Nietzsche, this master morality can only be formulated by the "higher types" of men, who are life-affirming and capable of formulating a "unifying project" (Leiter, 2005, pp. 116–122). In terms of cultural evolution, this seems in line with Boyd and Richerson's (2005, p. 13) postulate that societies require conformists and a certain degree of creators/innovators to evolve adaptively. These moral and cultural reforms would initially work on what David Hume defined as artificial virtues. Contrasting with natural virtues, the artificial ones are contingent to the social order and public interest and their virtue is not always self-evident. These virtues rely on institutions and require a general practice; they are extendedly social. Natural virtues are self-contained, cooperative, complete and are typical of small familial groups; such virtues might exist even without the presence of a societal extended order (Hardin, 2007, p. 45). Hence, some examples of artificial virtues would be the respect for private property, the respect towards one's government, the conformity towards the laws of nations, etc. While examples of natural virtues would be benevolence, prudence, wit, among others (Cohon, 2010). Hume seems to engage with the dichotomy present in the gene-culture coevolution theory, where natural innate tendencies—the natural virtues—interact with society's culture and morality—the artificial virtues. Importantly, these two types of virtues are not independent of one another, given that the cultural and moral framework selects for the numerical expansion or contraction of certain innate tendencies. Individual preferences therefore depend on this framework and on the coevolutionary process that generates it.

4.3.2 *The Importance of the Framers*

Once generated and accepted in some parts of society, individuals can impose morality from the top through the capture of government and power. Moral imposition takes place in hierarchical aristocratic moralities but also in egalitarian ones, as Christopher Boehm (1999) shows with his concept of "reverse domination" (i.e. egalitarianism is imposed from the top). Once institutionally established and enforced, any chosen moral framework is of extreme importance in shaping the preferences of individuals in a given group or society. An extensive amount of evidence of this malleability of preferences comes from experimental psychology and economics (Lichtenstein & Slovic, 2006a). As developed by Kahneman and Tversky (1981, 1984), Framing, "the idea that formally inconsequential changes in how opinions are presented have huge effects on judgments and decisions" (Lichtenstein & Slovic, 2006b, p. 23), is a vital component of how preferences arise. Thus, individuals may prefer A or B according to the way these options are presented (i.e. framed). A classical example of the impact of framing is the default position under which options are displayed. As Johnson and Goldstein (2003) showed, countries whose default position on organ donation is that everybody is a donor unless the person opts-out have much higher levels of donors than countries where the default rule is that nobody is a donor until the person opts-in. As a result, countries with similar cultures as Germany and Austria show very different percentages of organ donors (12 and 99.98%, respectively) because of the former having an opt-in default rule while the latter has an opt-out rule. In the second chapter, I already offered other examples of how framing decisively influences preferences when discussing preferences (Sunstein, 2006, pp. xv–xvi). The conclusion being that within the limits of innate preferential tendencies, the context, especially framing, shape preferences. Hence, preferences are not well defined a priori and before context (Tversky & Simonson, 1993). Framing is a simple form of presenting options while always leaving individuals the possibility of opting out or in, which is the normative position of Legal scholar Cass Sunstein and behavioural economist Richard Thaler (2003). Their normativity relies on libertarian paternalism. Yet, even when the possibility of opting out or in is not available (i.e. full paternalism), there is also an overall framing of choices, with the main difference that the impossibility of opting out puts potential "dissidents" outside of the legal sphere.

The acknowledgement that many individual preferences cannot be taken at face value appeals to a Nietzschean process of "revaluation of all values". An especially contentious issue is the erosion of the idea that individuals should have the liberty to choose their own interests without being manipulated by others (i.e. the sacredness of individual autonomy). Sunstein and Thaler remind us that to escape manipulation is practically impossible because most, if not all, options come already framed in a given form. Other individuals already framed most social options, both in government and in private institutions, as in the market. Prevalent framing is the consequence of humans being social animals; to escape human framing could mean absolute isolation.

These academics show that in most situations, the default rule of the framer has a tremendous influence on people's decisions and preferences. If the default position requires people to opt-into some program (e.g. savings plan), the enrolment rates are much lower than if the default rule enrols people automatically while giving them the option to opt out. Still, why not let individuals choose without a default rule (let's call this option "required active choosing")? As Thaler and Sunstein point out:

> required active choosing is attractive in some settings, but a little thought reveals that this is not at all a way out of the dilemma. On the contrary, required active choosing is simply another option among many that the employers (the framers) can elect. (Sunstein & Thaler, 2006, p. 242)

Empirical evidence shows that required active choosing increases the level of enrolments in relation to the opt-in default rule but considerably decreases such a level in relation to the automatic enrolment (opt-out) one (Choi, Laibson, Madrian, & Metrick, 2002). Required active choosing ignores the ones that would prefer to not choose, e.g. to leave the choice in the hands of more competent people, or that simply prefer to follow the general default trend (Sunstein & Thaler, 2006, pp. 239–248). Hence, this activity of framing by planners in diverse scenarios, both in public and private life, is almost impossible to avoid, even when explicit default rules are absent.

The evidence of this remarkable tendency for individuals to follow their group authoritative norms seems to confirm Jonathan Haidt's (2012, p. 313) assertion that group morality "binds and blinds" (i.e. facts become less relevant than to preserve or follow the group identity). Experimental psychologists have identified cognitive biases confirming that individuals have difficulties operating as independently based rational optimisers. It is possible to name some of the most relevant ones: the "status quo bias", which is the widespread tendency to support the current state of affairs rather than deep change (Kahneman, Knetsch, & Thaler, 1991); the "system justification", i.e. the tendency to support one's political regime even when one would have individual reasons to change it (Banaji, Jost, & Nozek, 2004); "in-group bias", the tendency to favour the group one belongs to in relation to other groups in terms of behaviour and general thinking) (Doria & Taylor, 1981); the "bandwagon effect", the tendency for individuals to accept an idea or belief the more popular and spread it becomes in a group (Nadeau, Cloutier, & Guay, 1993).

The shifting of a broad range of preferences in entire groups is an interesting feature of evolutionary adaptation or maladaptation. For example, regarding the maladaptive problem of sub-replacement fertility levels, political and moral framing could have a deep impact on society. Specifically, a simple framing that emphasises the virtues and prestige of parenthood in relation to career-oriented lives could have strong adaptive effects.

Neuroscientists have also assessed the impact of the framers. Here is how psychologists S. Lichtenstein and P. Slovic describe the results of a neuro-scientific study (Mclure et al., 2004) on preference construction: The researchers

> described a study in which subjects indicated their preferences for the taste of Pepsi versus Coca-Cola while undergoing functional magnetic resonance imagery (fMRI) that monitors blood flow in the brain. When the drinks were unlabelled and subjects used their sense of taste alone to choose a preferred drink, a consistent neural response in the ventromedial prefrontal cortex correlated with the expressed preferences. When subjects were told they were drinking Coca-Cola, the hippocampus responded along with the dorsolateral region of the prefrontal cortex, and preference for Coca-Cola increased. This finding suggests that different parts of the brain are involved when affect (here, brand name) is evoked. (Lichtenstein & Slovic, 2006b, p. 30)

This finding also suggests that preferences rely on certain predispositions (e.g. tastes), on the influence of social symbols, on group identity and on the preservation of reputation within groups. With preferences, there are several innate "buttons" being pressed, and one of them can be the desire to keep one's reputation and one's harmony within a group, which combines with other instinctive taste "buttons". The desire for reputation is a potential reason for the strong impact of framers on individual preferences. Political scientist Timur Kuran (1997) acknowledges this widespread tendency to maintain one's reputation and harmony within society. The central claim of his "preference falsification theory" is that people express preferences that are seen as acceptable in their societies instead of expressing what they really want. Thus, he portrays such a phenomenon as the main reason why the fear of innovation and intellectual stagnation can be prevalent. But do real preferences exist? As we have seen, there maybe be a priori tendencies, but they only take their final shape when involved in a particular context. For example, the feeling of guilt or shame for a given innate preference is not uncommon when such a preference does not conform to socially accepted norms. In fact, it becomes difficult to say if a person prefers what he or she instinctively wants or if the real preference is in fact the rejection of such a preference (e.g. guilt or shame). This difficulty arises because there are a priori tendencies or instincts to desire certain objective situations which are in tension with equally a priori tendencies for group conformity and reputational self-monitoring.

The shift in the preferences of a collective is a logical consequence of a moral shift in the political and social institutions that authoritatively frame social choices. These shifts can be incremental, but they are most visible when arising through what resembles Kuhnian paradigm shifts. Thomas Kuhn (1996) postulated that science advances through "paradigm shifts", where a particular paradigm with a set of methodological rules and assumptions is replaced by a different one. Because both individuals who are conformist and individuals who are revolutionary compose scientific communities, when a paradigm is no longer capable of explaining a vast amount of scientific observation, the revolutionary elements begin working on a different paradigm. When some scientists find a "better" paradigm and persuade enough colleagues, communitarian peer pressure ensures that most scientists adhere to the new paradigm and the paradigm shift is complete. Thus, "normal science" returns until a new revolutionary shift arises. Moral and cultural shifts can operate in a similar fashion. When a social or group morality is no longer serving the interests of the social group, especially in competition with others, the less conformist elements in those groups produce new ways of dealing with the current problems. These new ways are often rejected and fought against by the establishment, which sees them as disruptions of group norms, but, when strong enough, these new ideas spread, first through pressure groups, and eventually to political society. When finally reaching political society, leaders adjust the framing process to serve this new morality, which will shift group preferences in a new direction.

4.3.3 *The Limits of Behavioural Uniformity*

Given the individual tendencies for both conformity and innovation, both tendencies were probably necessary for social groups to shift and adapt to new challenges according to the need of changing environments. But because innovations can also contain maladaptive cultural pathologies, the "conservative" position towards conformity to current social norms can also be valuable. This might explain the existence of these different tendencies within groups, especially at the level of larger societies. Of course, different groups might have different percentages of innovators and conformists, which also affect the "character" of the group. Both change and conformity to the in-group increase the differences between groups, thus creating stronger forces of selection at the group level.

Even though moral framing is vital in shaping the preferences of a collective, the limits of group uniformity through the framing of rules depend on the types that constitute groups and also on their evolutionary history. Individuals within groups can maximise their fitness at the cost of the group. Yet, rational egoists and their attempts to free ride are not the only constraints to the achievement of group uniformity. The conditional cooperators will only cooperate if the framed rules allow for the punishment of free riders (Ostrom, 2000; Turchin, 2006). Sometimes certain rules coming from a particular moral point of view are difficult to implement due to contrary natural tendencies acquired by the individual's group evolutionary history. For example, the attempt by the Israeli kibbutzin to impose rules decreeing that children must be raised in common without special attention from the biological parents was not successful. These parents could never fully accept such a rule even when committed to the communitarian cause and continued to desire a special influence on and proximity to their own offspring (Shepher, 1971). Important legacies of our evolutionary past like the tendency to care for one's biological children (i.e. kin selection) is a difficult feature to overcome, and strong preferences like these will not be easily overcome by framing a new group morality from the top. Unlike sterile ants who work for their group and their reproductive queens (Wilson, 1971), humans are not as integrated into a larger group, given that they still have reproductive self-sufficiency (i.e. as a couple). Conversely, many societies forbid polygamy, and that is not as "natural" as it may seem, given the existing fitness incentives for males to reproduce with more than one female. Yet, the west has successfully restricted such tendencies for polygamy, tendencies that might generate social instability because of the many childless and dissatisfied men polygamy produces.

The different moral types not only help to explain how a new morality arises but they also explain how others may or may not accept new moralities. Some types are better "equipped" to operate under particular social norms than others. When a given group morality becomes too difficult to follow for many elements due to their innate traits, it is possible that such a group would break into several sub-groups because of the high costs of maintaining uniformity. For instance, following Haidt's typology, if the average "care foundation" or "liberty foundation" is stronger than the "loyalty foundation" in a specific population, to escape an imposed morality may become a priority in relation to adapting to group norms. The extent to which new groups take form depends on the willingness of individuals to fight for a new morality for their group. Namely, if the lack of identification with their group overcomes the desire to transform existing moral norms, individuals may form new groups.

4.3.3.1 Group Identity

Group identification seems to be another feature that is difficult to change by framing a new morality. By investigating the "genetic seeds" of group conflicts and warfare, Paul Shaw and Yuwa Wong (1989) identified that language, phenotype, homeland, religion and a myth of common descent were important features in determining the strength of group identification. The more uniform those characteristics are the stronger the group identity is. Hence, to create group uniformity through moral framing without these features seems to be difficult and improbable. Even the evolution of altruism has limitations; on the "limits of altruism", political economist Paul Rubin writes:

> (For natural selection to take place at the level of the group), groups practicing altruism must grow faster than other groups. I call altruistic behaviour that would lead to faster growth "efficient altruism". This often consists of cooperation in a prisoner's dilemma. Altruistic acts such as helping a temporarily hungry or injured person would qualify as efficient altruism. Efficient altruism would also require monitoring recipients to avoid shirking. (Rubin, 2000, p. 9)

Put differently, for altruism to be efficient it will tend to remain within the group and require strong monitoring of free riding.

These innate traits that come with the evolutionary legacy of individuals show the limits of imposing moralities that are too distant from these natures, even though the exact limits are of difficult assessment. The likelihood of an individual to adhere to a framed group morality depends not only on the level of group identification but also on what "buttons" such morality is pressing and their sensitivity. Moralities usually press different moral buttons or foundations. An individual might not like a particular feature being imposed on the in-group, but his or her button that aims at maintaining reputation and conformity might be more sensitive or stronger than the button that makes him or her dislike such a particular imposition. This process makes the individual "accept" or at least conform to such a morality. Christopher Boehm (2012, Chapter VII) uses a similar logic to explain why "genetic free riders" did not completely go away from the current human gene pool even though societies constantly punished them throughout group evolution. For him, the answer to the question of how free riding genes remain in human gene pools is simple: many free riders use their consciences to restrain themselves and their fear of punishment is stronger than their will to free ride. Because they can contain their free riding tendencies and anticipate the loss of reputation, free riders suffer no punishment and therefore escape social control. Boehm's explanation suggests that weakly expressed free riding genes can remain in the population at significant levels in the same way that altruistic genes also remain and spread when compensated. Probably social controls such as capital punishment, ostracism or expulsion would have to be extremely tight and the monitoring mechanisms very deep to eliminate free riding genes.

However, for a group to develop such anti-free riding moral rules it requires the existence of a considerable number of self-sacrificing altruists who can enforce such rules. A particular morality can never merely depend on the fear of punishment or of loss of reputation, even though this conformity may allow free riding to persist within a population. Considerable numbers of "genuine" altruists are always necessary to solve collective action problems and to create a working moral framework for any group.

The question of the limits of group conformity and of the power to shape preferences deserves more future philosophical and scientific research. Yet, for the moment, the main point to emphasise is that the context can largely shape preferences, but only until a certain point; such a point being the pre-wired behavioural, evolutionary legacy. Beyond that point, the monitoring costs of the framing procedure become increasingly higher.

References

Abbot, P., Abe, J., Alcock, J., Alizon, S., Alpedrinha, J., Andersson, M., et al. (2011). Inclusive Fitness Theory and Eusociality. *Nature, 471*(7339), E1–E4.

Adorno, T., Frenkel-Brunswik, E., Levinson, D., & Sandford, R. (1950). *The Authoritarian Personality*. New York: Harper & Row.

Alford, J., Funk, C., & Hibbing, J. (2005). Are Political Orientations Genetically Transmitted? *American Political Science Review, 99*, 153–167.

Amodio, D., & Jost, J. (2012). Political Ideology as Motivated Social Cognition: Behavioral and Neuroscientific Evidence. *Motivation and Emotion, 36*, 55–64.

Banaji, M., Jost, J., & Nozek, B. (2004). A Decade of System Justification Theory: Accumulated Evidence of Conscious and Unconscious Bolstering of the Status Quo. *Political Psychology, 25*(6), 881–919.

Billy, J., Kasarda, J., & West, K. (1986). *Status Enhancement and Fertility: Reproductive Responses to Social Mobility and Educational Opportunity*. New York: Academic Press.

Block, J., & Block, J. H. (2006). Nursery School Personality and Political Orientation Two Decades Later. *Journal of Research in Personality, 40*, 734–749.

Boehm, C. (1996). Emergency Decisions, Cultural Selection Mechanics and Group Selection. *Current Anthropology, 37*, 763–793.

Boehm, C. (1999). *Hierarchy in the Forest: The Evolution of Egalitarian Behavior Cambridge*. Cambridge, MA: Harvard University Press.

Boehm, C. (2012). *Moral Origins: The Evolution of Virtue, Altruism, and Shame*. New York: Basic Books.

Borgerhoff-Mulder, M. (1988a). Behavioral Ecology in Traditional Societies. *Trends in Ecology & Evolution, 3*, 260–264.

Borgerhoff-Mulder, M. (1988b). Kipsigis Bridewealth Payments. In L. Betzig, M. Borgerhoff-Mulder, & P. Turke (Eds.), *Human Reproductive Behavior: A Darwinian Perspective* (pp. 65–82). Cambridge: Cambridge University Press.

Bowman, C., & Kraybill, D. (2001). *On the Backroad to Heaven: Old Order Hutterites, Mennonites, Amish, and Brethren*. Baltimore: Johns Hopkins University Press.

Boyd, R., & Richerson, P. (1985). *Culture and the Evolutionary Process*. Chicago: University of Chicago Press.

Boyd, R., & Richerson, P. (2000). Climate, Culture, and the Evolution of Cognition. In C. Heyes & L. Huber (Eds.), *The Evolution of Cognition* (pp. 329–346). Cambridge, MA: MIT Press.

Boyd, R., & Richerson, P. (2005). *Not by Genes Alone: How Culture Transformed Human Evolution*. Chicago: The University of Chicago Press.

Boyd, R., & Richerson, P. (2008). Gene-Culture Coevolution and the Evolution of Social Institutions. In C. Engel & W. Singer (Eds.), *Better Than Conscious?*

Decision Making, the Human Mind, and Implications for Institutions (pp. 305–325). Cambridge, MA: MIT Press.

Buchanan, J. M. (2000). Group Selection and Team Sports. *Journal of Bioeconomics, 2*, 1–7.

Buss, D. M. (1999). *Evolutionary Psychology: New Science of the Mind.* Boston: Allyn and Bacon.

Choi, J., Laibson, D., Madrian, B., & Metrick, A. (2002). Defined Contribution Pensions: Plan Rules, Participant Decisions, and the Path of Least Resistance. In J. Poterba (Ed.), *Tax Policy and the Economy* (Vol. 16, pp. 67–113). Cambridge, MA: MIT Press.

Coale, A., & Watkins, S. (1986). *The Decline of Fertility in Europe.* Princeton: Princeton University Press.

Cohon, R. (2010). Hume's Moral Philosophy. *The Stanford Encyclopedia of Philosophy.* Retrieved from http://plato.stanford.edu/archives/fall2010/entries/hume-moral.

Cosmides, L., & Tooby, J. (1992). Cognitive Adaptations for Social Exchange. In J. H. Barkow, L. Cosmides, & J. Tooby (Eds.), *The Adapted Mind: Evolutionary Psychology and the Generation of Culture* (pp. 163–225). New York: Academic Press.

Cosmides, L., & Tooby, J. (2001). *What Is Evolutionary Psychology? Explaining the New Science of the Mind.* New Haven: Yale University Press.

Darwin, C. (1871). *The Descent of Man and Selection in Relation to Sex.* New York: Appleton.

de Waal, F. (2006). *Primates and Philosophers: How Morality Evolved* (S. Macedo & J. Ober, Eds.). Princeton: Princeton University Press.

de Waal, F. (2014). Natural Normativity: The "Is" and "Ought" of Animal Behavior. In F. de Waal, P. Churchland, T. Pievani, & S. Parmigiani (Eds.), *Evolved Morality: The Biology and Philosophy of Human Conscience* (pp. 49–71). Leiden: Brill.

Doria, J., & Taylor, M. (1981). Self-Serving and Group-Serving Bias in Attribution. *The Journal of Social Psychology, 113*(2), 201–211.

Fehr, E., & Gächter, S. (2000). Cooperation and Punishment in Public Goods Experiments. *The American Economic Review, 90*(4), 980–994.

Feilden, T., Firth, C., Kanai, R., & Rees, G. (2011). Political Orientations Are Correlated with Brain Structure in Young Adults. *Current Biology, 21*(8), 677–680.

Fitszimons, G., Jost, J., & Kay, A. (2004). The Ideological Animal: A System Justification View. In S. Greenberg, S. Koole, & T. Pyszezynski (Eds.), *Handbook of Experimental Existential Psychology* (pp. 263–282). New York: Guilford Press.

Gintis, H. (2000). Strong Reciprocity and Human Sociality. *Journal of Theoretical Biology, 206*(2), 169–179.

Gintis, H. (2012). *On the Evolution of Human Morality*. Retrieved from http://socialevolutionforum.com/2012/06/27/herbert-gintis-on-the-evolution-of-human-morality-comment-on-steven-pinker/.

Glaser, J., Jost, J., Kruglanski, A., & Sulloway, F. (2003a). Exceptions That Prove the Rule—Using a Theory of Motivated Social Cognition to Account for Ideological Incongruities and Political Anomalies: Reply to Greenberg and Jonas. *Psychological Bulletin, 129,* 383–393.

Glaser, J., Jost, J., Kruglanski, A., & Sulloway, F. (2003b). Political Conservatism as Motivated by Social Cognition. *Psychological Bulletin, 129,* 339–375.

Graham, J., Haidt, J., & Nosek, B. (2009). Liberals and Conservatives Rely on Different Sets of Moral Foundations. *Journal of Personality and Social Psychology, 96*(5), 1029–1046.

Haidt, J. (2012). *The Righteous Mind: Why Good People Are Divided by Politics and Religion*. London: Allen Lane.

Haidt, J., & Kesebir, S. (2010). Morality. In S. Fiske, D. Gilbert, & G. Lindzey (Eds.), *Handbook of Social Psychology* (5th ed., Vol. 2, pp. 797–833). Hoboken, NJ: Wiley.

Hamilton, W. D. (1975). Innate Social Aptitudes of Man: An Approach from Evolutionary Genetics. In R. Fox (Ed.), *Biosocial Anthropology*. London: Malaby Press.

Hardin, R. (2007). *David Hume: Moral & Political Theorist*. Oxford: Oxford University Press.

Harpending, H., & Cochran, G. (2015). Assortative Mating, Class, and Caste. In T. Shackelford & R. Hansen (Eds.), *The Evolution of Sexuality* (pp. 57–67). New York: Springer.

Hatemi, P., Gillespie, N., Eaves, L., Maher, B., Webb, B., Heath, A., et al. (2011). A Genome-Wide Analysis of Liberal and Conservative Political Attitudes. *Journal of Politics, 73,* 271–285.

Heckathorn, D. (1990). Collective Sanctions and Compliance Norms: A Formal Theory of Group-Mediated Social Control. *American Sociological Review, 55,* 366–384.

Heckathorn, D. (1993). Collective Action and Group Heterogeneity: Voluntary Provision vs. Selective Incentives. *American Sociological Review, 58,* 366–384.

Hill, K., Hurtado, A., & Kaplan, H. (1984). Food Sharing Among the Ache Hunter-Gatherers of Eastern Paraguay. *Current Anthropology, 25,* 113–115.

Hostetler, J. (1993). *Amish Society*. Baltimore: Johns Hopkins University Press.

Irons, W. (1979). Cultural and Biological Success. In N. Chagnon & W. Irons (Eds.), *Evolutionary Biology and Human Social Behavior* (pp. 257–272). North Scituate: Duxbury Press.

Johnson, E., & Goldstein, D. (2003). Do Defaults Save Lives? *Science, 302,* 1338–1339.

Jost, J. (2006). The End of the End of Ideology. *American Psychologist, 61*(7), 651–670.

Kahneman, D., & Tversky, A. (1984). Choices, Values, and Frames. *American Psychologist, 39,* 341–350.

Kahneman, D., Knetsch, J., & Thaler, R. (1991). Anomalies: The Endowment Effect, Loss Aversion, and Status Quo Bias. *The Journal of Economic Perspectives, 5*(1), 193–206.

Kaplan, H., & Hill, K. (1985a). Food Sharing Among Ache Foragers: Tests of Explanatory Hypotheses. *Current Anthropology, 26,* 223–245.

Kaplan, H., & Hill, K. (1985b). Hunting Ability and Reproductive Success Among Male Ache Foragers. *Current Anthropology, 26,* 131–133.

Keeley, L. (1996). *War Before Civilization: The Myth of the Peaceful Savage.* New York: Oxford University Press.

Kraybill, D., & Olshan, M. (1994). *The Amish Struggle with Modernity.* Hanover: University Press of New England.

Kuhn, T. (1996). *The Structure of Scientific Revolutions* (3rd ed.). Chicago; London: The University of Chicago Press.

Kuran, T. (1997). *Private Truths, Public Lies: The Social Consequences of Preference Falsification.* Cambridge, MA: Harvard University Press.

Labov, W. (2001). *Principles of Linguistic Change: Social Factors.* Oxford: Blackwell.

Leiter, B. (2007). Nietzsche's Theory of the Will. *Philosopher's Imprint, 7*(7), 1–15.

Leiter, B. (2005). *Nietzsche on Morality.* London; New York: Routledge.

Lichtenstein, S., & Slovic, P. (2006a). *The Construction of Preference.* Cambridge; New York: Cambridge University Press.

Lichtenstein, S., & Slovic, P. (2006b). The Construction of Preference. In S. Lichtenstein & P. Slovic (Eds.), *The Construction of Preference* (pp. 1–41). Cambridge; New York: Cambridge University Press.

Mclure, S., Li, J., Tomlin, D., Cypert, K., Montague, L., & Montague, R. (2004). Neural Correlates of Behavioral Preference for Culturally Familiar Drinks. *Neuron, 44,* 379–387.

Mill, J. S. (1859). *On Liberty.* London: John W. Parker and Son.

Nadeau, R., Cloutier, E., & Guay, J. (1993). New Evidence About the Existence of a Bandwagon Effect in the Opinion Formation Process. *International Political Science Review, 14*(2), 203–213.

Nietzsche, F. (2003b). *On the Genealogy of Morals* (K. Ansell-Pearson, Ed.). Cambridge: Cambridge University Press.

Nietzsche, F. (2003a). The Anti-Christ. In R. Hollingdale (Trans.), *Twilight of the Idols and the Anti-Christ* (pp. 123–200). London: Penguin Books.

Norenzayan, A. (2014). Does Religion Make People Moral? In F. de Waal, P. Churchland, T. Pievani, & S. Parmigiani (Eds.), *Evolved Morality: The Biology and Philosophy of Human Conscience* (pp. 229–249). Leiden: Brill.

Nowak, M., Tarnita, C., & Wilson, E. O. (2010). The Evolution of Eusociality. *Nature, 466*(7310), 1057–1062.

Nowak, M., Tarnita, C., & Wilson, E. O. (2011). *A Brief Statement About Inclusive Fitness and Eusociality*. Retrieved from http://www.ped.fas.harvard.edu/IF_Statement.pdf.

O'Hara, D. (1999). *The Art of Reading as a Way of Life: On Nietzsche's Truth*. Evanston, IL: Northwestern University Press.

Olson, M. (1971). *The Logic of Collective Action: Public Goods and the Theory of Groups*. Cambridge, MA: Harvard University Press.

Olson, M. (1982). *The Rise and Decline of Nations: Economic Growth, Stagflation, and Social Rigidities*. New Haven: Yale University Press.

Olson, J., Vernon, P., Harris, J., & Jang, K. (2001). The Heritability of Attitudes: A Study of Twins. *Journal of Personality and Social Psychology, 80*, 845–860.

Ostrom, E. (2000). Collective Action and the Evolution of Social Norms. *The Journal of Economic Perspectives: EP* (A Journal of the American Economic Association), *14*(3), 137–158.

Peter, K. (1987). *The Dynamics of Hutterite Society: An Analytical Approach*. Edmonton: University of Alberta Press.

Plotkin, H. (1994). *Darwin Machines and the Nature of Knowledge*. Cambridge, MA: Harvard University Press.

Queller, D. (2012). *Two Languages, One Reality*. Retrieved from http://edge.org/conversation/the-false-allure-of-group-selection.

Rogers, E. (1983). *Diffusion of Innovations* (3rd ed.). New York: Free Press.

Rubin, P. (2000). Group Selection and the Limits to Altruism. *Journal of Bioeconomics, 2*(1), 9–23.

Salter, F. (2003). *On Genetic Interests: Family, Ethny, and Humanity in an Age of Mass Migration*. Frankfurt am Main; New York: Peter Lang.

Shaw, P., & Wong, Y. (1989). *Genetic Seeds of Warfare: Evolution, Nationalism, and Patriotism*. Boston: Unwin Hyman.

Shepher, J. (1971). Mate Selection Among Second-Generation Kibbutz Adolescents and Adults: Incest Avoidance and Negative Imprinting. *Archives of Sexual Behavior, 1*, 293–307.

Sober, E., & Wilson, D. S. (1998). *Unto Others: The Evolution and Psychology of Unselfish Behavior*. Cambridge, MA: Harvard University Press.

Sunstein, C. (2006). Preface. In S. Lichtenstein & P. Slovic (Eds.), *The Construction of Preference*. New York: Cambridge University Press.

Sunstein, C., & Thaler, R. (2003). Libertarian Paternalism Is Not an Oxymoron. *University of Chicago Law Review, 70*, 1159–1202.

Sunstein, C., & Thaler, R. (2006). Preferences, Paternalism, and Liberty. In S. Olsaretti (Ed.), *Preferences and Well-Being* (pp. 233–265). Cambridge, UK: Cambridge University Press.

Turchin, P. (2006). *War and Peace and War: The Rise and Fall of Empires.* New York: Penguin Books.
Tversky, A., & Kahneman, D. (1981). The Framing of Decisions and the Psychology of Choice. *Science, 211*(4481), 453–458.
Tversky, A., & Simonson, I. (1993). Context-Dependent Preferences. *Management Science, 39*(10), 1179–1189.
Vanhanen, T. (1999). *Ethnic Conflicts Explained by Ethnic Nepotism.* Stamford, CT: Jai Press.
von Hayek, F. A. (1979). *Law, Legislation and Liberty* (Vol. III). London: Routledge.
Willer, R. (2004). The Effects of Government-Issued Terror Warnings on Presidential Approval Ratings. *Current Research in Social Psychology, 10,* 1–12.
Wilson, E. O. (1971). *The Insect Societies.* Cambridge, MA: Belknap of Harvard University Press.
Wilson, E. O. (1998). *Consilience.* New York: Knopf.
Wilson, D. S. (2002). *Darwin's Cathedral: Evolution, Religion, and the Nature of Society.* Chicago: The University of Chicago Press.
Wilson, D. S. (2012). *Clash of Paradigms: Why Proponents of Multilevel Selection Theory and Inclusive Fitness Theory Sometimes (But Not Always) Misunderstand Each Other.* Retrieved from http://socialevolutionforum.com/2012/07/13/david-sloan-wilson-clash-of-paradigms-why-proponents-of-multilevel-selection-theory-and-inclusive-fitness-theory-sometimes-but-not-always-misunderstand-each-other/.
Wilson, D. S., Sheldon, K., & O'Gorman, R. (2008). For the Good of the Group? Exploring Group-Level Evolutionary Adaptations Using Multilevel Selection Theory. *Group Dynamics: Theory, Research, and Practice, 12*(1), 17–26.
World-Bank. (2013). *Fertility Rate, Total (Births per Woman).* Retrieved from http://data.worldbank.org/indicator/SP.DYN.TFRT.IN/countries?order=wbapi_data_value_2012+wbapi_data_value+wbapi_data_value-last&sort=desc.
Zuckerman, P. (2008). *Society Without God.* New York: New York University Press.

CHAPTER 5

Reassessing Liberal Democracy's Shortcomings and Their Institutional Market-Enhancing Solutions

5.1 Liberal Democratic Shortcomings Reassessed

As documented in Chapter 3, public choice theorists identified several structural problems in contemporary liberal democracies (Buchanan & Tullock, 1999; Caplan, 2006; Tullock, Seldon, & Brady, 2002). These problems not only prevent the satisfaction of citizens'/voters' preferences but also create the conditions for such maximisation of preferences to fail. As a result, by severely reducing the democratic elements of choice and preference satisfaction, liberal democracies fail to achieve the goal of enabling the autonomous self-rule of individuals. The fixes to these shortcomings that extensively come out of public choice literature are market solutions in the classical liberal tradition (Buchanan, 2000; Pennington, 2011). I will now re-examine the extent to which rational/public choice theorists have accurately diagnosed these problems under this new naturalistic and evolutionary perspective.

Based on multilevel selection theory (Wilson & Wilson, 2007), I argued in Chapter 2 that a plurality of behavioural assumptions should replace the canonical public choice postulate of the parity of assumptions. Namely, instead of assuming that individuals have the same behavioural tendencies in markets and politics, as a canonical public choice does, one should instead assume that different behavioural types operate in markets and politics. This pluralist assumption means that both contexts might have different types operating in them. Hence, models of types as the one of Elinor Ostrom (2000, pp. 142–143)—conditional

F. N. Faria, *The Evolutionary Limits of Liberalism*, Palgrave Studies in Classical Liberalism, https://doi.org/10.1007/978-3-030-31496-5_5

cooperators, willing punishers and rational egoists; or the types of Peter Turchin (2006, pp. 98–99)—knaves, moralists and saints; or Jonathan Haidt's (2012) ones—liberals vs conservatives; or the types suggested before in this book—group-philia versus group-phobia—are all possible type models that one can use to analyse and compare institutions. Curiously, even though endorsing the public choice parity of assumptions, Geoffrey Brennan and James Buchanan (2000, pp. 72–73) seem to hint at some form of types model. In particular when claiming that majoritarian electoral systems seem to attract individuals with certain morals and ideologies who are likely to operate in specific ways, namely to believe in redistribution, to make the government grow, etc. F. A. Hayek (1944, Chapter X), another classical liberal like Buchanan, goes along the same line when claiming that, in centralised institutions of coercion (e.g. the state), it is the worst who are more likely to get on top, i.e. the most unscrupulous and inhibited in dictating values to others. Thus, even if these claims reveal the suspicion towards state power that characterises the classical liberal tradition, one can find authors in this ideological field hinting at models of behavioural pluralist types. These authors sometimes depart from the "sameness" of rational egoists that is so prevalent in rational/public choice analysis.

When reanalysing the public choice insights on institutions such as markets and politics, there are important points to include. Most relevantly, the different behavioural types, the role of morality/culture, the behavioural types that are likely to shape institutions and the capacity of political/moral framers to shape mass preferences in society. Among others, the evolutionary traits of group conformity and widespread cognitive biases found by experimental social scientists are also relevant in this endeavour. With this in mind, I will now reanalyse the public choice diagnostic of the shortcomings of liberal democracy, starting with the principal–agent problem.

5.1.1 The Principal–Agent Problem

Put simply, the principal–agent problem is the obstacle that prevents the interests of political representatives from being aligned with the interests of the voters/citizens. This problem is present when the agents (the politicians) have more information or/and skills than the principals (the voters) who hire the agents. Especially under universal rational egoistic assumptions, the agents will concentrate the benefits on themselves at the cost of the principals because of the agents' advantages in information or/and skills. Even the existing mechanisms that aim at solving this problem merely mitigate it instead of solving it. Specifically, these mechanisms are part of a social contract that institutes incentives based on punishments and gains to make sure the principals control the agents. But informational privileges always seem to give an extra advantage to agents even under the best contracts (Brennan & Hamlin, 2004, p. 100). Even though firms in the market can suffer from such a problem (e.g. shareholders not being able to control the benefits of managers and CEOs), the idea that the decentralisation and exit options of markets are better than politics at overcoming this problem is prevalent in public choice theory (Pennington, 2011).

By shifting from this assumption of universal rational egoism to assuming a pluralism of types, one should highlight the different nature of these two institutions—markets and politics. While the market narrows down the preferences of its participants to choices that maximise utility within the price system (e.g. profit maximisation for companies or affordable products for consumers), political action can itself be the engine that shapes and creates preferences in society—including the preference for societies where markets fulfil preferences. If one imagines different behavioural types other than the rational egoists operating in both these institutions, the difference between markets and politics becomes clear. In the marketplace, self-sacrificing, group-oriented altruists might solve the principal–agent problem by attaining leading managerial positions within companies without using their superior knowledge against the interests of the shareholders. Remembering the importance of morality in creating group cohesion, a particular meta-morality strengthens the group's behavioural tendency. The ones with a higher knowledge-based power impose a meta-morality on the group and also on themselves (e.g. honour). Still, in the marketplace, even though business company leaders can create certain non-pecuniary values, the ultimate value of profit and pecuniary aims cannot disappear because of the need to "survive" among other economic challengers in the market. This "meta-value" is external to any business company or to the ones working in a company because such a meta-value is being institutionally created by political powers that assign property rights and the capacity to legally and morally generate wealth (Wintrobe, 1998, pp. 160–161). Because the nature of profit as a meta-value is intrinsic to market activity, preferences for pecuniary rewards become institutional imperatives.

The profit imperative might also explain why the principal–agent problem is difficult to solve in this context. It is likely that rational egoist types, interested in material gains, end up operating in leading managerial positions; and even supposed altruists in those positions would probably be merely conditional cooperators, not really engaging in self-sacrifice if no non-pecuniary group higher values are or can be in place.

In contrast, the political realm is unrestricted in terms of the meta-values it can institutionalise. This difference implies two decisive points: the first is that politics can attract all behavioural types and offer ground for them to operate, and, second, that it has a capacity to shape preferences at a large scale, unhindered by ultimate profit motives. For sure, there are limitations that all rulers face in order to stay in power. Namely, they need enough internal support and resilience in relation to other antagonistic political societies. But rulers can achieve such goals via the valorisation of diverse goals and morals. In terms of the principal–agent problem, the political realm can offer a higher capacity to solve such a problem than the realm of business companies. The political realm has a relative advantage because individuals can use framing operations to shape and align (to the extent possible) the preferences of citizens with the preferences of representatives. The extent to which one can solve the principal–agent problem depends on the capacity that representatives have to shape and align the preferences of the ones being represented with their own. This may be more evident in autocratic regimes, which can offer a higher range of values and goals, but it is equally valid for actual liberal democracies, which, as James Buchanan (2000, p. 19) highlighted, are the creation of elites. These elites impose the theoretical primacy of liberalism over democracy by instituting human rights or other rights that aim at protecting the losing minorities from democratic majorities. By instituting such meta-values, the framers also shape and shift the preferences of the individuals living within a polity. It is perhaps not a coincidence that social values (e.g. marriage laws, gender relations) are more liberal in 2015 than they were 30 or 40 years before in those same western liberal democracies (Scott & Clery, 2013; Social, 2013, pp. 5–11).

It is worth remembering that there are limits to the process of shaping preferences. It is likely that some people will never accept certain policies or values regardless of framing effects. This is because of some types being so at odds with the framers that conformity does not operate to align preferences with what is being framed. Even the idea that markets can solve the principal–agent problem better than politics because decentralisation allows for exit options and brings principals close to their agents (Pennington, 2011) depends on the types operating in these contexts. As we have seen, group moralities shape preferences, and decentralisation itself is the consequence of a particular group morality. Unlike Mancur Olson's (1971) postulates in his logic of collective action, certain groups may solve collective action problems better than other groups because of the former having more altruists than the latter. This is valid even if one group is bigger than the other. Potentially, a big, and even centralised group of altruists can solve collective action problems better than small groups of rational egoists. Such an understanding puts a question mark on the idea that market decentralisation helps to solve the principal–agent problem better than a centralised political entity. The question here is one of what types of individuals are operating in particular contexts, leading to different answers according to the observation of such types. With liberal democracies, some polities will solve or mitigate the principal–agent problem better than some other polities and the differences rely on the behavioural/moral types that operate in them. It depends on the cohesiveness and on the level of integration of the group in question. Ultimately, it may be possible to solve the principal–agent problem, but, as aforementioned, the satisfaction of certain preferences reduces fitness because of maladaptive ideas. If maladaptiveness becomes intrinsic to liberal democracies, the institution and the elements operating in these institutional venues will not prevail through time and resolving the principal–agent problem will therefore be temporary.

In sum, the process of elitist moral framing might solve the principal–agent problem. This process can shape mass preferences and can align the preferences of the principals with the ones of the agents.

5.1.2 *The Aggregation Problem*

The aggregation problem is a crystallisation of the principal–agent problem when applied to democratic practice. It relies on Kenneth Arrow's (1951) famous impossibility theorem, which postulates it is impossible to design a voting system that is not highly vulnerable to dictatorial rule or to skilful manipulation. The theorem also claims it is impossible to design a voting system that is not the result of arbitrary ordering produced by voting cycles. In this sense, it is not possible to account for a common will. As William Riker (1982, p. 241) claimed, the concept of common will does not exist if it cannot be measured.

From the perspective of experimental psychology and economics, Sunstein and Thaler come to a similar conclusion to the one of Arrow: that framing is impossible to avoid, which means the elitist manipulation of preferences is unavoidable. From their work, one can infer that the best we can hope for regarding the success of liberal democracy is a libertarian paternalism where elites benevolently orient mass preferences, but where these benevolent elites still leave the masses ample room for choice (Sunstein & Thaler, 2003). Still, once again, this process might in fact be a form of aggregating previously shaped mass preferences in a way that generates a Durkheimian collective consciousness (i.e. shared beliefs and ideas that serve as a collective, unifying force) (Durkheim, 1997). Such a process of preference shaping and maximisation would not reach every single individual, but it would create enough moral common ground within the group to make disagreements a matter of secondary and less important choices. In the language of James Buchanan's political philosophy, such disagreements would take place at lower levels, under the meta-rules or meta-values (Brennan & Buchanan, 2000). This capacity to shift preferences depends on the types present in a group and the extent to which they identify with the in-group. Therefore, cognitive biases like the status quo bias (Kahneman, Knetsch, & Thaler, 1991), the bandwagon effect (Nadeau, Cloutier, & Guay, 1993) or the in-group bias (Doria & Taylor, 1981) make sure that the concept of "common will" that Kenneth Arrow put in question can exist beyond a context where individuals have a priori given preferences.

Interestingly, Anthony Downs (1957) explained why parties would align themselves with the median voter. His explanation emphasises the force of competition for votes. But, by understanding the way elitist framing shapes preferences, it seems that the preferences of the median voter are themselves the result of acts of framing by cultural and political elite agents. Hence, when trying to understand why the central parties become similar to each other in their policies, it is as important to comprehend the way elites shape preferences as it is to understand the party competition for the votes of the median voter. The characteristics of the median voter itself and its actual existence are not a coincidence but a product of cultural and political framing of the dominant elites. To the extent that competition also has an important role, it is the one between groups, as in multilevel selection theory, which is the reason why the tendency for a collective consciousness to arise is so prevalent.

The evolutionary legacy of traits for conformity and for the imitation of the successful (Boyd & Richerson, 2005, Chapter V) solidifies the process where the aggregation of preferences is a group process in a permanent adjustment to what is being framed. Perhaps the reason political theorists Geoffrey Brennan and Alan Hamlin (2004, pp. 105–106) downplay the importance of Arrow's impossibility theorem in demolishing any collective system of accounting preferences is that they understand the importance of the moral element in shaping those preferences. This understanding is perhaps the instinctive reason behind their recommendation that Arrow's problem should be perceived as a moral challenge aimed at liberal values; namely, that the problem should be perceived as a way to minimise dictatorial and manipulative possibilities and to maximise freedom of choice. They base their normative position on the notion that it is possible to create a collective consciousness through cultural and political institutions that helps to fulfil the goals of public preference maximisation. But such an institutional creation is already a framing process aiming at maximising preferences not so much by allowing a priori preferences to be satisfied but by shaping preferences for them to fit with those framed institutions. Put differently, individuals may satisfy their preferences because those preferences mutate to fit the supplied framework of norms. The mutation is especially relevant if the forces of between-group competition are stronger than the within-group ones. The aggregation problem becomes more one of transformation of preferences than one of simple aggregation.

5.1.3 *Rational Ignorance*

Rational ignorance is a public choice concept that explains many, if not most problems of liberal democracy through the idea that individuals are rationally ill-informed about politics. For voters, it is rational to know little about politics because the costs of getting informed are superior to the benefits that may come from it. The costs of acquiring political knowledge in order to cast an informed vote are higher than the likelihood of ever making a difference with one's vote and therefore of changing the result of a major election. This makes the democratic process one where rent-seekers capture the government and shift policies toward their own interests, concentrating benefits on themselves and dispersing the costs on the rationally ignorant voters/citizens.

Given the widespread political ignorance of the masses (Delli Carpini & Keeter, 1996), the tendency for group conformity exacerbates this problem by making people conform to the interests of those who capture the government through rent-seeking. In short, the rent-seeking groups that take control of government policy will also justify such policies as being in the interest of the citizens, framing them in moral language and within moral values to achieve. Rent-seeking producers can justify a tariff that benefits them by appealing to "national interest"; or certain rent-seeking social groups can justify their institutional participation quotas in terms of "equality of opportunities". Interestingly, the observed tendency for individuals to imitate the successful ones of their societies will also help to institutionalise the preferences of the successful rent-seekers, spreading their values and preferential culture. Yet, once again, this rent-seeking process creates the paradox of mass preferences shifting toward successful rent-seekers. Even if the values of such rent-seekers primarily aim at serving the interests of these particular sub-groups, society might institutionalise and emulate their values. Therefore, paradoxically, rational ignorance may be a catalyst for a general maximisation of rent-seeking-shaped preferences.

It may be argued that it is possible to measure the welfare inefficiency that such rent-seeking framing may bring. But this measurement will hardly tell the whole story about social and political preferences because the satisfaction of preferences includes trade-offs. These trade-offs may include less economic efficiency in exchange for other issues such as ideal models of society and the fulfilment of values. For instance, people may prefer to exchange economic freedom and higher economic growth for a larger welfare state, thus fulfilling the value of equality; or people may prefer to restrict cultural imports to preserve the specific traditions of their society.

The miracle of aggregation, as suggested by political economist Donald Wittman, (1995) postulates that democracy will work efficiently because the uninformed 90% slit votes 50–50 and then the informed 10% will cast the decisive vote. Yet, this hypothesis relies on the false assumption that voters vote randomly. In fact, if the voters' preferences depend on elite framing and are also the product of moral types in society, it is very unlikely that voting is random. In addition, the miracle of aggregation already assumes that electable parties offer good governmental options. If these good options are not available, even the informed 10% would make no difference in electing competent governments. In reality, the act of voting has a strong moral component, and it is far from being random. As public choice theorist Bryan Caplan (2004b, p. 470) reveals, political opinions and preferences of voters are characterised by biases, prejudices and also by a strong resistance to empirical evidence when others contest their views. This resistance to evidence highlights that morality confers behavioural uniformity and cohesion to groups, which is the reason why there is a tension between empirical reality and conformity to group morality—when the latter is at odds with the former.

5.1.4 *Rational Irrationality*

By documenting that the average voter has strong opinions about politics even though he/she is rationally ignorant, Caplan explains political democratic failure with the concept of "rational irrationality". The concept entails the idea that the strong preferences of ignorant voters are the main reason they ask for inefficient policies. In the voting booth, it is rational to be irrational because the cost of voting is insignificant and the single vote has no substantial impact on election outcomes. Hence, when voting, they indulge in their prejudices and biases without being corrected by reality—while the marketplace would correct the voters if they had bought a bad product. Some of Caplan's examples of these biases are the anti-market bias, the anti-foreign bias and the make-work bias (Lomasky, 2008, p. 470), all of which can be explained by multilevel selection.

Regarding the anti-market bias, individuals see free markets as promoters of individual competition, which generates many inequalities and social changes. Therefore, the free market is not an institution that directly promotes the group. Even though one may argue that markets can be Pareto efficient (i.e. that they make individuals better off while making nobody worse off), people's general outlook of the market is one where each individual simply takes as much as possible for himself or herself, with little regard for the group. And many consequences of power changes come from such a process. Indeed, markets might have no group borders, which makes them look less socially appealing to group minded individuals.

The inclination for collectiveness is the same reason that makes individuals display the anti-foreign bias identified by Caplan.

This bias expresses the commonly identified in-group bias (Doria & Taylor, 1981), which evolved because those who had a better sense of community/group cohesion were better able to survive in the competition between groups. Protectionist measures, either in terms of economic protectionism, cultural protection or migration protectionism, as Caplan shows, are thus policies which individuals commonly prefer. Traditionally, groups require some degree of protectionism to maintain high degrees of social trust and to ensure that altruism evolved and remained while free riding has diminished. Groups that are considerably open have no boundaries, which weakens the sense of trust in one's community because of the sense that anyone can be an outsider, therefore lowering social trust (Putnam, 2007).

Finally, the observed make-work bias, which is the tendency to prefer full employment policies, can be seen as a consequence of this search for group cohesion. Even though societies oriented towards economic growth have the potential to generate more wealth by retaining productive jobs while eliminating the less productive ones, such a process can be harmful to the aforementioned cohesion. The vast unemployment caused by the disappearance of jobs that are no longer productive can generate, among others, social riots or social/class division of previously cohesive groups or societies, which can then lead to coups and changes of political systems. But a sense of group fairness is equally an important factor. An egalitarian takeover, where egalitarian elites impose a system of tribal egalitarianism through "reverse dominance" (Boehm, 1999), relies on a natural sense of fairness and group cohesion (i.e. the need to prevent the group/tribe from breaking apart). Groups can also work hierarchically, yet the existence of a very large percentage of the population that is unoccupied and has no hierarchical utility for the group can be a large source of tensions. Because many regard living on welfare as free riding, i.e. as something traditionally punished, it is no surprise that individuals often prefer full employment to welfare state "charity". When one has a job, there is a sense of contributing to the group, while if one engages in the prolonged practice of being a welfare receiver, others can regard such a practice as free riding, which may be punishable. Ultimately, these biases are part of what F. A. Hayek (1979, p. 174) saw as the tribal (egalitarian) instincts, suggesting that individuals should overcome these "groupish" instincts to give rise to the great market society. If these biases are present in democracy too and constitute, according to Caplan, a failure of democracy caused by rational irrationality, the solution could be to institutionalise a more "Hayekian" moral framing to change these prevalent preferences. But these biases are profound and have a particular evolutionary function. It is difficult to erase or transform them by framing.

Caplan's (2006, Chapter III) claim that the efficiency of policies based on prejudices is at odds with the opinions of most well-informed specialists in economics highlights that policies under liberal democracy fail because polities deliver too little power to specialists and too much power to the democratic biases of voters. Yet, even if one accepts the argument that the economic efficiency of the policies based on biases is inferior to the ones recommended by most economic specialists, it does not mean specialists have an encompassing knowledge. Most economists deal with the satisfaction of preferences and not with the evolutionary maximisation of fitness. In fact, economic growth does not correlate with maximisation of fitness and in the current western world, there is actually a negative correlation between those two (World-Bank, 2013). Thus, economically efficient policies can undermine the fitness of individuals and, in the long run, of the very own institutions causing fitness minimisation. This is a particular problem that arises from radical specialisation and from the delivery of certain policies to specific specialists. Namely, the problem of tackling a question from a certain perspective while lacking an understanding of the unexpected consequences that specialists from other disciplines may identify. Notwithstanding, the recommendations of Caplan's economic specialists are also in line with the liberal democratic *telos* of individual happiness and preference satisfaction, which, not coincidently, is a product of the prevalent western collective morality.

Notably, liberal elites already frame liberal democracies along the lines of Bohem's (1999) "reverse domination". One can regard these elites as specialists that set the constitutional boundaries, narrowing down the choices that citizens can make. Liberal elites produce the framing that will shape the preferences of the political participants in society. In addition, many important features of democracies remain outside of democratic accountability because of the belief that specialists have better knowledge than the masses of voters (e.g. central banks). The mass group/tribal biases of rational irrationality are perhaps incompatible with upheld liberal democratic values, but it is also not exactly clear to what extent is it possible to alter these evolutionary tendencies. The ones more capable of shifting policies in their favour are also the ones more likely to shape preferences, yet always within the limits of the existing types or sub-groups in the social realm. The capture of public policy by groups leads us to the phenomenon of rent-seeking and its importance.

In conclusion, it may be possible to overcome the problem of rational ignorance because political agents have the power to shape the preferences of individuals and therefore the power to make the preferences of rationally ignorant voters more in line with government policies. Still, by identifying persistent biases, rationally irrationality shows the eventual limits that such a process of preference transformation can have.

5.1.5 Rent-Seeking and the Logic of Collective Action

Rent-seeking is the process through which well-organised interest groups capture government, either through legal lobbying or illegal means, to attain their own preferred policies, regardless of the cost imposed on voters/citizens. Gordon Tullock believes that the activity of extracting rent through rent-seeking has a negative social value and the most common example of such a process is the one concerning tariffs and protectionism (Tullock et al., 2002, p. 43). As he puts it, by investing resources to get the government to impose a tariff on Korean cars, the U.S. automobile industry is restricting choice and making the citizens of the United States worse off. His conclusion follows from the logic of comparative advantage.

Yet, Tullock's argument seems to fall short of a complete analysis. Are the citizens of the United States clearly worse off in such a case? From a strict Pareto efficient economic analysis based on comparative advantage theory, it seems so. However, when one introduces evolutionary group competition in the equation, one must ask what the political consequences are of allowing each group to specialise in the production of products that confer a comparative advantage. As a radical but illustrative example, most polities or nations will want to have the best means of military defence and to be as autonomous as possible in the production of such weapons. It seems irrational that any nation or polity can show a strong preference for allowing other nations to have an almost monopoly on the production of weaponry merely because those other nations have a comparative advantage in specialising in it. This flows directly from the logic of group selection forces: these polities/nations probably do not want to take the risk of being attacked and conquered by antagonistic heavily armed nations while being almost unarmed because of having specialised in some other non-military field. A comparative advantage would mainly work in a world with no group interests or selection. Yet, one may counter-argue that national defence is an exception to the rule of comparative advantage, precisely because of its particularity. Still, beyond weaponry production, many more products and services are important in situations of group conflict. Some examples could be food supply, transportation vehicles, among several others. This, of course, is not to say protectionism is always beneficial, but, under group competition, some degree of autonomy confers any group the means to maintain cohesion and self-defence. In terms of preferences, an economic analysis based on preference satisfaction would validate Tullock's assertion that the U.S. citizens would be worse off with a tariff on Korean cars. But in terms of fitness, they could be better off if such a tariff meant that the United States would keep its production of cars, which could be helpful in a war economy in case of conflict. Here, once again, the tension between the maximisation of the universal satisfaction of preferences can collide with the maximisation of group fitness.

If humanity made up a group, then relative gains would be achievable, perhaps without protectionism. Yet, the fact that humans have relatively mastered the earth to the point where no other species offer direct competition makes it unlikely that humanity can become a group. Given this absence of direct competition, the main threat to humans are other humans, and groups arise accordingly. However, following a group selectionist logic, humanity could become a group if another non-human group offered effective competition. Even natural dangers like hurricanes and droughts can foster temporary cooperation, but they are unlikely to be strong enough to transform humanity into a group that suppresses competition at lower levels of selection. Hence, under the current situation, with the current knowledge, the formation of groups is mostly unavoidable.

It is then not always clear that rent-seeking is a process that makes people worse off, in particular if one goes beyond a strict economic account of the pros and cons. Importantly, rent-seeking can be a way to frame policies and shape preferences. Many in society emulate the values and practices of the most successful rent-seekers because of the pervasive status quo bias and the tendency to emulate the successful. The successful rent-seekers may search for their own material gain and "sell" it to the public in terms of "moral language" (e.g. rational egoists) (Brennan & Hamlin, 2004, pp. 119–120). But they can also lobby and self sacrifice for values they truly believe should be the ones of society (e.g. lobbying for actions to stop/prevent climate change; lobbying for affirmative action, such as women's quotas). This lobbying activity leads us to question the types of individuals that can become successful rent-seekers and exert their influence in society.

By conceiving political power as a monopoly rent, Geoffrey Brennan and James Buchanan shed light on the type of individuals likely to be successful rent-seekers and hold positions of power:

> Suppose that a monopoly right is to be auctioned; whom will we predict to be the highest bidder? Surely we can presume that the person who intends to exploit the monopoly power most fully, the one for whom the expected profit is highest, will be among the highest bidders for the franchise. In the same way, positions of political power will tend to attract those persons who place higher values on the possession of such power. These persons will tend to be the highest bidders in the allocation of political offices. (Brennan & Buchanan, 2000, p. 72)

In other terms, the intensity of preferences becomes an important feature to understand who the successful rent-seekers are. The rent-seekers who merely search for material gains must believe in the inherent goodness or desirability of such a materialistic aim. In the same way, those who aim at instituting certain values to underpin policies in society or in their group must also have faith in those values. As Brennan and Buchanan suggest, only with intense preferential beliefs will the rent-seeker apply all efforts and resources and bid the highest values to achieve the desired goals. When comparing both beliefs, especially in the light of multilevel selection theory, it is more likely that the intensity of beliefs in group values trumps a simple belief in material wealth, even though the second is also a moral belief—the belief in the moral goodness of achieving wealth. Yet, the first belief is group-oriented while the second is not necessarily so, i.e. it can be mostly an individual goal. This means the former is explicitly political while the latter does not have to be. But rent-seeking is political by nature and power becomes necessary for individuals to achieve goals. Values, ideologies and religions can make individuals endure the hardest sacrifices to defend their beliefs, and rent-seeking should not be the exception. According to multilevel selection theory, groups made up of altruistic individuals have a clear advantage over those groups whose members are rational egoists (Wilson & Wilson, 2007). Thus, groups unified by a strong belief, with members who devote their lives to certain collective causes, will probably outcompete those groups whose members are merely interested in material wealth. Free riders would plague the groups of the latter types, which would produce few if any public goods. Liberal democracies have instituted the pursuit of wealth as part of the moral good of achieving happiness, and that is why material rent-seekers legitimately operate in the political sphere. But above such materialistic seeking types, there was a group of individuals that fiercely challenged the prior non-liberal European *ancien régime*. The prevalence of rent-seeking in societies may happen because group political values have a higher intensity. After all, individuals can alternatively pursue wealth in the market place. The pervasiveness of rent-seeking strengthens the idea that economic actors capture the government not merely to make an extra-profit but also because of power itself and the higher goal of instituting values and shaping preferences.

Karl Marx wrote, "the ideas of the ruling class are in every epoch the ruling ideas (…). The class which has the means of material production at its disposal, has control at the same time over the means of mental production" (Marx & Engels, 2004, p. 64). Because of his historical materialism, Marx saw values and beliefs as a justification for rulers to keep the means of production and he also sees political power as a tool of dominance for the aim of material or wealth "conservation". This vision seems to be somehow a-historical because it ignores how those in power reached such a position. Could it be that rulers reached the power position because of the motivational strength of a real belief in certain values, which then they espouse on society, shaping its general preferences? Because a belief in nothing, in nihilism, seems to be unlikely as a motivator of action, the idea that political power can be captured by the sole desire for material wealth seems implausible, and it is fruitless as a group strategy. Even the moral goodness of achieving profit is often a means to achieve values and ideologies like liberalism, equality, liberty or happiness; that is, profit-seeking is subjected to "higher" moral goals. Still, the rational egoists who merely seek profit without believing in those "higher" values do exist (Ostrom, 2000, pp. 142–143; Turchin, 2006, pp. 98–99), it is just that those are probably secondary rent-seekers.

5.1.5.1 *Two Levels of Rent-Seeking*

It is then possible to identify two levels of rent-seeking: one level is paradigm changing, with agents who capture monopoly power to institute a new paradigm of moral/political values. The second level is where rent-seekers operate within an established moral paradigm and want to achieve material gains, perhaps falsely paying lip service to the prevalent moral paradigm. Alternatively, such secondary rent-seekers may want to deepen the values of the established regime. The ones that change paradigms have a revolutionary rent-seeking attitude (e.g. the bourgeoisie in the French revolution) and often change the paradigm by climbing through the institutions. As Gordon Tullock (2005, pp. 44–46) showed, most revolutionary leaders or elements come from within the polity. The most motivated agents, with a higher intensity of beliefs, will be the ones self-sacrificing the most to reach power. A considerable degree of self-sacrifice is necessary because a great political power requires a life of permanent risk or danger. For example, Joseph Stalin was never completely at ease when sleeping because of fear of assassination (Tullock, 2001, p. 143). Even under liberal democracy, a leader or elements of government are not in the most hedonistic and safest places in society (e.g. John F. Kennedy). The rent-seekers operating on the second level may be simple rational egoists. They may be economic agents searching for favourable policies to maintain or acquire economic rents. But in this second level, there are also rent-seekers motivated by the fulfilment of the established moral rules. With western liberal democracies, examples of moral rent-seekers would be groups that fight for the deepening of freedom and equality like feminist interest groups, human rights NGO's, among many others. All these groups at the second level have the capacity, and often the liberty, to influence or capture public policymaking. Not merely because such groups can be small and well organised, like Mancur Olson would predict, but also because they are driven by morals, which allows them to overcome collective action problems more easily, problems like free riding.

These groups are successful because their quasi-religious beliefs allow them to solve free riders problems—and groups of altruists beat groups of egoists (Wilson & Wilson, 2007). A strong belief makes people restrain their own free riding actions in order to act morally and therefore individuals have a positive notion of themselves as members of a moral collective. Even the materialistic wealth seeking rational egoists may rationalise their desires and sublimate them with a general belief in a morality that sees the pursuit of money as morally good (e.g. wealth seeking liberty under liberal democratic values).

5.1.5.2 On the Logic of Collective Action

As aforementioned, the idea that group morality and strong beliefs can solve collective action problems challenges the classic "logic of collective action" by Mancur Olson (1971). His model shows that, by assuming universal rational egoism, only small groups can mobilise because big groups cannot solve the free riding problem. This process leads to the exploitation of democracy and of the preferences of the majorities by small, well-organised, rent-seeking interest groups. Yet, as I showed before, a big group of strongly believing moral group altruists can mobilise more successfully towards the goal of rent-seeking than smaller groups of rational egoists. The most likely reason scholars often associate rent-seeking with smaller groups is that smaller groups are logistically easier to organise than big groups. But the final effect can be similar to having a big group acting because of the influence that such a small group would exert on the formation of preferences of the remaining population. This outcome, of course, is underpinned by the prevalent phenomenon of individuals imitating the successful elites with whom they identify (i.e. in-group bias, along with status quo bias and conformity). Against Jean-Jacques Rousseau's idea that it is impossible to represent the will of the people (Inston, 2010, p. 129), elite framing shows that such an identification with the ruling power of a particular group is real because of mass preferences being shaped and uniformised. Flags, values, shared myths are all examples of mechanisms of group identification, through which group members identify with political representatives. So the reason why rent-seekers are numerically small and elitist may not be a matter of size, maybe it is just unnecessary to be a large group to capture and maintain power. Moreover, unlike in small hunter-gatherer tribal groups, in large societies power hierarchies are almost impossible to avoid for logistic reasons. Altruistic representation is then possible for two main reasons: (1) power holders can be moral group altruists, for instance, Glaeser, Porta, Lopez-De-Silanes, & Shleifer (2004) provide ample evidence of welfare-enhancing governmental policies; and (2) power holders can shape mass preferences and become revered or legitimate. Another reason is that the intensity of a belief is probably stronger in smaller, concentrated groups. There is here an important difference between these "moral" rent-seekers and the rational egoists of material/economic rents, which is that Mancur Olson's logic of collective action applies much better to the latter. Indeed, if the world was only composed of rational egoists, Olson's logic of collective action would have universal application. But this is not the case because of the existence of other behavioural types. However, Olson's model is useful to analyse sub-groups composed of rational egoists, of which the best candidates are in fact economic/material rent-seekers that operate at this second level of rent-seeking.

5.1.5.3 Rent-Seeking Is Not Necessarily a Shortcoming

The standard notion that rent-seeking is a detrimental phenomenon that stifles production or innovation and generates scarcity or higher prices is one that applies to economic actors (Tullock et al., 2002, p. 44). Economists often assume these actors to be rational egoists. Still, because not all rent-seekers are of an egoist kind, it is less certain that this conclusion is universally true. As an example, it is possible to conceptualise agents who believe in innovative and productive societies, who will make the necessary sacrifices and investments for these types of societies to arise. Mancur Olson (1982) famously claimed that liberal democracies will tend to accumulate rent-seeking distributional coalitions, such as protectionists, restrictionists and "enemies" of economic growth. This accumulation continues at least until liberal democracies economically stagnate and are "rescued" by a fierce liberalising revolution. Yet the example of Margaret Thatcher in the 1980s UK shows that political elites can pursue market-oriented policies without the need for revolutions. In this case, individuals made a change through reforms and through the use of moral language, emphasising self-reliance, the moral virtues of entrepreneurship, etc. (Vinen, 2010). Hence, when one accounts for a non-rational egoist (i.e. "altruistic") moral type of rent-seekers who aim at capturing political power, the idea that rent-seeking is always detrimental to society seems misguided. Searching for monopoly power is not necessarily a waste of resources per se or an unmistakable problem for liberal democracy.

Rent-seeking does not have to be a severe problem for liberal democracies as long as it continues to operate at the second level, under the framework set by liberal democratic agents. There are counterbalancing forces at this second level of rent-seeking where "moral liberals" counteract the action of rational egoists and vice versa, ideally achieving a certain balance. These democracies are endangered mostly by rent-seeking at the first level, where groups of individuals with non-liberal values and ideas capture power and frame non-liberal democratic institutions. Still, liberal constitutionalism protects its democracies from illiberal revolutions by marginalising antagonistic actors or ideas, thus preventing competitors from taking part in institutional deliberation (Hughes, 2010, Chapter I). However, if the second level balance between rational egoists and moral liberal rent-seekers does not create social harmony or general preference satisfaction, especially at the moral level, challengers may start to operate at the first level of rent-seeking, challenging the liberal democratic paradigm.

Such a potential failure to satisfy general preferences may come from the inability to generate material wealth through economic growth, but interpreting world phenomena depends on morality (Haidt, 2012). It is possible that slower economic growth under a particular group framework satisfies general preferences, with elites moralising the reasons behind such a slower growth. It may also maximise fitness. Conversely, fast economic growth does not positively correlate with fitness enhancement and the satisfaction of proximate material preferences can lead to unsustainability (e.g. low birth rates, etc.). Thus, the general perception of the satisfaction of preferences will compare empirical reality with the framed moral values of a given political and cultural society.

Brennan and Hamlin (2004, pp. 119–120) are correct when claiming that individuals vote mainly for moral and expressive reasons. Given the widespread political ignorance, values are the ultimate instrument of analysis that resonates at an instinctive/emotional level. There is some empirical evidence showing that people also vote instrumentally, like when individuals vote for a candidate with good chances of winning the election instead of voting for an ideal candidate with few chances of victory (Christiano, 2004, p. 139). Yet such a process continues to operate at a moral level. The reason is that, when someone opts for a candidate that is not ideal but has good chances of winning, there is usually an important challenger from another group or party; a challenger that one wants to see defeated because of representing such antithetical visions that one opts for a candidate with closer moral/political visions. Unsurprisingly, moral analysis continues to be crucial for the analysis of political and social preferences.

Ultimately, rent-seeking, with its logic of concentrated benefits and diffused costs, will mostly depend on the strength of institutionalised moral values that justify or condemn the allocation of those costs and benefits. Above all, rent-seeking groups and the types that constitute them are crucial for the definition of such values.

In sum, rent-seeking is not necessarily a detrimental process for the satisfaction of preferences in liberal democracies because postulating the harmfulness of rent-seeking is mainly valid when one assumes universal self-interest/egoism. When assuming a pluralism of types that also includes morally (liberal) "altruistic" rent-seekers who aim at fulfilling liberal values, rent-seeking can become a process through which individuals satisfy preferences; especially because of the potential capacity that rent-seekers have to shape mass preferences and align them with the preferences of governmental representatives. All in all, when analysed from a behaviourally pluralist perspective, it is possible to conclude that the shortcomings of liberal democracy are much less severe than what public choice theorists acknowledged. With the appropriate altruistic types, liberal democracy reveals a high potential to satisfy preferences.

5.2 Reassessing the Autocratic Market Solution

In rational/public choice literature, market autocracy—as a solution for the shortcomings of liberal democracy—does not possess the normative strength that, for example, a contractarian approach has. This absence of normative support relies on the assumption that altruistic/benevolent autocrats are not a likely possibility. Hence, the best that public choice theorists write in favour of autocracy is that in the autocratic regime there is a considerable capacity to curtail some democratic shortcomings, but not without creating other problems. I will now reanalyse such insights from the pluralist/naturalistic/evolutionary perspective to create alternative interpretations to public choice models of autocracy. Namely, I assess if an autocracy can generate a market-oriented and preference maximising polity. First, I will discuss the main rational/public choice models of autocracy. Afterwards, I discuss the market under autocracy.

5.2.1 *The Rational/Public Choice Models of Autocracy*

The main rational/public choice models of autocracy that I explored in this book were Olson's "stationary bandit" and Wintrobe's "repression versus loyalty". Both models operate on the behavioural assumption that autocrats are self-interested and assume a narrow (or thick) version of rational self-interest. These models assume that autocrats are mostly interested in power or/and wealth and that self-sacrificing altruistic autocrats who care about the welfare of their people are essentially a fantasy (i.e. non-existent). Olson (1993) is clearer in assuming this position, while Wintrobe (1998, p. 95), who has a more pluralistic model with different types of autocrats, states that altruistic autocrats (e.g. timocrats) probably do not exist. By shifting away from such a narrow (or thick) version of rationality and by allowing for a plurality of behavioural types—like pro-group altruists—I reanalyse the rational/public choice insights on the question "is autocracy a good framework for the preference maximising market?". This re-evaluation comes to different conclusions, or at least to conclusions that differ in their theoretical underpinnings.

The central tenet of Olson's model is the claim that, in the state of nature, bandits will plunder populations at will because these populations cannot build counter defence systems. Populations cannot defend themselves due to the difficulty of solving collective action problems inherent to large-scale populations. In contrast, these bandits operate in small groups and can hence solve their collective action problems to plunder as much as possible. The thieves then become stationary to plunder the same population regularly, offering their subjects the conditions to produce wealth, such as security and public goods. Thereafter, the thieves can extract this wealth through taxation, therefore maximising their gains. Yet, one may contest Olson's logic on two important points: (1) The materialistic motivation of plundering groups seems to be unreal or too simplistic; and (2) populations, or sub-segments of them, could solve collective action problems in terms of collective security if they had enough altruistic types willing to self-sacrifice for the group. Following the multilevel selection logic, groups that contain more altruists will not succumb to these hypothetical roving bandits because of having the capacity to produce a self-defence group. Given that these groups with more altruists will maximise their fitness and be evolutionarily selected in conflicts with other groups (Wilson & Wilson, 2007), it is not certain that roving bandits would always be "free" to settle down. The outcome would depend on the types existing in the population. Moreover, the role of morality in helping groups solving collective action problems and allowing for collective mobilisation is absent in Olson's model. Dominant groups are likely to come together around a set of beliefs that not only justify the groups' dominance but that also help group members to unite around those beliefs. Believing in a set of values helps members to punish free riders and deviant elements. Hence, one must insert the existence of "roving bandits" in a moral context, in a morality that would see such a plundering dominance as a means to fulfil a particular set of values. Yet, there is a plurality of possible moralities that unite groups, and the maximisation of wealth is merely one of them or, most likely, a simple aspect, while some moralities even preach a detachment from material desires (e.g. Buddhism or Catholicism). From an evolutionary perspective, it is unlikely that autocratic states arise because of the mere desire to maximise wealth. There is a good reason to believe that competition with other groups is a strong force behind such hierarchical and pro-group dispositions; namely, groups require leadership to organise and make collective decisions, sometimes under pressure, which is a common and perhaps necessary strategy to maximise group fitness under collective competition, especially in the face of all the shortcomings of voting collective decisions.

Still, as Olson predicts, small elites are usually the ones solving collective action problems. But this is considerably less because of their small size, which allows for tight control of members, and more because of an intense belief in a particular morality that propels action towards political power. Hence, the reason big groups are less likely to mobilise, even when they have many altruists, is that elites have to first shape and nudge their group's moral preferences to unite the group around such beliefs—a process which relies on mass traits like conformity and status quo biases. Later on, these elites can mobilise the masses towards war or other mass collective events, but prior leadership is essential in the definition of moral goals. Instead of the small versus large groups explanation by Olson, this is a strong evolutionary reason for the historic prevalence of autocratic elitist rule and mass group conformity.

Of course, this reason does not rule out that autocracies may contain less altruistic types or that such systems can resemble Olson's wealth maximiser or even that they can be predatory. The nature of autocracies mostly depends on behavioural types. The evolutionary perspective just shows the limitations of the "stationary bandit" model. Ronald Wintrobe tried to overcome such limitations by replacing Olson's assumption of wealth maximisation by a form of power struggle. For Wintrobe (1998, Chapter II), what defines the type of autocracy is the various methods an autocrat uses to stay in power. Depending on the way autocracies use the tools of repression and loyalty, autocrats can be of a specific type (i.e. tinpots, tyrants, totalitarians and timocrats).

Yet, with the rejection of altruistic types, Wintrobe (1998, p. 95) ends up attributing to raw power the importance that Olson gave to wealth.

But even though power can be the desired aim in itself, it requires motivational content. Power for what? Power can only be complete with a design to fulfil. It is this design that helps to generate a morality that will make others believe in one's project. David Hume understood that no man rules merely by fear or force, but by persuasion. In his own words, the autocrat's "bodily force can reach but a small way, and all the further power he possesses must be founded either on our own opinion, or on the presumed opinion of others" (Hume, 1994, p. 18). Because of a strong economic vision of power, Wintrobe (2004, p. 77) claims that autocrats will buy off opponents for support, which is the reason why he thinks autocracies engage in more "pork barrel politics" than democracies. Yet, as Scott Atran and Robert Axelrod (2008) demonstrated, someone can only be "bought" when the differences are not of a moral nature (i.e. because certain values are sacred). Trying to buy off resilient moral opponents is nearly impossible and therefore repression is the only available tool of an autocrat. Hence, instead of types being defined by the use of repression and loyalty, one should define autocratic types by their behavioural tendencies, and the use of repression and loyalty will be a reflex of morality. This process will operate on the basis of upholding and framing group morality while punishing free riders or dissidents. Also, such a process is present in most existing regimes. Even western liberal democracies forbid several dangerous groups for the regime from freely exerting their political actions (Tronnberg, 2013). While it is tempting to claim that the use of repression is a mere function of power keeping, the morality behind it is also important, if not more so. Hence the controversial moral problems that liberal democratic institutions have in applying repression on dissident political thought and action while paradoxically claiming to uphold values like liberty or autonomy.

Perhaps because such a logic of framing and punishing is so prevalent, Wintrobe (1998, p. 94) acknowledges that, even though he does not believe that altruistic autocrats exist, even the altruistic type would have to use some repression to control the incentives to produce and prevent inefficiency or power loss. While this assertion is true, it is also important to understand that altruistic pro-group political behaviour does not aim at the satisfaction of preferences of all members, aiming instead to fulfil a particular moral framework (i.e. a conception of "good for group"). Yet, rational/public choice theorists like Wintrobe often reject the validity of altruistic claims of general welfare, i.e. claims of caring about citizens, because these claims are not Pareto efficient and do not see all preferences as morally acceptable. In such altruistic claims, some individuals have to be worse off if they present anti-group behavioural preferences at the moral level. As even Wintrobe (1998, pp. 77–78) acknowledges, the act of repression often increases the autocrat's popularity by creating a single popular mindset and group stability. Unsurprisingly, these are the evolutionary products of between-group competition features that select for altruistic pro-group individuals (Puurtinen & Mappes, 2009).

5.2.2 *The Market Under Autocracy*

Public choice authors such as Olson or Wintrobe are sceptical about autocracy being a better political framework for a preference-enhancing market. However, this scepticism may result from known methodological assumptions, which, if changed, can present different conclusions. Of special relevance in public choice literature is the question of knowing if autocracies are better at curtailing rent-seeking and redistributive governmental actions, which prevent the unfettered market from working efficiently.

While some authors, like Robert Barro (1996a, 1996b) or Stephan Haggard (1990), consider that autocracies have a higher capacity than democracies to stop these rent-seeking redistributive and inefficient processes, some others, like Ronald Wintrobe (2004, p. 85), believe that the opposite is true because autocrats have to buy off the main producers, i.e. interest groups, of the country and therefore these producers will have more power. But why should autocrats restrain rent-seeking? Either autocrats are altruistic and have the best in mind for their group or they simply believe that it is in their self-interest to restrain wasteful rent-seeking activity and to generate more wealth for them to tax. Yet, if one discards the existence of altruistic autocrats, as it is common in rational choice analysis, only the option of self-interest remains. However, better economic conditions could prolong the autocrat's regime by increasing the means that he or she could use, i.e. the tax revenue. But better economic conditions may lead to democratisation, which would end the autocrat's "reign" (Londregan & Poole, 1996). By excluding altruistic types, it becomes difficult to understand the incentives to curtail wasteful rent-seeking, in particular because the autocrat could benefit from buying off these interest groups or from joining these groups to better exploit the population, namely by concentrating benefits and dispersing costs.

In contrast, if one understands the autocrat as a moral type, understanding the values he or she holds can help to explain why the autocrat would restrain wasteful rent-seeking; or why the autocrat would allow some sorts of rent-seeking while excluding other sorts; or why the autocrat would value wealth creation over redistributive policies. Yet, one must apply the same logic to liberal democracies. Ronald Wintrobe explains that if politicians only accepted offers that serve the public, waste would be diminished. But because public choice theorists often assume that no altruistic public-oriented politician exists, waste is the predicted result of the rent-seeking process (Wintrobe, 1998, p. 154). If one assumes that democratic politicians can be public-minded, then altruistic politicians would only accept the offers of rent-seekers who serve the preferences of the public. The main difference between these two systems is that liberal democracy, because of its relatively higher degree of pluralist political participation, has the potential to attract several types of politicians. Some could be public-minded and some could simply enjoy the concentration of benefits through the dispersion of costs on the general public. The behavioural types that operate in liberal democracies would then determine the level of wasteful rent-seeking, which can be a mixed process of both altruists and rational egoists. Conversely, in autocracies, it is more likely that this process is stabler, whether towards wasteful rent-seeking/redistribution or toward shutting down these economically hurtful processes (i.e. privileging the unfettered market instead). This higher stability will depend on the moral behavioural types that run such an autocracy and on the institutionalised moral framework. Hence, market-oriented and wealth creation-oriented autocracies may have an advantage over democracies in providing an appropriate political framework for the market.

This conclusion is strengthened by the classic assumptions in public choice theory that small and well-organised producer groups dominate democracies (Becker, 1983; Olson, 1982; Stigler, 1971) and that open access to power for competing forces leads to waste. Hence, Wintrobe's claim that producer groups have more power in autocracies seems to be not only at odds with classic public choice, but also with historical narrative. After all, in the key event of 1789, the French bourgeoisie made a revolution against what they saw as a regime that was oppressive of their interests (Sewell, 1994).

The main difference comes from a moral perspective. While liberal democracies are relatively open because their morality proclaims that politics should not impose a particular view of collective happiness (i.e. the "good way of life"), such a particular vision can sustain autocracies because they are less pluralistic and smaller in their elitist power core. Moreover, given the absence of universal elections, autocratic leadership has to rely on a given moral vision and on loyalty to that vision as the representative of an identity group. This requirement is probably the main reason autocracies are more protectionist than liberal democracies (Aidt & Gassebner, 2010). Autocracies require a higher level of loyalty towards and from their socio-political group. Since group loyalty leads to the increase of group competing forces (i.e. evolutionary "between group" selection), it creates a general search for collective autonomy and for less dependence on other competing groups when autonomy is possible. Hence, the way autocrats deal with rent-seekers and redistribution is likely to express this search for group autonomy. The search for collective autonomy is a less prevalent phenomenon in liberal democracies, where moral pluralism, inclusiveness and universal individualism underpin policies that relatively deemphasize group competition and sometimes even group existence.

Still, even with more protectionist tendencies, Barro's (1996a, 1996b) findings suggest that autocracies have a slight advantage in relation to liberal democracies in terms of economic growth. Wintrobe (1998, p. 161) explains this advantage by emphasising the power that autocrats have to transfer property rights from labour to capital through repression (e.g. by preventing collective labour bargaining), which is a form of political redistribution. Yet, because liberal democracies often allow for the collective bargaining of wealth, they also transfer monetary rights from capital to labour. This comparison does not confirm that autocracies are more or less distributive or more or less free market-oriented than liberal democracies. It merely confirms a lighter conclusion: that Wintrobe (1998, p. 160) is correct when postulating that there is no such thing as "free market" in the absence of some form of political institution that assigns property rights and monetary earning rights. Polities shape property rights and earning rights in the same way as they shape preferences: through elite moral and political framing.

However, it is far from obvious that autocracies have higher economic growth than liberal democracies. When empirically comparing economic growth in autocracies and liberal democracies, Limongi and Przeworski (1993, p. 56) conclude that no regime is clearly superior in that regard and that, because of the diversity of results and regimes, there must be something else that explains results apart from democracy or authoritarianism. From a multilevel selection angle, this "something else" relates to the types that operate within a regime. But it also relates to the cultural and moral framework, to the products of elitist framing and to the selection under between and within-group forces. When figuring out whether autocracy is a better framework for the preference-maximising market than liberal democracy, it is important to emphasise the behavioural moral types that constitute the autocracy. Autocracy has the potential to solve the shortcomings of liberal democracies, like wasteful rent-seeking or inefficient redistribution. Yet, an autocracy can only solve these shortcomings if it contains many altruistic moral types and relies on a moral framework that holds market wealth creation and preference satisfaction as aims to achieve. In contrast, liberal democracies will have more difficulties solving these problems because of having more pluralistic types pulling in different directions. Still, the resilience of autocracies will always depend relatively more on group loyalty and group identity, which will drive these autocracies towards some form of protectionism. Hence, even though there is the political potential to build a "market society" to solve some "public choice" shortcomings of liberal democracy, group competition will always present limits to such a solution. From the perspective of creating a structure to satisfy "market preferences", an autocracy can solve some typical problems of liberal democracies, but it may also produce other issues that are less common in liberal democracies. Protectionism and collective autonomy are some of them.

In conclusion, under a behaviourally pluralistic approach, a market-enhancing autocracy is theoretically possible if managed by the right "market-oriented" moral types. Still, because autocracies require higher levels of group loyalty than liberal democracies, it is likely that autocracies will search for a certain autonomy and self-sufficiency, leading to anti-market policies. The autocratic drive towards collective autonomy can thus explain why autocracies tend to be more protectionist than liberal democracies.

5.3 Reassessing the Liberal Market Solution: Constitutional Political Economy

Following the liberal tradition of the social contract and applying the rational/public choice logic of constitutional political economy, James Buchanan (2000) proposes the social contract as the only rational solution to the problems of current liberal democracies. For him, the only liberal solution to the problems of current democracies that produce preference dissatisfaction is to create a social contract where the preferences of all individuals count and where value is strictly individualistic—i.e. nobody can force preferences on others in the name of a collective. The social contract would create a real liberal contractarian democracy of free and equal individuals maximising their preferences. Yet, when reanalysing the contract's main assumptions and logic from the evolutionary angle, this solution may present several shortcomings that can prevent the contract from being a true solution. Next, I will reanalyse the solution of the social contract from the evolutionary perspective. I also reassess the alleged "public choice" advantages of choosing in markets over choosing in liberal democratic/majoritarian politics regarding preference satisfaction.

5.3.1 The Moral/Social Contract

By conceptualising politics as "exchange" of preferences, Brennan and Buchanan (2000, Chapter II) idealise the social contract as an agreement by sovereign individuals on the institutions and rules that will prevail in their political society. Such an agreement must get unanimous consent and supply Pareto improvements resulting from a trade of preferences that will stop at equilibrium.

When assessing the potential for such a contract to materialise, it is perhaps not enough to claim that an agreement is unlikely because large-scale individualistic agreements are empirically not observable. As political scientist Russell Harding (1988, p. 514) pointed out, even political theorists do not agree on what individuals could or would agree on. It is also necessary to present an explanation for why this lack of agreement is so prevalent. Hence, from a multilevel selection perspective, perhaps the main reason why such large-scale contracts are unlikely or impossible is that a particular morality binds every group, especially of a political kind. For groups to implement such a morality, the punishment of deviants or free riders is necessary. This need makes it nearly impossible for people to establish contracts based on respecting the preferences of all individuals, especially if we are dealing with a population with many behavioural types or with strong allegiances to sub-groups. If the evolutionary process of the establishment of group morality works because of cultural and political elites capturing political power and framing the group moral framework

(Boehm, 1999), the common procedure of shaping mass preferences and punishing deviants becomes an essentially unavoidable phenomenon. Hence, groups will operate on the basis of conformity and punishment to maintain the necessary cohesion to compete with other groups. In theory, James Buchanan's liberal contract could take place among a group of liberal contractarians. Yet, following Durkheim, even though liberalism is a group morality, it is one that would be difficult to implement at a large scale because of the prevalent tendencies for "groupism" rather than for universal individualism (Caplan, 2004b, pp. 471–472).

Of course, non-liberal individuals could participate in the negotiation of such a social contract and the final results would be the ones at the equilibrium point of the trade of preferences. But this seems to disregard the strong variance in the intensity of preferences, making some preferences incompatible with some others. Thus, negotiations eventually break before reaching any equilibrium. For instance, a non-liberal elitist individual with collectivist/communitarian notions of morality would most likely never accept to live under a liberal contract where the punishment of moral deviants would target non-liberals. Such elitist non-liberal preferences would not attempt to achieve a liberal social contract because it would be paradoxical. The closest to a social contract would then be an organic and collective Burkean social contract, which would be, in the words of Edmund Burke, "a partnership not only between those who are living, but between those who are living, those who are dead, and those who are to be born" (Burke, 2005, p. 54). Ultimately, the non-aligned moral types would join cohesive sub-groups to fight for political dominance, and not necessarily through liberal means. This fragmentation would stifle the liberal social contract. The prevalence of such a contract depends on an elitist and paternalistic "framing" approach by the ones aiming for a liberal vision. Ultimately, new larger groups can arise from old sub-groups; but such a process of identity formation, when possible, requires previously framed institutions and transformations of mass preferences—i.e. changing of language, symbols of union, moral framework, etc.—to the point where new political and social identities arise. For example, the European Union is an attempt to create a European political identity from previous European sub-national affiliations.

Apart from the difficulties that different behavioural moral types and sub-group affiliations pose to the liberal social contract, knowing that preferences are never well-formed until they are framed adds to the problem of the contractarian approach (Tversky & Kahneman, 1981).

That many behavioural/moral types could take part in the social contract already presupposes that some liberal elite has previously shaped preferences to the point where all individuals want to enter the contract with a liberal disposition. This process questions the extent to which the contract is not an elitist manipulation. After all, the United States is today one of the most individualistic countries in the world (Rothwell, 2010, pp. 65–84), yet its constitution results from elites that instituted liberal democracy via a non-contractarian approach. As a result, the established constitutional liberal framework likely shaped the current individualistic preferences in the United States. Even James Buchanan (1999a, pp. 370–371) understood the need of a moral framework prior to the social contract when he asked for the development of a truly liberal ethical revolution (i.e. a civil religion). He thought mobilisation for participation would not be possible in any other way because of collective action problems. Still, the main problem remains. Even if a particular morality could spread in a large population, the only way to make the entire population adhere to such a morality would be to institute political mechanisms to punish deviants. Yet, someone must put the mechanisms in place prior to the social contract by using non-liberal, non-contractarian means. Therefore, the logic of elitist manipulation appears inescapable.

5.3.1.1 The Feasibility of "Politics as Exchange"

The liberal preoccupation with elite manipulation seems to be present in the conception of the "veil of uncertainty", which is the hypothetical position where individuals decide the meta-rules of the social contract. In this position of uncertainty, Brennan and Buchanan (2000, p. 35) postulate that rational individuals would not choose to elect a dictator because the costs would probably be too high in relation to benefits. However, the opposite could also be true: under uncertainty, the costs of having open access to political office, where worse politicians could rise, could be higher than to have a strong, powerful leader. To elect a competent autocrat could be a rational decision made by individuals who would want to diminish the problems of "open access" politics by concentrating power in one visible entity, problems such as rational ignorance or imperfect information. What uncertainty gives us in this situation are several possible political solutions, but it is not obvious that this uncertainty would lead to Buchanan's anti-elite preferences. Perhaps only a previously nudged anti-elite set of preferences could shift these "meta-decisions" in Buchanan's direction. Yet, such a previous nudging would be a paradox because people would keep choosing liberal arrangements as long as they were being illiberally manipulated.

A decision where contractual participants would hand power over to a specific individual or to a set of individuals via a process of "politics as exchange" would put liberal contractualism into question. Hence, Buchanan unsurprisingly postulates that uncertainty leads individuals to fear elitist power. The perpetuation of such a model would only be possible if this fear is real. Only by maintaining such anti-elite preferences can liberalism and democracy be blended and therefore underpin the general framework of politics as exchange (Vanberg, 2013, p. 21). Yet, the fact that groups or sub-groups often have incompatible internal positions is a strong catalyst for individuals to break from the politics of exchange to one of authority (i.e. supporting leaders that would apply certain group principles). In addition, the multilevel selection process of moral groups punishing free riders or anti-group elements makes it difficult, if not impossible, to give equal positions to anti-group or free rider elements and to pro-group elements, especially if a given behavioural morality is to prevail and evolve. To be sure, competing or antagonistic groups can also negotiate with each other, but even if groups could achieve Pareto improvements for everything else measurable, the ultimate question of fitness cannot be easily solved because of its relative nature. As David Sloan Wilson (2002, p. 38) points out, it is less important how well an organism (e.g. group) reproduces, what is important is that it reproduces and survives better than competing organisms (e.g. groups). Thus, Pareto improvements coming out of "politics as exchange" between groups could not solve the problem of fitness being a relative or differential concept. Theoretically, the best that groups could achieve would be strict equality of fitness maximisation, but such a process is practically impossible because of natural inequalities, especially without a higher power supervising the natural world. Even if possible, this egalitarian aim would imply mechanisms of control that would go way beyond the liberal threshold.

Constitutional political economists prefer using a narrow version of rational choice theory, which assumes all individuals to be knaves, because, as James Buchanan (2008, p. 290) postulates, this is a way to prevent knaves from achieving power, even if some individuals can be altruists. Hence, to prevent knaves from achieving political power, citizens must constitutionally limit this power. But limiting political power also prevents competent altruists from having enough capacity to rule for the common good of a political group. As a result, it is unclear if the benefits of allowing altruists to rule compensate for the risks of having knaves in power. Still, even though political power is always limited—ultimately by revolutions or even by group extinction—individuals do not always show a belief in limited government. They often prefer strong powerful leaders that represent the group (Fisher, 2013), an organisational model which has been prevalent throughout history. However, the cultural and institutional nudges of political institutions can reinforce both preferences for limited governments and for strong rulers.

The conceptualisation of the social contract under the veil of uncertainty relies on a central premise: that it is possible for individuals to engage in a large-scale dialogue where the trade of preferences occurs under real conditions of inequality and leads to an optimal equilibrium point (Buchanan, 1959, p. 136). This dialogue aiming at shaping preferences has limitations of several kinds. However, the most relevant may be that several moral types operating in different groups often talk past each other. They confirm the observed phenomenon of morality "binding and blinding" (Haidt, 2012, p. 313). Put differently, to provide group cohesion, morality can blind individuals to antithetical perspectives of out-group members. Given the ubiquitous presence of the "confirmation bias" (Nickerson, 1998), individuals search for information that confirms their beliefs while ignoring opposite perspectives or evidence. These natural/evolutionary shortcomings of universal justification dialogue are problematic for deliberative liberal democrats, even when they postulate deliberation merely for meta-rules, as it is the case of James Buchanan (1959, p. 136) or John Rawls (1993). Once again, the thick moral homogeneity required for the social contract is not only difficult to achieve, it also requires a previous process of preference shaping and within-group selection.

Even though deliberative democrats advocate deliberation and exchange of justificatory arguments by free and equal individuals to end the reinforcement of the existing inequalities of power in society (Gutmann & Thompson, 2004, p. 16), these unequal distributions serve as a guide of behaviour for those within a group (Boyd & Richerson, 2005, p. 13). Because of ever-changing environmental circumstances, elements of groups developed the tendency for conformity and for the imitation of the successful, which is a tendency behind the prevalence of the status quo bias. In this sense, it is easier to shift the preferences of individuals by displays of success and power than it is to persuade individuals on equal grounds through simple dialogues. Because there is an epistemic problem in contractualist decision-making—i.e. the "veil of uncertainty"—following and imitating the successful is a traditional way of overcoming the asymmetries of knowledge. Since this happens mostly within groups with a collective identification (Labov, 2001), the polarisation between the sub-groups of a polity becomes more acute and any social contract dialogue presents its limits.

5.3.1.2 Choosing the "Free" Market?

Even considering the possibility that homogenous political groups agree on the meta-rules, would rational individuals choose to deliver most choices to the economic free market because of the high decision costs of unanimous collective decisions and of the high external costs of majority collective decisions (Buchanan & Tullock, 1999)? Judging by the identified "anti-market bias", which Bryan Caplan (2006, p. 30) characterises as a systematic bias, it is uncertain that individuals would prefer the marketplace, with its individualistic method of satisfying preferences. As discussed beforehand, because the "groupish" evolutionary legacy of humans drives the anti-market bias, and given the fitness benefits of groupishness, it may not be irrational to choose methods that are more collective-oriented than the market appears to be. Still, individuals must always consider the high external and decision costs of majoritarian and unanimous decision-making when trying to solve collective action problems. James Buchanan and Gordon Tullock (1999) believe that qualified majority voting would be the rational choice of individuals for lower level decisions. Buchanan and Congleton (2006, pp. 13–59) also believe that the more important a decision is, the closer to unanimity people would want it to be. Yet, not only would it be problematic to identify the most important decisions—all methods, majoritarian, deliberation or unanimity present problems in this regard—but also qualified majority voting has the potential to prevent many collective decisions from being made. Therefore, a traditional solution to cut the cost of these methods of collective decision-making is to come closer to the Hobbesian social contract (Hobbes, 1975), where individuals hand over power to a powerful entity that represents the political group. Group identification, trust in an altruistic leadership and general conformity to the status quo are then traits that provide the means to cut these costs while still aiming at the best arrangement for the individuals in a group, especially one in evolutionary competition with other groups.

Perhaps the choice of such leadership arrangements is less based on dialogue and exchange of preferences and more based on observation, emulation and conformity to displays of success. For instance, anthropological evidence suggests that no human society exists without some form of hierarchical leadership (Boehm, 1999; Lewis, 1974) and social psychological research shows that most groups structure themselves around a particular leadership, even when these groups begin leaderless (Bass, 1954). Yet, there are always risks and costs to pay when choosing bad representatives who will have a considerable amount of power. This is the reason why the destiny of groups depends so much on good leadership. Political leadership is especially important under the logic of group competition. In particular, bad leadership can make groups lose in such a competition (i.e. under the prevalence of mass conformity and imitation). It is not simple to assess if it is in the interest of rational individuals to limit power, thus building an open political process, or to choose powerful representatives. Both options cut the costs of some sort while increasing the costs of some other sort. Ultimately, it is difficult to know what rational individuals would choose in these hypothetical social contracts, but the fact that these social contracts are not in the empirical horizon suggests that this autonomous and purely individualistic method of choice is not part of the human evolutionary legacy. From the perspective of multilevel selection, strong individualistic decision-making did not serve the purpose of group evolutionary fitness maximisation.

5.3.2 *Preferences: Reanalysing the Market Advantages Over Liberal Democratic/Majoritarian Politics*

Market advantages flow directly from the individualistic postulate of preference maximisation. James Buchanan's (1999b) rational/public choice comparison of economic markets and democratic politics show that, in relation to choices made through voting, the market has: a higher degree of certainty, because it does not depend as much on the choices of others; a higher degree of responsibility, which is individual and not dispersedly collective; a higher degree of freedom from coercive majorities; and a higher degree of freedom to choose marginally due to escaping the problem of bundling better. Implied in these market advantages is the notion that voting must be a method to use only as a last resort when the social results of the market do not satisfy general preferences (Buchanan, 1999b, p. 87). But there is no way to measure the "common good" in terms of expressed preferences (de Condorcet, 1785) because of the problem of cycling, and systems of choice alter the results even when individual preferences are held constant (Buchanan & Tullock, 1999, p. 122). Then, it may not even be possible to understand if there is such a point where one can say the market is not generating a social ordering that satisfies general preferences. Perhaps voting is to be avoided altogether.

However, group competing forces are real. These forces are the likely reasons why although mechanisms to assess "the common will" may be intangible (Arrow, 1951), collective interests are important even within public choice analysis, even if limited to the minimum as James Buchanan (1999b, p. 87) suggests. Collective decisions that individuals cannot produce on the margin will exist because of this group notion. Public goods, like the building of a street lighting system or going to war (collective security), will be prevalent. This collective need is often justified in terms of being "good for the group/society", not simply good for individuals, many of whom could oppose these collective decisions. The prevalence of moral collectiveness confirms that agents in groups regularly take decisions not by satisfying all individual preferences but by punishing deviants or free riders from the institutionalised moral framework, like in public goods games (Ostrom, 2000). Because of the evolutionary need of ancient humans groups to adapt to different environments and to dangerous competition from other groups, shifts of collective behaviour were necessary (Boyd & Richerson, 2000). Hence, to expect that such shifts would have unanimous consent and would satisfy all individual preferences is unreal (Boehm, 1999), especially because institutional framing has its limits when shaping preferences. This still leaves elitist/representative collective decisions or some form of majoritarian democracy as likely methods of collective decision-making. Still, to know exactly when to shift from beneficial market decisions at the margin to collective decisions is probably impossible to calculate, which shows the importance of elitist decision-making in defining these moments.

5.3.2.1 Choosing Among Products Created by Experts Versus Choosing the Experts

Brennan, Buchanan and Vanberg regard the negligible impact of a single vote in a large election as a major weakness of voting democracy, which creates incentives that lead to massive rational ignorance

(Brennan & Buchanan, 2000, p. 85; Buchanan & Vanberg, 2001). However, in the economic market context, individuals have the incentives to inform themselves because the satisfaction of their preferences (i.e. purchases) directly depends on being informed. James Buchanan and Viktor Vanberg then conclude that the economic context is overall superior in satisfying preferences. They confirm this superiority by claiming that democratic politics is analogous to choosing among experts and that the market is analogous to choosing among the products of the experts. Because of widespread rational ignorance about each specific area of knowledge, Buchanan and Vanberg (2001, p. 138) argue it is more likely that individuals can satisfy their preferences when choosing among products created by the experts than choosing the experts themselves. The average individual possesses no adequate knowledge to choose the best experts.

This epistemic reasoning shows much more than a superiority of markets over voting systems in terms of preference satisfaction when one applies the same reasoning to constitutional or foundational politics. Lacking knowledge in a particular field may not only undermine the postulates of voting democracy but also undermine the foundational social contract underpinning normative constitutional political economy (Buchanan, 2000). After all, it is unreasonable to assume that all participants would have the same knowledge of what politics should produce or of the best way to achieve this production. To allow all individuals to take part in such a contract means that the ones with worse or no knowledge of good politics could choose rules in the dark. Here, perhaps individuals would have incentives to inform themselves because of having veto power, but the rational attitude could again be one of rational ignorance. That is, ignorance could prevail even though every individual has veto power. If the uninformed take their veto privilege until the end, no contract succeeds. Perhaps the specialists in politics could persuade other individuals, but how would the ones with little knowledge recognise political experts? If the informed cannot recognise the best politicians in regular liberal democracies, one cannot expect them to recognise the "experts" during the social contract; especially because emotion, and not pure rationality, would likely lead this process. Moreover, the uninformed could accuse the experts of working against the interests of the less knowledgeable. Rational irrationality could also operate; systematic biases by the rationally ignorant could prevent the experts from persuading the uninformed. Another likely reason for the existence of rational ignorance is the known tendency to enter a dialogue passively, expecting to be persuaded by the best arguments. But, once again, there is no guaranty that experts would persuade other individuals, as the average individual could not recognise the knowledgeable ones. In conclusion, even if social contracts came into existence, the results would be far from being optimal, similar to when the average individual chooses expert politicians "in the darkness" of rational ignorance.

Perhaps more important than the obstacles that ignorance brings to the social contract are the problems that ignorance causes to the whole democratic process of choosing political frameworks and representatives. If it is better for specialists to provide products that the average individual can then choose, then specialists in politics should create the best frameworks under which individuals will make choices. Put differently, the specialists should then shape and restrict the realm of choice for the "good" of rational ignorant masses. This happens in reality. Elites framed current liberal democracies to promote a framework of liberalism and democracy—no individualistic social contract ever took place. Yet, such framing logic decisively affects the market too. Given that markets require moral and political institutions to underpin them, those specialists in politics will also define what individuals can choose in the marketplace and the best way to achieve it. Clearly, a specialist in politics will have normative positions that people may contest, but the same is valid for the marketplace, where many show dissatisfaction about the mass consumption of certain products and services because of collective concerns. Even the political free market position, which claims market agents should consume everything freely, is also a normative position. If it is better to let people choose among products and not between specialists, for the sake of comparative methodological coherence, one should apply the same logic to the selection of political specialists (i.e. the ones with the best knowledge and capacities to frame political institutions).

If individuals do not always choose the best for themselves in politics (Caplan, 2004a, 2004b), they also do not always choose the best for themselves in the marketplace. Prevalent cognitive biases often lead to sub-optimal results (Tversky & Kahneman, 1974). Even though markets may reveal a higher degree of responsibility in individual choice than voting politics (Buchanan, 1999b), many individuals have no information about the consequences of the products they consume. Consumers will operate more on the basis of imitation (i.e. consuming what others are consuming) (von Hayek, 1979, p. 166) and heuristics

(Tversky & Kahneman, 1974). That people use the information which is most readily available is something well documented (Redelmeier, 2005). Moreover, political supervisors already provide product safety, which removes further incentives for individuals to gain knowledge about consumption goods. Competing markets may assure that the most desired goods keep being produced while eliminating the least desired or competitive ones. But this efficiency does not mean that individuals are choosing the best for themselves, either at an individual level or at the level of their group in competition with other groups. Because of informational problems and cognitive biases, individuals not always consume the best alternative in the market. Still, as public choice theorists claim (Buchanan, 1999b; Caplan, 2006), the consumers' incentives and capacities to satisfy preferences are stronger than the ones from voters because of the direct consequences of the act of purchasing on preference satisfaction. For instance, it is easier to exchange one brand of juice for another than to change public policy through voting. Yet, there are cases in which individuals consume products that are physically damaging and reduce fitness, like tobacco or soft drugs, and that, most times, such consumption is more the result of a physical/psychological addiction than of rational decisions. Systematic biases akin to the logic of rational irrationality can strengthen these bad decisions. Like Caplan (2004b) claims to happen in voting politics, people also systematically ask for products that hurt their wellbeing just because the price of consuming them is low, and the consequences come late in the future. This tendency may apply to the consumption of some products like chocolate, salt, tobacco or similar others. The bad effects of the excessive consumption of these products mainly come in the longer run. Perhaps the reasons in the two contexts are different. In politics, people may truly believe that bad policies are good while in the market they may know that a product may hurt them, but instinctive bias, the social status of the product or the uncertainty of its effect drives them to consume a particular good. Whatever the reasons, many continue to consume these products regardless of the evidence of their hurtfulness provided by specialists. Still, one can understand the consumption of products and services that reduce fitness as standard satisfaction of preferences. But when one places such maladaptive individual choices within a large collective, they minimise group fitness, which hurts a group in competition with other groups. It is then not surprising that most, if not all groups or political societies restrict and enforce choice through paternalism, whether in the market or in political institutions (e.g. high taxes on tobacco, criminalisation of drugs, etc.).

5.3.2.2 Maximising Individual Preferences Can Be Maladaptive

The process of restricting choice and enforcing group norms relies on gene-culture coevolution (Boyd & Richerson, 2008), where norms apply selective pressure on populations to conform to rules, often through the punishment of deviants. This is a process identified by anthropologists Gregory Cochran and Henry Harpending (2009, Chapter IV), who postulate that elite "domestication" is a powerful force in human evolution. Namely, specific elites created norms that have shaped and still shape the behavioural types operating in groups. This elite "domestication" theory is also in line with Christopher Bohem's (1999) classic anthropological explanation of how human tribal groups traditionally adhere to certain norms; namely, through hierarchical imposition, sometimes by egalitarian-minded elites (i.e. "reverse domination") and sometimes by standard hierarchical ones. It can be maladaptive for individuals to permit the satisfaction of all or most preferences because such permission would mean that anti-group preferences, especially the ones that minimise fitness, would be legitimate. But anti-group moral legitimacy would weaken any group when in competition with others. Thus, an elite that enforces norms promoting pure individualism or no group allegiance would weaken the in-group in relation to out-groups.

5.3.2.3 Time Horizon and Priced Preferences

Public choice theorists are correct when they demonstrate that politics is inherently more uncertain from the point of view of individual choice because one faces a choice in the middle of many individuals whose vote one cannot control (Buchanan & Tullock, 1999, pp. 37–38). Hence, the time horizon in the market is longer than in politics because one can plan for the future, knowing when to save and when to spend, whereas in democratic politics it is virtually impossible to do so, especially for the long run. This impossibility to make long-term plans in politics is due to the dependence of the voter on other people's voting preferences (Brennan & Buchanan, 2000, p. 86). Moreover, the fact that preferences are priced in the market but not so much in the political realm strengthens the superiority of markets over voting politics in satisfying individual preferences (Buchanan, 1999c, pp. 90–102). In democratic politics, one cannot properly analyse costs and benefits when choosing, mainly because of the absence of priced information. This impossibility enlightens an important point within public choice theory, which is that rational decision-making is a product of the evaluation of known costs and benefits of several real options (Meadowcroft, 2013, pp. 77–78). Individuals can only satisfy their preferences under a contextualised process. Conversely, preferences based on infinite, hypothetical, uncosted and unpriced wishes do not really count. Thus, one cannot talk about not satisfying preferences if one desires to go to the moon while having no real means to do so and not knowing the costs and benefits of such an enterprise.

This conception of what it means to satisfy preferences naturally confers a tremendous advantage to the market, where prices always help to assess the costs and benefits of every preference. In other social realms and not only in politics, many preferences come not only unpriced but are also of a difficult assessment in terms of costs and benefits (i.e. family, personal relations, social capital). Cultural and political preferences, which ultimately shape politics and markets, are difficult to assess. What would be the exact costs and benefits of a given political and social world vision? The difficulties of such an assessment are overwhelming. Yet, individuals often strive towards moral abstract goals or follow their instincts without too much calculation of costs and benefits, perhaps because for many of these important moral and sentimental goals, the calculations are of impossible or even of irrelevant assessment. Most crucial, the function of morality in groups is to create social cohesion, the type of cohesion that makes individuals go to war to defend their groups and values without wasting much time calculating the costs of such actions. But, as philosopher Michael Sandel (2012) points out, the attempt to put a market price on every aspect of civic life erodes the moral meaning behind social institutions, and this meaning functionally creates cohesion. If we price every aspect of civil life, cooperation becomes strictly connected to the amount of wealth one has. Such materialist individualism breaks the bonds that connect communities because of behaviour and action depending on money and not so much on non-material moral norms. Hence, to prevent the breakdown of communities caused by public affairs depending on wealth (e.g. money classes), groups require norms, moralities, beliefs and traditions that do not depend on material wealth. Political scientist Robert Axelrod and anthropologist Scott Atran understood that trying to buy off sacred moral values is not only a terrible negotiation strategy but is also the origin of many political and social conflicts. The reason for these conflicts is that "sacred values differ from material or instrumental values in that they incorporate moral beliefs that drive action in ways dissociated from prospects for success" (Atran & Axelrod, 2008, p. 221). Ultimately, an abstract and non-priced morality is vital to maintain the cohesiveness of groups.

Even if the political process worked in such a way that voters could know the exact prices of all public projects, there would still be a tension between group and individual interests. The voters' acceptance of public investment depends on the way politicians present the investment to the electorate in the same way that life or death choices taken by medical patients depend on how doctors present the options (Tversky & Kahneman, 1981). If a question between two options is presented by emphasising the gains instead of the losses, individuals tend to favour gains. Hence, elitist manipulation, especially of the moral kind, would be present even if voters fully knew the prices of collective services. This manipulation not only worsens the public choice theorists perspective on majoritarian democracy but also complicates their proposed solution of pricing all government activity/spending in order for individuals to maximise preferences (e.g. earmark taxation) (Buchanan, 2001, p. 72). For a voter to know if a new bridge or road is good for the community, if it is good for oneself, if it should be built now or later, would very much depend on the way politicians present such a policy question to the public. To know if such a policy would be good for the group or for the individual chooser would continue to be difficult.

One may see this difficulty to assess public policies as one more reason to allocate most decision-making processes to the market. Even though the producers of goods also nudge and shape preferences through branding and social meaning, the individual has at least a direct connection between himself or herself and the consumer products, increasing the possibilities of preference satisfaction. Even in relation to the intensity of preferences, markets present higher possibilities of preference satisfaction because of their dispersed, marginal and individualistic nature, while voting politics inefficiently offers one vote to the uninterested and the same one vote to the extremely interested (Buchanan & Tullock, 1999, p. 134). This asymmetry of intensities is also a strong reason why rent-seeking becomes prevalent. In politics, the ones with a higher intensity of preferences have the incentives to capture power and shut it down as much as possible through the framing of institutions. The way to solve the political problem of the intensity of preferences is then through the capture of power by the few, which explains why political decisions have this elitist character. In theory, markets could solve the problem of preference intensities, but only if one analyses preferences through the price system (e.g. disregarding preferences that are uncosted). However, because morality is also important, politics becomes the vortex for the shaping of mass group preferences, a process resulting from competition at the group level (Sober & Wilson, 1998). Politics is thus a way to shift the moralities of groups; it has the evolutionary purpose of adapting collective behaviour to new environmental challenges, although not always efficiently (Boyd & Richerson, 2000, 2005, Chapter V).

5.3.2.4 Free Entry as the Ultimate Advantage

Particularly strong is the claim that markets have the ultimate advantage over voting politics because they possess "free entry" (Buchanan, 1999d, p. 108) while politics presents many obstacles to entry/participation. This advantage confers a more universal democratic quality to the market. Also, in a majoritarian democracy there is no exit option in the sense that regardless of the voting decision, the voter has to accept the collective decision. The lack of an exit option in majoritarian democracies leads to problems similar to the tragedy of the commons and to an oversupply of public goods (Buchanan, 1999c, pp. 71–87). Perhaps if there are severe obstacles to entry/participation in politics and if individual voting does not have a significant direct impact in public policies, the level of public goods is determined by those rent-seekers who capture government and not so much by popular demands. However, whether through mass demands or minority rent-seeking, democratic politics presents many difficulties in terms of preference satisfaction. In contrast, the "free entry" that characterises markets escapes these problems. Consumers can take part only in market activities where they can satisfy their preferences and producers can always present new products to the public, generating competition for the best ideas, products and services. Yet, a multilevel selection analysis of these characteristics can not only explain why these restrictive characteristics are prevalent in politics but also why the supposed public choice advantage that markets have, i.e. "free entry", may not be such a clear one.

The idea that liberal democratic/majoritarian politics presents difficulties in satisfying preferences because of its collective nature is not surprising. Group dynamics rely on a moral institutional framework and on punishment. Group dynamics do not rely on a framework where all, including "anti-group" elements, can legitimately pursue their preferences. In politics, there is hardly an "exit option" within the polity because of the within-group selective force (Wilson & Wilson, 2007) aiming at cohesion, conformity and behavioural homogenisation that fit the institutionalised norms. "Free entry", which is an alleged advantage in markets, can be problematic for group cohesion. This "free entry" is characteristic of an individualistic and borderless process that is undermined by the evolutionary forces of between-group competition. Notably, groups require limits and borders to exist as groups, even if these borders are not entirely closed or absolutely defined. Hence, not all elements will enjoy "free entry" if group cohesion is a goal. Groups will not welcome many products like tobacco, drugs, organ trade or even pornography, and will not accept all economic producers in their polities, especially out-group producers that may have rent-seeking aims. Social collectives may even fight the free promotion of ideas that appear to be anti-group. Because the free satisfaction of preferences in the market does not equate with maximisation of group fitness, the market advantage of "free entry" over the political process can become an evolutionary fitness disadvantage. If so, the free market is unlikely to persist as a moral/social institution. Paradoxically, perhaps the market's ultimate strength may also be an ultimate shortcoming.

In sum, "politics as exchange" (i.e. the social contract) is incompatible with the multilevel selection logic of group competition because of the detrimental effects that the act of respecting all preferences has on group cohesion. The elitist moral punishment of dissidents, which aims at keeping groups cohesive and operating as units, is incompatible with a procedure that values and maximises all preferences (e.g. the social contract), including anti-group preferences. However, when comparing the market advantages over liberal democratic/majoritarian politics regarding preference satisfaction, the market reveals a high potential to satisfy individual preferences. This high potential is due to the intrinsically individualistic mechanism of choices that the market represents. In contrast, democratic politics have more obstacles because of the difficult nature of collective choices. Markets strengthen this logic because, when operating in the marketplace, individuals tend to become closer to the self-interested "homo economicus" (Ariely, 2008) and altruism becomes less relevant for the maximisation of preferences.

Although markets reveal a high potential to satisfy individual preferences, especially due to their choices being individualistic by nature, liberal democracy has a considerably higher potential to satisfy preferences than classic public choice theorists tend to acknowledge. Both liberal democracy and markets reveal a high potential regarding preference satisfaction. But how desirable and sustainable is the ethic of the liberal satisfaction of preferences from an evolutionary perspective?

References

Aidt, T., & Gassebner, M. (2010). Do Autocratic States Trade Less? *World Bank Economic Review, 24*(1), 38–76.

Ariely, D. (2008). *Predictably Irrational: The Hidden Forces That Shape Our Decisions.* New York: HarperCollins.

Arrow, K. J. (1951). *Social Choice and Individual Values.* London: Chapman & Hall.

Atran, S., & Axelrod, R. (2008). Reframing Sacred Values. *Negotiation Journal, 24*(3), 221–246.

Barro, R. J. (1996a). Democracy and Growth. *Journal of Economic Growth, 1,* 1–27.

Barro, R. J. (1996b). *Getting It Right: Markets and Choices in a Free Society.* Cambridge, MA: MIT Press.

Bass, B. (1954). The Leaderless Group Discussion. *Psychological Bulletin, 51*(5), 465–492.

Becker, G. (1983). A Theory of Competition Among Pressure Groups for Political Influence. *Quarterly Journal of Economics, 98,* 371–400.

Boehm, C. (1999). *Hierarchy in the Forest: The Evolution of Egalitarian Behavior Cambridge.* Cambridge, MA: Harvard University Press.

Boyd, R., & Richerson, P. (2000). Climate, Culture, and the Evolution of Cognition. In C. Heyes & L. Huber (Eds.), *The Evolution of Cognition* (pp. 329–346). Cambridge, MA: MIT Press.

Boyd, R., & Richerson, P. (2005). *Not by Genes Alone: How Culture Transformed Human Evolution.* Chicago: The University of Chicago Press.

Boyd, R., & Richerson, P. (2008). Gene-Culture Coevolution and the Evolution of Social Institutions. In C. Engel & W. Singer (Eds.), *Better Than Conscious? Decision Making, the Human Mind, and Implications for Institutions* (pp. 305–325). Cambridge, MA: MIT Press.

Brennan, G., & Buchanan, J. M. (2000). *The Reason of Rules: Constitutional Political Economy.* Indianapolis, IN: Liberty Fund.

Brennan, G., & Hamlin, A. P. (2004). *Democratic Devices and Desires.* Cambridge, UK: Cambridge University Press.

Buchanan, J. M. (1959). Positive Economics, Welfare Economics and Political Economy. *Journal of Law and Economics, 2*, 124–138.

Buchanan, J. M. (1999a). The Ethics of Constitutional Order. In *The Logical Foundations of Constitutional Liberty* (Vol. 1, pp. 368–373). Indianapolis: Liberty Fund.

Buchanan, J. M. (1999b). Individual Choice in Voting and the Market. In *The Logical Foundations of Constitutional Liberty* (Vol. 1, pp. 75–89). Indianapolis: Liberty Fund.

Buchanan, J. M. (1999c). *Public Finance in Democratic Process: Fiscal Institutions and Individual Choice*. Indianapolis: Liberty Fund.

Buchanan, J. M. (1999d). Rent Seeking and Profit Seeking. In *The Logical Foundations of Constitutional Liberty* (Vol. 1, pp. 103–119). Indianapolis: Liberty Fund.

Buchanan, J. M. (2000). *The Limits of Liberty: Between Anarchy and Leviathan*. Indianapolis: Liberty Fund.

Buchanan, J. M. (2001). *The Economics of Earmarked Taxes Debt and Taxes* (pp. 71–89). Indianapolis: Liberty Fund.

Buchanan, J. M. (2008). Constitutional Political Economy. In C. K. Rowley & F. Schneider (Eds.), *Readings in Public Choice and Constitutional Political Economy* (pp. 281–295). New York: Springer.

Buchanan, J. M., & Congleton, R. D. (2006). *Politics by Principle, Not Interest: Towards Nondiscriminatory Democracy* (1st digitally printed pbk. ed.). Cambridge; New York: Cambridge University Press.

Buchanan, J. M., & Tullock, G. (1999). *The Calculus of Consent: Logical Foundations of Constitutional Democracy*. Indianapolis: Liberty Fund.

Buchanan, J. M., & Vanberg, V. (2001). Constitutional Choice, Rational Ignorance and the Limits of Reason *Choice, Contract, and Constitutions* (pp. 127–148). Indianapolis, IN: Liberty Fund.

Burke, E. (2005). *Reflections on the Revolution in France*. New York: Digireads.com.

Caplan, B. (2004a). Rational Ignorance. In C. K. Rowley & F. Schneider (Eds.), *The Encyclopedia of Public Choice* (Vol. 2, pp. 468–470). New York: Kluwer Academic Publishers.

Caplan, B. (2004b). Rational Irrationality. In C. K. Rowley & F. Schneider (Eds.), *The Encyclopedia of Public Choice* (Vol. 2, pp. 470–472). New York: Kluwer Academic Publishers.

Caplan, B. (2006). *The Myth of the Rational Voter: Why Democracies Choose Bad Policies*. Princeton: Princeton University Press.

Christiano, T. (2004). Is Normative Rational Choice Theory Self-Defeating? *Ethics, 115*(1), 122–141.

Cochran, G., & Harpending, H. (2009). *The 10,000 Year Explosion: How Civilization Accelerated Human Evolution*. New York: Basic Books.

de Condorcet, M. (1785). *Essay on the Application of Analysis to the Probability of Majority Decisions*. Paris: De L'Imprimerie Royale.
Delli Carpini, M. X., & Keeter, S. (1996). *What Americans Know About Politics and Why It Matters*. New Haven, CT: Yale University Press.
Doria, J., & Taylor, M. (1981). Self-Serving and Group-Serving Bias in Attribution. *The Journal of Social Psychology, 113*(2), 201–211.
Downs, A. (1957). *An Economic Theory of Democracy*. New York: Harper & Row.
Durkheim, E. (1997). *The Division of Labor in Society* (W. D. Halls, Trans.). New York: Free Press.
Fisher, M. (2013). Most Russians and Pakistanis Say They Prefer a Strong Ruler Over Democracy. *The Washington Post*. Retrieved from The Washington Post website: http://www.washingtonpost.com/blogs/worldviews/wp/2013/01/11/most-russians-and-pakistanis-say-they-prefer-a-strong-ruler-over-democracy/.
Glaeser, E., Porta, R., Lopez-De-Silanes, F., & Shleifer, A. (2004). Do Institutions Cause Growth? *Journal of Economic Growth, 9*, 271–303.
Gutmann, A., & Thompson, D. (2004). *Why Deliberative Democracy?* Princeton, NJ: Princeton University Press.
Haggard, S. (1990). *Pathways from the Periphery: The Politics of Growth in the Newly Industrializing Countries*. New York: Cornell University Press.
Haidt, J. (2012). *The Righteous Mind: Why Good People Are Divided by Politics and Religion*. London: Allen Lane.
Hardin, R. (1988). Constitutional Political Economy—Agreement on Rules. *British Journal of Political Science, 18*(4), 513–530.
Hobbes, T. (1975). *Leviathan*. London: Dent.
Hughes, G. (2010). *Political Correctness: A History of Semantics and Culture*. Malden, MA: Wiley-Blackwell.
Hume, D. (1994). *Hume: Political Essays* (K. Haakonssen, Ed.). Cambridge: Press Syndicate of the University of Cambridge.
Inston, K. (2010). *Rousseau and Radical Democracy*. London: Continuum International Publishing Group.
Kahneman, D., Knetsch, J., & Thaler, R. (1991). Anomalies: The Endowment Effect, Loss Aversion, and Status Quo Bias. *The Journal of Economic Perspectives, 5*(1), 193–206.
Labov, W. (2001). *Principles of Linguistic Change: Social Factors*. Oxford: Blackwell.
Lewis, H. (1974). *Leaders and Followers: Some Anthropological Perspectives*. Reading, MA: Addison-Wesley.
Limongi, F., & Przeworski, A. (1993). Political Regimes and Economic Growth. *The Journal of Economic Perspectives, 7*(3), 51–69.

Lomasky, L. (2008). Swing and a Myth: A Review of Caplan's *The Myth of the Rational Voter*. *Public Choice, 135*(3–4), 469–484.
Londregan, J., & Poole, K. (1996). Does High Income Produce Democracy? *World Politics, 49*, 1–30.
Marx, K., & Engels, F. (2004). *The German Ideology*. New York: International Publishers Co.
Meadowcroft, J. (2013). *James M. Buchanan* (Vol. 17). New York; London: Bloomsbury Academic.
Nadeau, R., Cloutier, E., & Guay, J. (1993). New Evidence About the Existence of a Bandwagon Effect in the Opinion Formation Process. *International Political Science Review, 14*(2), 203–213.
Nickerson, R. (1998). Confirmation Bias: A Ubiquitous Phenomenon in Many Guises. *Review of General Psychology, 2*(2), 175–220.
Olson, M. (1971). *The Logic of Collective Action: Public Goods and the Theory of Groups*. Cambridge, MA: Harvard University Press.
Olson, M. (1982). *The Rise and Decline of Nations: Economic Growth, Stagflation, and Social Rigidities*. New Haven: Yale University Press.
Olson, M. (1993). Dictatorship, Democracy and Development. *The American Political Science Review, 87*(3), 567–576.
Ostrom, E. (2000). *Collective Action and the Evolution of Social Norms* (Vol. The Journal of Economic Perspectives: EP; a Journal of the American Economic Association).
Pennington, M. (2011). *Robust Political Economy: Classical Liberalism and the Future of Public Policy*. Cheltenham: Edward Elgar.
Putnam, R. (2007). E Pluribus Unum: Diversity and Community in the Twenty-First Century. *Scandinavian Political Studies, 30*(2), 137–174.
Puurtinen, M., & Mappes, T. (2009). Between-Group Competition and Human Cooperation. *Proceedings of the Royal Society B, 276*, 355–360. https://doi.org/10.1098/rspb.2008.1060.
Rawls, J. (1993). *Political Liberalism*. New York: Columbia University Press.
Redelmeier, D. (2005). The Cognitive Psychology of Missed Diagnosis. *Annals of Internal Medicine, 142*(2), 115–120.
Riker, W. (1982). *Liberalism Against Populism: A Confrontation Between the Theory of Democracy and the Theory of Social Choice*. Oxford: Freeman.
Rothwell, D. (2010). *In the Company of Others, an Introduction to Communication*. New York: Oxford University Press.
Sandel, M. (2012). *What Money Can't Buy: The Moral Limits of Markets*. New York: Farrar, Straus and Giroux.
Scott, J., & Clery, E. (2013). Gender Roles: An Incomplete Revolution? *British Social Attitudes*. Retrieved from Natcen Social Research website: http://www.bsa.natcen.ac.uk/media/38457/bsa30_gender_roles_final.pdf.

Sewell, W. (1994). *A Rhetoric of Bourgeois Revolution: The Abbé Sieyes and What Is the Third Estate?* London: Duke University Press.

Sober, E., & Wilson, D. S. (1998). *Unto Others: The Evolution and Psychology of Unselfish Behavior*. Cambridge, MA: Harvard University Press.

Social, T. P. (2013). Women in Developing Countries. *Flash Eurobarometer, 372*, 1–33. Retrieved from European Commission website: http://ec.europa.eu/public_opinion/flash/fl_372_en.pdf.

Stigler, G. (1971). The Theory of Economic Regulation. *Bell Journal of Economics and Management Science, 2*(1), 3–21.

Sunstein, C., & Thaler, R. (2003). Libertarian Paternalism Is Not an Oxymoron. *University of Chicago Law Review, 70*, 1159–1202.

Tronnberg, F. (2013). *State Regulation of Anti-democratic Parties: A Comparative Study of Germany, Spain and Sweden*. Master Thesis in International and European Affairs, Linköpings. Retrieved from http://www.ohlininstitutet.se/wp-content/uploads/2008/09/Frida-Tronnberg.pdf.

Tullock, G. (2001). Monarchies, Hereditary and Non-hereditary. In W. F. Shughart & L. Razzolini (Eds.), *The Elgar Companion to Public Choice* (pp. 140–157). Cheltenham: Edward Elgar Publishing.

Tullock, G. (2005). *The Social Dilema of Autocracy, Revolution, Coup D'Etat and War*. Indianapolis: Liberty Fund.

Tullock, G., Seldon, A., & Brady, G. L. (2002). *Government Failure: A Primer in Public Choice*. Washington, DC: Cato Institute.

Turchin, P. (2006). *War and Peace and War: The Rise and Fall of Empires*. New York: Penguin Books.

Tversky, A., & Kahneman, D. (1974). Judgment Under Uncertainty: Heuristics and Biases. *Science, 185*(4157), 1124–1131.

Tversky, A., & Kahneman, D. (1981). The Framing of Decisions and the Psychology of Choice. *Science, 211*(4481), 453–458.

Vanberg, V. (2013). *James Buchanan's Contractarianism and Modern Liberalism*. Freiburger Diskussionspapiere zur Ordnungokonomik. Department of Economic Policy and Constitutional Economic Theory. University of Freiburg. Retrieved from http://www.econstor.eu/handle/10419/88108.

Vinen, R. (2010). *Thatcher's Britain: The Politics and Social Upheaval of the 1980s*. London: Pocket Books.

von Hayek, F. A. (1944). *The Road to Serfdom*. London: Routledge.

von Hayek, F. A. (1979). *Law, Legislation and Liberty* (Vol. III). London: Routledge.

Wilson, D. S. (2002). *Darwin's Cathedral: Evolution, Religion, and the Nature of Society*. Chicago: The University of Chicago Press.

Wilson, D. S., & Wilson, E. O. (2007). Rethinking the Theoretical Foundation of Sociobiology. *The Quarterly Review of Biology, 82*(4), 327–348.

Wintrobe, R. (1998). *The Political Economy of Dictatorship*. Cambridge, UK; New York, NY: Cambridge University Press.

Wintrobe, R. (2004). Dictatorship. In C. K. Rowley & F. Schneider (Eds.), *The Encyclopedia of Public Choice* (Vol. 1, pp. 77–91). New York: Kluwer Academic Publishers.

Wittman, D. A. (1995). *The Myth of Democratic Failure: Why Political Institutions Are Efficient*. Chicago: University of Chicago Press.

World-Bank. (2013). *Fertility Rate, Total (Births per Woman)*. Retrieved from http://data.worldbank.org/indicator/SP.DYN.TFRT.IN/countries?order=wbapi_data_value_2012+wbapi_data_value+wbapi_data_value-last&sort=desc.

CHAPTER 6

The Market: Evolutionary Limits and Possibilities

6.1 On Hayek's Evolutionary Account of Market Superiority

I will now focus on the impact that free markets and the adjacent ethic of the liberal satisfaction of preferences have on the evolutionary fitness of groups. To appraise such an impact, I assess the most relevant evolutionary defence of the institutional superiority of the market order: F. A. Hayek's model of cultural group selection.

By regarding the market as a discovery process, F. A. Hayek (1945) generated a theoretical framework in which the process of preference satisfaction depends on the "knowledge problem". Specifically, because individuals have epistemological problems in knowing what their wants or needs are and how or if they can satisfy these needs, the market process is the best way for individuals to maximise their options of consumption by trial and error, which allows for a discovery process of preference maximisation. This means that a market-driven higher economic growth, i.e. more goods and services available, is a mechanism that helps individuals to discover their subjective preferences. Such economic growth makes the preferred goods and services expand while eliminating the less desired ones via economic competition. Hence, for Hayek (2009), the free market is a process that, through the general absence of government intervention, allows for the conservation of the unique information which prices contain, information that is too complex to be understood from an individually rational perspective. The free market

F. N. Faria, *The Evolutionary Limits of Liberalism*, Palgrave Studies in Classical Liberalism, https://doi.org/10.1007/978-3-030-31496-5_6

is what economic historian Karl Polanyi defined as a market economy, which, in his own words, "implies a self-regulating system of markets; in slightly more technical terms, it is an economy directed by market prices and nothing but market prices" (Polanyi, 2001, p. 45). However, this economic market does not exist in a political vacuum, as economist Viktor Vanberg reminds us, the market "is always a system of social interaction characterized by a specific institutional framework, that is, by a set of rules defining certain restrictions on the behaviour of market participants" (Vanberg, 1986, p. 75). Thus, the free market results from an institutional political arrangement that aims at conserving market prices; it is not an unhampered process of supply and demand disconnected from an institutional framework.

Within liberal theory, Hayek's model of cultural group selection departs from an atypical anthropological moral position. He rejects Hobbesian primitive individualism (Hobbes, 1975), that is, he rejects the idea that in the state of nature there are only individuals in a permanent struggle with one another. For Hayek: "the savage is not solitary, and his instinct is collectivist" (von Hayek, 1988, p. 12). Hayek's central postulate is that individuals are dealing with two opposing systems of morality (Miller, 1989, p. 313). One moral system relies on the small tribe morality, which is constituted by instincts of group altruism and solidarity. The evolutionary system selected these instincts because humans lived most of their lives in small bands of hunter-gatherers. In particular, such instinctive traits were helpful in conferring cohesion and common goals to groups under inter-group competition. Hence, these instincts became overwhelmingly prevalent because of evolutionary pressures at the group level. The other opposing system of morality is the "great society" morality. It is one that evolved gradually in the last 500 or 100 generations (Beck, 2011, p. 414). In the words of political theorist David Miller, this new system of morality reflects "the growing interdependence of individuals across wide tracts of space and consists in those rules which allow extended cooperation via trade and markets—rules of property, contract and so forth" (Miller, 1989, p. 313). Thus, the first type of morality is instinctual and the second type is artificial. This mimics David Hume's distinction between natural virtues, which are innate tendencies typical of small family groups, and artificial virtues, those mediated through institutions that allow for an enlarged social order and are not always self-evident (Hardin, 2007, p. 45). Because the second type of morality is less intuitive, it is always in danger of being disrupted by a rebellious natural small group morality. Karl Polanyi had previously identified such a Hayekian idea in what he called "double movement" (Polanyi, 2001, p. 79), which is a constant struggle between market forces and spontaneous anti-market movements defending society from the disruptions that free markets bring to social structures and norms. This struggle between anti-and pro-market forces has been a regular presence in the western world in the last 200 years. Hayek (1988) often calls "socialism" to these reactions against the extended market order, although, as David Miller (1989, p. 312) remarked, "socialism" is a term that does not capture the complex nature of these challengers.

For Hayek, a very important reason for why natural morality constantly reacts against the morality of the great (market) society is that we have been civilised in the market order against our wishes. That is, individuals had to repress their natural morality and instincts to achieve the modern stage, but these instincts are still largely present. Yet, why would human groups want to discard their natural morality to live in a counter-intuitive market morality? Hayek's answer relies on cultural group selection theory. He postulates that those groups that embraced such an artificial moral (market) order were better able to reproduce and increase in numbers, prevailing in the forces of between group competition and displacing groups that did not embrace the "great society" moral framework. In Hayek' words: "We may not like the fact that our morals have been shaped mainly by their suitability to increase our numbers, but we have little choice in the matter" (von Hayek, 1988, p. 134).

Hayek claims to understand the reasons why so many individuals dislike a market order that is more based on individual competition than on group altruism. As the historian of science Naomi Beck notes, Hayek

> maintained that the various steps in the transition to market economy—such as recognition of private property through land enclosures, allowance of competition with fellow craftsmen in the same trade and lending money for interest—were all breaches of solidarity which governed the small group. (Beck, 2011, p. 415)

Hence, human groups and individuals had no wish to embrace this market-based civilisation and ended up being "civilised" against their wishes (Beck, 2011, p. 415); Hayek is clear about why it happened: "It was the price (we) had to pay for being able to raise a larger number of children" (von Hayek, 1979, p. 168). Therefore, for Hayek, these violations of tribal natural morality became traditions with tacit knowledge that evolved because they allowed those who practise them to grow in numbers and supplant those who did not. Such violations, like long-distance trade, are the product of individual path-breakers that became evolutionarily successful, that were favoured by cultural group selection and that passed on their practices to the next generations through imitative learning (Beck, 2011, p. 417). The market order is then the best way to coordinate actions at a large scale and with high numbers of people, increasing the carrying capacity of the groups that practise extended market order norms. Thus, Hayek considers the natural instincts of the tribe to be inadequate to succeed in the evolutionary process. According to him, societies should not have common goals but rather rely on a spontaneous individualistic market order. As Hayek puts it: "The abstract society rests on learnt rules and not on pursuing perceived desirable common objects" (von Hayek, 1979, p. 168). For Hayek, individuals do not understand the advantages of modern market morality. Market morality led to the expansion of these individuals because its norms "enabled those groups practicing them to procreate more successfully and to include outsiders" (von Hayek, 1988, p. 16). In other words, moral preferences for group altruism, solidarity or redistribution are of no importance for modern market civilisation. If individuals applied these instinctual moral preferences to the modern order, they would condone millions to death and impoverishment by destroying the material foundation that arose because of the suppression of such "tribal" moral preferences (von Hayek, 1988, p. 120). Thus, Hayek concludes, "such demands for justice are simply inappropriate to a naturalistic evolutionary process… *Evolution cannot be just*" (von Hayek, 1988, p. 74).

Overall, even though Hayek's model of group selection is of a cultural kind and operates on a Lamarckian process of transmission of acquired social and institutional norms, his model's impact on group fitness is in line with the natural (genetic) selection at the group level (Wilson & Wilson, 2007). Apart from some minor details and interpretations, several contemporary authors observed that Hayek's model of cultural group selection is in line with current evolutionary theory (Feldmann, 2005; Rubin & Gick, 2004; Stone, 2010; Zywicki, 2000); especially with the revival of group selection in the form of multilevel selection theory. Yet, just because his general model of group cultural selection is appropriate according to current evolutionary theory, it does not mean that his conclusion about market superiority is true; namely, his conclusion that the market institutional order is an evolutionary winner because it allows for higher procreation and expansion of numbers. For him, the market order is a group fitness maximiser. Some academics criticised Hayek's group selection model regarding its alleged incompatibility with methodological individualism (Vanberg, 1986), but, as evolutionary economist Geoffrey Hodgson (1991, p. 79) claims, Hayek should not be criticised for postulating that selection takes place at the level of groups, but for normatively asserting that free markets are evolutionary winners. Notably, Hayek's claim that free markets are evolutionary winners because they allow for the maximisation of the number of individuals in groups is akin to claiming that free markets are fitness maximisers at the group level. If such a claim is not empirically solid, one must call the normative side of the model into question; one can no longer see the market liberal order as evolutionarily superior to other institutional frameworks.

The current data challenge Hayek's main postulate. As several authors pointed out (Miller, 1989; Witt, 1994), the populations with the most developed market economies and higher abundance of material goods and services have fertility rates that are not only much lower than those from less-developed economies but that are also contracting. Put differently, more developed market economies show strong reductions of their native populations while less developed ones show tremendous increases (Haub, 2012). In the words of economist Ulrich Witt:

> Even when the population-increasing effect of development aid is taken into account, the huge differences in population growth rates between the less-developed countries and those countries with the most-productive and most-diversified market systems do not seem to be compatible with Hayek's conjecture. It appears that it is not so much a difference in the efficiency of the rules of conduct (…) that determines differential population growth rates, but rather something like individual preferences of habits. A highly developed and economically most successful order is just as compatible with a preference of its members for a small number of children as are less-developed orders with a preference of their members for large numbers of children. (Witt, 1994, p. 184)

Curiously, not only less developed market economies appear to maximise population fitness better than more developed economies, but also systems that are extensively anti-free market seemed to have done better. David Miller presents the example of the communist Soviet Union:

> Do we find population reductions and widespread impoverishment (in non-market economies)? In fact, over the period since 1917, the Soviet population has more than doubled, from about 130 million at the time of the Revolution to over 260 million in the 1980s; and the level of personal consumption has also risen very substantially (...). Hayek's claim appears to be conclusively refuted. (Miller, 1989, p. 315)

Miller (1989, p. 315) adds that the products imported from western market economies by the Soviet Union were paid by exports, which shows that the reason why the system worked, at least in terms of fitness, was not because of western charity. Moreover, in the very same Russia, a drastic collapse in fertility rates and population growth came after the communist regime (in 1991) and after the Russians established a market-oriented economy. Contrary to Hayek's claim, there seems to be evidence that the free market economy has a negative impact on fertility rates and on population growth. There is also evidence that fertility rates in Russia only increased (*Economic-Times*, 2008) after the government publicly declared its intentions to increase them and successfully invested in the process (Hill, 2012, p. 17). This shows the importance that government framing has on fertility rates and population growth/contraction, to an extent that Hayek did not acknowledge. For example, the one-child policy in China shows the capacity of governments to influence birth rates. But we can find other examples, like in Egypt, which is another country that practised population fertility controls and that successfully increased birth rates through political framing (Fahim, 2013). Interestingly, the contact with the material abundance that results from markets is slowing down the population growth of developing countries (Plumer, 2013). For instance, economists Robert Jensen and Emily Oster studied this subject in India and found out that "the introduction of cable television is associated with increases in women's autonomy and decreases in fertility" (Jensen & Oster, 2009, p. 1057). On the same topic, a study on Brazil by Ferrara et al. (2012) shows that exposure to soap operas that typically portray small families alters social norms, which leads women to prefer fewer children. Of course, one single factor may not completely account for such changes in fertility rates, but it seems unequivocal that the market expansion and production of these products is contributing to the changes in social norms and preferences, which impact on birth rates. Yet, regardless of this impact in developing countries, it is important to still acknowledge the extraordinary difference between well-developed market economies and developing economies in terms of relative fitness: as the population reference bureau reveals,

> World population grew to 7.06 billion in mid-2012 after having passed the 7 billion mark in 2011. Developing countries accounted for 97 per cent of this growth because of the dual effects of high birth rates and young populations. (Haub, 2012)

Judging by modern data, it thus seems that the market has a negative effect on fertility and population growth, which refutes Hayek's claim that the free market is a fitness maximiser and an evolutionary winner. However, such a refutation does not convince everyone. Economist Horst Feldmann claims that Hayek was correct and that modern demographic trends are in line with his theory of market superiority. He notes that, according to Hayek, "the process of population growth will slowly come to an end when all fertile regions of the earth are similarly densely occupied" (Feldmann, 2005, p. 26); and, most importantly, he adds that Hayek

> also stresses that the steepest increases in the population never occurred in the highly developed market economies, but in developing countries that were in process of introducing market economy institutions. In these countries, people were already benefiting from the market economy (for example, in the form of better medical coverage), but had not yet fully adapted their behavior and traditions, especially their reproductive customs; these are customs that change only gradually. Thus Hayek's argument is much more sophisticated than his critics claim. (Feldmann, 2005, p. 27)

As Feldmann correctly notes, cultural norms and customs decisively influence reproductive tendencies. Yet, once again, this seems to run counter to Hayek's main claim about free markets being group fitness maximisers. In practical terms, markets are reaching the developing world and pushing its customs towards low birth rates. This push towards low fertility implies that markets end up being fitness minimisers instead of fitness maximisers. Even if it is true, as Hayek claims, that free markets generate the necessary wealth to aid group fitness, the fact that these markets apply pressure on populations to change reproductive customs in a fitness reducing way undermines his logic.

Feldmann's (2005, p. 28) argument that the collapse in population growth of developed countries happens because they are reaching a high settlement seems unsustainable. Even economically developed countries that are not densely populated suffer from low fertility rates. For example, the lowly populated United States has fertility rates below replacement levels for almost all its ethnic groups, growing in population mostly because of recent immigration (Hamilton, Martin, & Ventura, 2013). In the same way, Russian authorities have been trying to tackle the problem of market-induced low fertility rates despite being one of the least densely populated countries in the world (Demoscope.ru, 2009). Still, population density should not be a problem for Hayek (1988, pp. 120–126) because he thought the Malthusian danger was of no importance in the modern great society. Hayek (1984) did not seem to worry much about the exhaustion of resources. He mostly highlighted the creative strength of competition as a discovery process, not being visibly concerned with the depletion of resources (Beck, 2011, p. 421). Hayek seemed to believe that the creative forces of free markets would create conditions to overcome scarcity, therefore allowing for an undefined and potentially unlimited increase in population numbers. Hence, population contraction caused by high density should be just one more obstacle that the market allows groups to overcome.

Although Hayek emphasised the question of fertility, a population can also grow via integrating migrants from other groups. There are at least two major reasons why integrating migrants has limited effects on the capacity to raise large numbers of children. One is that, as political ethologist Frank Salter explained, the mass migration from groups into other groups drastically reduces the relative fitness of the receiving population (Salter, 2004, 2007). Second, if market societies receive elements in high numbers from other groups that are culturally less market-oriented, these newcomers can change the market morality of the native population.

There is also a highly relevant question about Hayek's model: what would happen when the market and market institutions become equally present in all places of the world after being naturally selected because of its superior fitness-based characteristics? Evolutionary group selection would not cease to take place and it is unlikely or even impossible that all groups would then grow at exactly the same level because such an equilibrium depends on too many variables. The answer is that cultural and moral norms beyond the market would then make the difference in the process of group selection. Norms that are fitness maximisers would prevail in the natural selection at the group level while norms that are fitness minimisers would be displaced along with their groups. This natural selection of norms explains why the European population dramatically increased in numbers after the event of the industrial revolution (Piketty, 2014, p. 79) and after the spread of free markets. While the material abundance of food and medical assistance allowed for an increase in numbers, the traditional socio-religious morality that placed prestige in child rearing and in large families was still intact. The result was a population explosion that allowed Europeans to spread throughout the globe. As Horst Feldmann reminds us, when Europeans spread towards Anglo-America, "the native population, whose institutions were inferior to those of the West (market wise), was displaced, in many cases through the use of force, which is evidence of Hayek's hypothesis of group selection" (Feldmann, 2005, p. 27). Yet, such a European institutional superiority responsible for creating the group competitive strength of sheer high numbers disappeared when individualistic market norms replaced older traditional norms (e.g. the prestige of large families) (Boyd & Richerson, 2005, Chapter V), a process that progressively led to western below-replacement fertility rates. One can extend this process beyond the western world, given that the most wealthy and developed market economies of the world show relatively low levels of fertility (Haub, 2012).

Evolutionary scientists Robert Boyd and Peter Richerson (2005, Chapter V) show how western "great society" is characterised by the evolution of selfish cultural variants that have a detrimental impact on group fitness (e.g. on fertility rates). They show that modern market society led to a stage where the most successful individuals are the ones that invested in their professional careers at the expense of investing time and resources in raising large families. Because these high-status successful individuals (e.g. politicians, businessmen, professors) are the ones framing institutional social values, selfish cultural/moral variants of an anti-fertility nature have evolved and spread through mass general imitation of the socially successful. Such variants that focus on professional prestige while diminishing the prestige of large families and parenthood are then responsible for this maladaptive behaviour (Boyd & Richerson, 2005, p. 149).

6.1.1 The Importance of Meta-morality

It is possible to identify and separate market norms like private property, contracts and free trade from social meta-group norms to which market norms obey. In this sense, there is an important problem for Hayek's claim that market morality is evolutionarily superior. When market morality becomes the meta-group norm instead of being merely subjugated to other fitness maximising moralities, such as those that confer prestige to large families above professional success, fertility rates tend to collapse. Put differently, when market individualistic norms replace group fitness- enhancing norms at the meta-level, group fitness is gravely affected. Hayek may not fail in claiming that markets allow for the creation of the necessary wealth to raise more children, but he seems to fail in understanding what happens to groups if their meta-morality becomes a market morality, which decisively undermines his normative claim of market evolutionary superiority. Because Hayek claims that social groups should not operate on the basis of common goals, i.e. as a collective unit, but rather on an individualistic, spontaneous order, the path opens up for market norms to become society's meta-norms. Yet, only political action can ensure the group selection process of punishing free riders and deviants from group goals. The market thus allowed for an initial increase of fitness and those who were successful in this process replaced former traditional group norms by market norms. Yet this happened at the cost of dissolving or weakening group goals while instituting individualism, and this individualism is producing reverse fitness effects. As Durkheim (2009, p. 29) postulated, individualism is a product of meta group norms.

Notably, Hayek did not seem to understand the consequences coming from a discovery process that aimed at satisfying preferences. This discovery process allowed for the discovery of production mechanisms that generated comfort and wealth, which might aid in raising more children. But such a process also meant the discovery of many other preferences that will have priority over sheer reproduction. Professional fulfilment or hobbies may all gain precedence over raising children, especially because of the high costs involved in raising the young ones. As economist Robert Frank (2011) demonstrated, because the interests of groups and of individuals often diverge, individualistic economic competition often leads to "arms races" that cause great harm to groups and to individuals in the long run. In this case, to maintain a similar level of wealth and status to other members in our social group requires a constant investment in professional careers. Thus, increasingly fewer individuals will pay the price of having a lower relative status or wealth to raise more children, even though there has never been so much wealth available in absolute terms. The Hayekian discovery process also meant to discover the preference satisfaction for everything beyond reproduction, for everything beyond fitness.

Karl Polanyi also realises that markets can be a mechanism to increase group fitness until the point where market morality becomes the meta-morality, thus replacing more traditional moralities. He postulates that markets, throughout history, have traditionally been embedded in higher group/communal moralities, whether of a religious or civic kind, and that market forces disrupt these values that aim at communal cohesion. The same logic is present in Hayek's model (i.e. the transition from tribal morality to modern market morality). However, Polanyi explains that market values can become meta-values while subjugating communitarian values to the needs of the market, therefore inverting the traditional moral order:

> Ultimately, that is why the control of the economic system by the market is of overwhelming consequence to the whole organisation of society: it means no less than the running of society as an adjunct to the market. Instead of economy being embedded in social relations, social relations are embedded in the economic system. (Polanyi, 2001, p. 60)

It is this inversion of values that decisively contributes to the atomisation of preferences; that is, to the satisfaction of preferences that are not shaped by explicit political and cultural collective aims. Because people traditionally make most, if not all restrictions on social behaviour in the name of the common good of a particular group identity (religious, ethnic, etc.), when market morality becomes the meta-morality, individuals can satisfy all preferences that are group fitness minimisers without political punishment. A meta-morality is especially relevant when acknowledging that the context and elite framers shape preferences, which are not well defined a priori (Kahneman & Tversky, 1984; Tversky & Kahneman, 1981). By ignoring such a process of preference formation, Hayek inferred that better material conditions were enough to allow for the maximisation of group fitness, given that the natural drive towards reproduction would remain strong even under the triumph of market meta-morality over traditional morality. Yet, such a steady, strong reproductive drive does not have empirical support because group morality and the framing of institutions shape reproductive preferences. To acknowledge that the triumph of market morality would lead to sub-replacement fertility rates and to an eventual group selective displacement of the peoples who practise market-based morals would have created fatal problems for his model. However, there may be a favourable selection for market processes within the process of cultural group selection because, as Hayek claimed, markets have shown the capacity to generate material conditions that allow for better circumstances to raise relatively more children. Still, such markets would have to be embedded in other meta social group norms and they would require strong supervision to prevent a market individualistic morality from ascending to the level of meta-morality. This combination of traditional social meta-norms and embedded markets would have been a better candidate for evolutionary superiority in the competing process of group selection than Hayek's free market postulate. To be sure, an embedded market is not a free market, given it is constantly being supervised to fit a higher fitness-maximising meta-morality. Contra Hayek, the unrestricted satisfaction of preferences in the market place is a poor candidate for survival in a cultural group selection competition.

Unsurprisingly, computer simulations have confirmed the tribal morality's evolutionary advantage in relation to the individualistic liberal morality, revealing that tribal cooperation is more adaptive than universalist cooperation. In particular, evolutionary simulation models intending to recognise the most adaptive cooperation strategies have steadily shown that in-group favouritism or ethnocentrism is a strategy which beats cooperative universalism in the long term (Axelrod & Hammond, 2006; Hartshorn, Kaznatcheev, & Shultz, 2013).

6.2 Tension Between Social Norms and Market Norms

It can be difficult to find a balance between a traditional meta-morality and a market morality, especially given the opposing forces that the two represent. This permanent tension is the essence of Polanyi's (2001, p. 136) "double movement" and Hayek's (1988) conflict between tribal morality and great society's market morality. In particular, behavioural psychologist Dan Ariely investigated the tension between market norms (or market morality) and social norms (non-market morality). Here is how he describes the two:

> We live simultaneously in two different worlds (…) one where social norms prevail, and the other where market norms make the rules. The social norms include the friendly requests that people make of one another. Could you help me move this couch? Could you help me change this tire? Social norms are wrapped up in our social nature and our need for community (…) you may help move your neighbour's couch (…) and reciprocity is not immediately required. (…) The second world, the one governed by market norms, is very different. (…) The exchanges are sharp-edged: wages, prices, rents, interests and costs and benefits. Such market relationships are not necessarily evil or mean— in fact, they also include self-reliance, inventiveness and individualism—but they do imply comparable benefits and prompt payments. When you are in the domain of market norms, you get what you pay for. (Ariely, 2008, p. 68)

Ariely's empirical work shows that these two moralities belong to different worlds and that they mix badly, one crowd out the other. As Ariely (2008, Chapter IV) points out, to apply market morality to situations where non-market social morality still applies usually generates hostile reactions. Examples of this moral misapplication are when a man tries to offer money to his mother-in-law for traditionally preparing Thanksgiving dinner or when a man offers money to his wife or girlfriend in exchange for sex. Overall, when money is applied to contexts where it is not welcome, individuals usually reject it and relationship problems arise. Yet, he found evidence for the strong effect of market norms in the erosion of social norms. The classic study by Uri Gneezy and Aldo Rustichini (2000) about a day-care centre in Israel is a good example of this phenomenon. These researchers found out that the day-care centre's policy of applying a fine to parents who arrived late to pick up their children was not a good deterrent and the fine even produced worse effects. Why? Because before the fine was implemented parents felt ashamed when they violated a moral social norm (i.e. the norm of not to coming late and not wasting other people's time). But after the fine was implemented, parents felt they now had the legitimacy to come late since they were financially compensating others for it. What happened was that a social norm was replaced by a market/pecuniary norm and therefore behaviour began to be interpreted according to the latter. Understanding the failure of such a policy, the day-care centre removed the fine some weeks later. Yet, most interestingly, the parents did not return to the old social norm. In fact, they not only continued to pick up their children late, but there was also a slight increase in the number of tardy pickups. In conclusion, as Ariely wrote:

> This experiment illustrates an unfortunate fact: when a social norm collides with a market norm, the social norm goes away for a long time. In other words, social relationships are not easy to re-establish. Once the bloom is off the rose – once a social norm is trumped by a market norm –it will rarely return. (Ariely, 2008, p. 77)

Perhaps they can return, but it is a slow process of building trust and punishing/shaming free riders, which requires time. The day-care centre experiment documents the fragility of non-market social norms. In addition, Ariely (2008, Chapter IV) displays a vast number of empirical cases which document that people will work tremendously hard for social causes rather than for money. For instance, in lab experiments, individuals who are asked to do a boring favour work harder than those who receive money; also, lawyers who reject to work at a cheaper price for retirees often accept to work for free if such a request comes in the form of a non-market moral cause. This willingness to work for moral causes explains why rent-seeking for moral causes can be as efficient at achieving political goals and solving collective action problems as rent-seeking for pecuniary aims. Perhaps moral rent-seeking can even be more efficient. What is particularly interesting in Ariely's (2008, p. 72) documented evidence is that the moral worlds of market and social norms are so much in tension that it is enough to mention pecuniary rewards for a particular activity to crowd out social norms. Because people enter the market morality mode, asking them for cheaper prices than the price system dictates makes them feel exploited, while not mentioning money at all keeps people in the social morality realm. It is possible to observe this process in most circumstances. Also interesting is the experimental finding that offering gifts instead of money is more likely to keep us in the social morality world, but thinking of money as a reward is more likely to make individuals more self-reliant and less communal (i.e. less likely to think and cooperate as a whole). Thus, thinking of money approximates individual behaviour to the standard homo economicus. Additional evidence shows that group identity is crucial in defining what people will do for non-monetary causes. For example, if someone volunteers to help moving other people's furniture, a feeling of exploitation and moral indignation will arise if the others moving that same furniture are being paid. Hence, pecuniary rewards affect all individuals even when some are trying to keep themselves in the social morality realm. Individuals cannot be indifferent to the norms being used within the group they operate in. Finally, there are situations where this tension becomes acute. Companies that rely more on creativity and problem solving than on mechanical work try to deemphasise pecuniary rewards and emphasise collective goals and causes, but because of market competition, this is difficult to maintain, and budget rationalisation, with cuts and bonuses, is an almost inescapable reality. Agents of security like the police or the military are perhaps the ones who face this tension most acutely. In some of their activities, they must risk their lives to stop violent criminals or enemies. While it is possible to pay extremely high wages in order for security agents to risk their lives, it is difficult to know how much their lives are worth, probably one's life has no pecuniary price. It is also difficult to know if high wages would motivate security agents in those life-threatening moments. The most common and probably most efficient way of solving this difficulty is to instil a notion of honour and struggle for higher causes (e.g. the common good, the moral rightness). Hence, at the limit, in extreme situations, non-market moral causes show an inevitable appeal (Ariely, 2008, pp. 73–86). Ariely sums up the conclusion of his findings: "Money, as it turns out, is very often the most expensive way to motivate people. Social norms are not only cheaper, but often more effective as well" (Ariely, 2008, p. 86).

This body of evidence confirms once again that preferences are undefined a priori and that group context and moral framing are decisive elements in shaping what people desire. The evidence also shows how easily market norms crowd out non-market social norms because of the former's pervasive power. This crowding out effect is the most likely reason why, at least in western societies, market norms grew to points never acknowledged in history, occupying now a superior and leading place in society (Polanyi, 2001). F. A. Hayek recognises the current dominance of market norms, but he considers it a positive development, even though, as he points out, the replacement of social norms by market norms happens against the people's will and natural sense of group morality (Beck, 2011, p. 415). Yet, Hayek not only failed to understand the negative impact that market norms and the individualistic free satisfaction of preferences can have on group fitness, but he also ignored that the group selection process cannot end. In this sense, the groups that create non-market norms regulating the detrimental effects of market norms on fitness will have an evolutionary advantage. Perhaps evolutionary economist Geoffrey Hodgson (1991, p. 80) is closer to this moral synthesis when he claims that an evolutionary winning strategy would be a mixed economy. But immediate or proximate preferences of individuals will always depend on the prevailing meta-moralities. General satisfaction always depends on these moralities. Even high inequality can satisfy people if the accepted meta-morality justifies it. Hence, individuals can gladly suffer a visible reduction in group fitness if a meta-market morality justifies such a reduction. Because morality "binds and blinds" (Haidt, 2012, p. 313), individuals analyse empirical evidence and real-world problems under a moral light which influences observation.

When market morality ascends to society's meta-morality, it continues to be a group morality, but because it empties the group of an explicit identity by acknowledging merely individuals, group cohesion suffers. The loss of group cohesion can be fatal under the evolutionary logic of group selection. As the main logic of multilevel selection tells us, "selfishness beats altruism within groups, but altruistic groups beat selfish groups" (Wilson & Wilson, 2007). Groups that suppress egoists (i.e. free riders) and increase the number of altruists will operate better as a unit and will therefore displace competing groups that do not show the capacity to mobilise or cooperate as "one". What follows from multilevel selection theory, even within the context of the Hayekian "great (market) society", is that the formation of identity groups is mostly unavoidable. Such groups can more easily shift the allocation of resources through political and economic control than the single/isolated economic agent (e.g. the consumer or producer). Political economist David Skarbek (2014) documented the inevitability of group formation. He showed that, even in prisons, individual prisoners create coalitions based on social identity. The reason behind this tendency flows directly from multilevel selection theory: isolated individuals cannot efficiently protect themselves nor will they be able to get advantages in attaining important resources and therefore must integrate into a group that is strong and cooperative enough to compete with other groups for similar goals. Once again, in terms of preferences, this process of group formation implies the punishment of free riders and of preferences that are not good for the group, even if such preferences are good for the "selfish" individual. It is because of the inevitability of group formation that a non-market social meta-morality becomes essential in controlling the anti-group preferences that individuals satisfy through a free market process.

6.3 Can the Market Be a Suitable Alternative for the Shortcomings of Liberal Democratic Politics?

We now come to discuss a central question of the book using the insights produced throughout this endeavour. Can the market be a suitable alternative for the shortcoming of liberal democratic politics in respect of preference satisfaction? Under the evolutionary approach I developed, the answer to this question is negative. The free market cannot be a suitable alternative for the shortcomings of liberal democracies because it creates problems of its own that do not seem to be an improvement over the failures of liberal democracy. Most relevantly, following the logic of multilevel selection (Wilson & Wilson, 2007), the free satisfaction of preferences present in the market liberalism is not conducive to the maximisation of group relative fitness, which weakens the sustainability of social groups and their institutions. A market morality ascending to the meta-level of society and underpinning most of the other social norms erodes group goals and cohesion. Yet, the reason why free markets create such problems is also present in liberal democracies. Both are being underpinned by liberalism at the meta-moral group level. I will now discuss how institutional liberalism, with its liberal satisfaction of individual preferences, can be maladaptive for groups.

6.3.1 *The Liberal Factor*

Political and economic thinker Joseph Schumpeter understood the prevalence of morality over mere institutional means when he wrote that "democracy is a political method, that is to say, a certain type of institutional arrangement for arriving at political – legislative and administrative – decisions and hence incapable of being and end in itself" (Yeager, 2001, p. 246). It is mostly because of this weak inner moral content that western democracies must become something more. They become liberal democracies. Because western societies created constitutional democracies based on liberal principles operating at the meta level, democracies work under liberal values as a social *telos*. The same is valid for the market. The market is a simple mechanism to satisfy preferences, but it is the infusion of liberal values that confers the desirability and goodness to such an aim.

Interestingly, from the evolutionary perspective developed in this book, enlightened liberalism as a moral phenomenon reveals feeble anthropological bases. The moral goodness of individualism or of the sovereignty of the individual at the basis of liberalism collides with the evolutionary logic of multilevel selection. Under multilevel selection, groups with individuals capable of operating for the good of the group, often at the cost of the individual, are likely to become evolutionary winners that maximise group fitness. Some main tenets of liberalism are also at odds with this evolutionary approach. For instance, Thomas Hobbes (1975) conception of self-interested and atomised individuals clashing in the state of nature, which strongly influenced subsequent liberal thinkers, is untenable because of the now known long human evolutionary past spent as collaborative tribal hunter-gatherers, something that even Hayek (1988, p. 12) pointed out. Other thinkers coming out of the tradition of liberal enlightenment founded their moral normativity on dubious anthropological concepts, as it is the case of John Locke's (1995) "blank state", the notion that individuals are born without innate knowledge and that all knowledge comes from experience, which largely goes against the hereditary logic of biological evolution (Pinker, 2002). Immanuel Kant's apology of individual autonomy, a priori reasoning, universalist morality and the rejection of group tradition/authorities as a moral basis places the rational individual at the centre of the moral world (Uleman, 2010). Yet, as philosopher Alasdair MacIntyre (2007, Chapter X) notes, not only is this purely individualistic production of universalist rational morality a fiction, this liberalism implies a form of unacknowledged domination, unlike other moralities that assume authority. Such a liberal framework has the effect of dissolving traditional social and cultural relationships. As Emile Durkheim (2009, p. 29) postulated, liberalism is the product of a social collective, and, following Christopher Boehm's (1999) "reverse domination" theory, it is also the product of reverse domination by liberal/egalitarian elites. But liberalism ultimately weakens group cohesion by not providing sufficient moral norms for groups to become cohesive units. This cohesion is an integral part of attaining evolutionary superiority when groups compete with other groups.

Jonathan Haidt's study of moral foundations suggests that liberalism does not use a complete set of moral foundations. Haidt's (2012, pp. 153–154) empirical studies reveal that liberals only use three foundations out of a possible six. Liberalism mostly focuses on the moral foundations of liberty, care and fairness, while lacking essential moral foundations for groups like authority, sanctity and loyalty. Whereas conservative-minded individuals use all six foundations, liberals merely stress three. This liberal understanding of morality represents an incomplete use of the necessary moral foundations for groups to function adaptively as units. Not only are the moral foundations of authority, sanctity and loyalty necessary for group mobilisation in an urgent situation of conflict, i.e. between-group selection, they also serve the purpose of shaping the behaviour and preferences of groups. These "non-liberal" foundations help to create a moral system of collective discipline that selects for certain pro-group behavioural types (i.e. within-group selection). By lacking a complete set of moral foundations, liberalism cannot strengthen groups and select for pro-group individuals.

Even the Hayekian apology of liberalism, which relies on group selection and on the evolution of social norms, seems to sanction traditional norms only if such traditions rest on the convention of market liberalism, which he finds superior to all other conventions. From Hayek's perspective, liberalism, i.e. individualism, comes from an evolved tradition, a tradition that destroys or displaces illiberal group traditions. Market liberalism thus displaces all tribal customs not operating on a small scale, face-to-face basis, such as the family. Hayek's position depends on the belief that the liberal "tradition" is evolutionarily superior and will therefore prevail regardless of what men may feel about it. But not only can Hayek not present convincing evidence that market liberalism maximises group fitness, he also wrongly deemphasises the role of cultural and political elites in establishing liberalism as a new group morality. While Hayek presents a narrative of a gradual evolution of social norms towards liberalism, Karl Polanyi (2001, Chapter II) shows that market liberalism was imposed through a top-down elitist process, similar to the "reverse domination" process of Christopher Boehm (1999), where counter-elites take control and establish a more egalitarian morality.

Hayek's bottom-up narrative may contain some truth. However, the relatively abrupt eighteenth-century European transformation of a traditional group morality, with its embedded markets, into the market (Hayekian) liberal society owes more to top-down elite framing and moral paradigm shifts than Hayek cared to emphasise. While explaining the elitist action that enabled the construction of the free market society, first in England and then in the rest of Europe, Polanyi notes that "land is tied up with the organization of kinship, neighbourhood, craft, and creed – with tribe and temple, village, guild and church" (…) (Polanyi, 2001, p. 187) and

> the lords and nobles were upsetting the social order, breaking down ancient laws and custom, … sometimes by means of violence, often by pressure and intimidation. They were literally robbing the poor of their share in the common (…) the fabric of society was being disrupted. (Polanyi, 2001, p. 37)

Regardless of how one describes these actions, positively or negatively, Polanyi (2001) presents historical evidence to show that what Hayek calls "tradition" came about not merely by the "natural" evolution of social norms but by an elitist and conscious state-oriented action. In sum, liberalism is more of an elite construction than Hayek's bottom-up explanation of how norms evolve leads us to believe.

6.3.1.1 Multilevel Selection and Market Liberalism

Law professor Todd Zywicki (2000) directly assessed the viability of market liberalism under the group selectionist model of multilevel selection (Wilson & Wilson, 2007). His conclusion is in agreement with Hayek's postulate of market evolutionary superiority by claiming that "the result of inter-group cultural competition resulted in the preeminence of individual liberty, constitutional government and free markets" (Zywicki, 2000, p. 90). He corroborates and justifies this evolutionary superiority by recalling that "the fundamental difficulty confronting advocates of group selection theories is the need to protect (the group) against parasites and free riders" (Zywicki, 2000, p. 91) and concludes that there is no better system at fulfilling this need than market liberalism. Reaching an antagonistic conclusion, Geoffrey Hodgson had already criticised this Hayekian market superiority by noting that Hayek

> ignores the possibility that selection may also be working at the level of structure and substructure, creating a diversity not simply of groups and agencies but also of types of economic system or subsystem, as well as a diversity of market forms. (…) Hayek should be criticized (…) for

> failing to incorporate additional processes of selection (…), involving the selection of different types of institution, including both market and non-market forms. (…) Evolutionary selection must involve different types of ownership structure and resource allocation mechanisms, all coexisting in a mixed economy. (Hodgson, 1991, p. 79)

Yet, Zywicki rejects this criticism by claiming that no other system, especially mixed economies with different systems of resource allocation, can punish free riders as efficiently as market liberalism. He criticises Hodgson's position by claiming that

> by empowering the recipients of government largess, he (Hodgson) is giving free riders the power to determine the allocation of wealth within society and undermining the process of wealth creation (…). Given the clear potential for free riding and opportunism associated with the welfare state and a mixed economy, it is doubtful that such regime would be successful in a between-group competitive process. (Zywicki, 2000, pp. 91–92)

In other words, the presence of rationally egoist rent-seeking and state predation are responsible for the clear advantage of markets over politics in promoting group cooperation and punishment of free riders. Ultimately, Zywicki claims that welfare states are vulnerable to free riding and to parasites living off the good of the group. This is especially relevant because, as evolutionary economist Paul Rubin (2000) notes, evolved altruism can only be beneficial if it is finite; that is, if it helps others of the same group who also contribute to the common good. Such a contribution is of particular importance when the in-group is in competition with out-groups. For instance, it may be important to help an injured member of the group who has the duty to contribute with his/her share after the recovery. The tendency to help individuals that will not or cannot contribute to the group is unlikely to be evolutionarily selected under strong group competition. Hence, Zywicki (2000, p. 92) concludes, market liberal groups are likely to supplant groups under welfare states.

We can divide the assessment of Zywicki's claims in two conceptual fields: the nature of politics and the nature of free markets. The claim that political activities are more susceptible to parasitical free riding than free markets, thus making markets the evolutionary winners, ignores the different role of these two contexts in shaping groups.

While a political entity operates for a particular group, defining who belongs to the collective and who can take part in the organisational process, market liberalism has or tends towards an individualistic nature of aims and goals, especially because it is potentially endless in its scope and reach. Free markets are "groupless" or tend towards "grouplessness". Hence, if one defines a free rider as someone who takes advantage of the common pool of resources in a public good situation, it is easier to claim that market liberalism is a better system at preventing free riding than politics because something groupless is by definition less susceptible to free riding. Yet, given that groups are a fundamental force of natural selection and it is impossible to abolish them, abolishing group mechanisms to stop free riding seems paradoxical and nonsensical. It is through some form of politics and through the constitution of group identities and aims that groups operate. So the challenge of stopping free riders is political. The political realm is the one that cannot fade away.

It is in politics that the focus of suppressing free riding and anti-group elements will determine the evolutionary success of groups. In this sense, the behavioural moral types operating in the political realm determines the success of politics in this suppression. Public choice theorists often overlook the importance of type-based moral pluralism because they hold an unrealistic vision of self-interested rational egoists operating in politics and markets: the standard parity of assumptions commonly used in public choice theory. The process of suppressing anti-group elements in politics rests on the adoption of a moral framework, backed up by religion or not, which political and social authorities enforce on the governed group (Boehm, 1999; Norenzayan, 2014). Such a process involves punishment at all levels, from socially shaming deviants to heavy penal castigations. The efficiency of the punishing process will depend on the types operating in politics and on their capacity to shut down the aims of free riders, anti-group elements and rational egoists. Hence, the more self-sacrificial elements providing public goods there are and the more "willing punishers" providing second order public goods exist, the better a political system will operate for the good of the group under inter-group competition. Sacrificing oneself to engage in the punishment of group deviants is a second order public good (Heckathorn, 1993; Turchin, 2006, p. 93). Therefore, the different degrees and quantities of moral behavioural types within systems can, to a large extent, explain why some political systems are more stable and cohesive than others and even why some welfare states are more prone to abuse by free riders than others.

Still, for groups to maximise fitness, the satisfaction of preferences in markets requires a political orientation of what individuals should prefer. This political orientation largely defeats the liberal principle that politics should not impose any notion of the "good life" (Rawls, 1993, p. 19). Again, Hayek's assertion that free markets, with their superior wealth creation, increase the carrying capacity of populations ignores the importance of political framing in shaping the preferences of individuals in groups. Naomi Beck also highlights the problem of Hayek disregarding the active role of altruism and human agency in shaping culture, as well as in shaping individual preferences:

> he [Hayek] advocated disregarding natural inclinations toward solidarity and altruism. But Hayek's conclusions seems to place too much faith in the beneficial effects of market forces and to unjustly deprive human agency of a decisive and positive role in shaping culture and society. (Beck, 2015, p. 83)

Hence, the increase of a population's carrying capacity only results in positive evolutionary fitness if individuals have preferences that are fitness maximisers (e.g. having large families, willingness to defend one's group, avoiding physical and psychological behaviours that are fitness reducers, etc.). The individual left alone to discover his or her preferences without group/authoritative moral guidance tends to develop all sorts of maladaptations (Boyd & Richerson, 2005, Chapter V). The most relevant of these is the development of a maladaptive individualist hedonism that does not obey to nor is restricted by any higher group goal. Emile Durkheim famously revealed this maladaptive trend when he wrote that "man cannot become attached to higher aims and submit to a rule if he sees nothing above him to which he belongs. To free him from all social pressure is to abandon him to himself and demoralize him" (Durkheim, 2005, p. 357).

More recently, the field of experimental psychology and economics has been confirming Durkheim's point. For instance, behavioural psychologists George Loewenstein and Dan Ariely intensely tested the behaviour of individuals under cool states and hot states. The cool states are those in which we think rationally because we are not under pressure or not having our most basic instincts activated, instincts like sexual arousal, hunger, etc. The hot states are those in which such basic instincts are fully active or primed. These scientists concluded that individuals generally have a very poor self-control and that people are often unable to know themselves under different states, especially given that individuals claim to want antagonistic aims when in cool and hot states (e.g. to claim that certain sexual practices are wrong while in the cool state but approving them during the hot state) (Ariely, 2008, Chapters V and VI). After such a diagnostic of average poor self-control, Ariely tested several ways to achieve the best results under this behavioural reality. The results revealed that the best way to prevent the failures associated with poor self-control is through the application of authoritative framing of rules and respective punishment. By establishing deadlines and penalties, individuals could, to a large extent, achieve better results than if left to themselves. For example, referring to tests made with university students where some students had no tight deadlines to deliver essays while others did, Ariely concludes that the best results come from those who had authoritatively been given a rigid deadline: He concludes: "What do these results suggest? First, that students do procrastinate (big news); and second, that tightly restricting their freedom (equally spaced deadlines, imposed from above) is the best cure for procrastination" (Ariely, 2008, p. 115).

Interestingly, this experiment also found that simply offering students a way to pre-commit to deadlines and penalties already helped, even though not as much as an authoritatively given deadline.

These insights from experimental psychology help to understand the main problem of the liberal satisfaction of preferences in markets. Because of a liberal moral antagonism to authority and to community control of the individual (Haidt, 2012, pp. 153–154), market liberalism cannot provide the group cohesion and goals that are required for the maximisation of group fitness in inter-group competition. While the market itself has an in-built system of economic punishment which promotes a certain degree of self-reliance, it atomises preferences in many directions that are fitness minimising; from the consumption of physically hurtful products, like alcohol, unhealthy food or drugs, to preferences for hobbies or careers over large families (Boyd & Richerson, 2005, Chapter V). Market liberalism also gradually removes the sense of "we", the sense of belonging to a collective entity whose collective destiny one shares and for which one will make sacrifices. The free satisfaction of preferences too often primes the hot state over the cool state, which means that, on the consumer side, it is likely that individuals will engage in fitness minimising activities when primed by product marketing. On the producer side, keeping up with the permanent individualistic economic competition requires total dedication to professional careers over family and community life. Most interestingly, the tension between free markets and the need for welfare states (Zywicki, 2000) arises mostly out of the liberal rejection of authoritative and communal guidance of the good life, which implies that not much, if anything, should be restricted for individuals. In fact, the pressure for the existence of large welfare states could diminish if individuals were less free to satisfy preferences in their hot states. Surely, while not every individual will reveal the same level of low self-control, mostly all require some form of communitarian control. As David Hume (1994, p. 18) noted, no man can lead without persuading others. Hence, even leaders take advice from their groups and are bounded by group expectations.

6.3.1.2 Liberalism in Democracy and Markets

While the liberal moral element underpinning free markets seems to be responsible for their evolutionary shortcomings, the same liberal element can explain most of the shortcomings of liberal democracy, namely the ones analysed during this dissertation (e.g. rent-seeking, rational ignorance, etc.). The notion that liberal democracy constitutionally exists to enable the free satisfaction of individual preferences produces the same atomisation and lack of group cohesion that market liberalism does. As mentioned before, this cohesion is necessary for groups under inter-group evolutionary competition (Wilson & Wilson, 2007). The main behavioural types operating in liberal democracies are moral rent-seekers, such as classical or social liberals, who aim at fulfilling liberal values, and pecuniary rent-seekers, who aim at concentrating benefits while dispersing costs (Tullock, Seldon, & Brady, 2002). Moral rent-seekers aim at deepening the fulfilment of meta-liberal values by reforming and adjusting the polity to allow for a freer and universal satisfaction of preferences, while pecuniary rent-seekers, even when restricting the satisfaction of preferences through given policies (e.g. protectionist tariffs), often "sell" their intents to the voters in liberal language (Brennan & Hamlin, 2004, pp. 119–120). These rational and egoistic pecuniary rent-seekers are the ones that public choice scholarship identifies as tremendous obstacles to a free satisfaction of preferences within liberal democracies (Tullock et al., 2002). In public choice literature, the prevalence of rational egoists is a key reason why the free market has tremendous advantages over current liberal democratic politics in terms of preference satisfaction

(Buchanan, 1999, p. 56; Buchanan & Vanberg, 2001, p. 137). Dan Ariely's (2008, p. 72) experiments confirm that pecuniary aims put people in the individualistic market morality mode, therefore behaving more like the rational homo economicus. Hence, when public choice theorists consider individuals to be the same in politics and markets, it is only natural that markets show a higher capacity to satisfy preferences, given that politics can use physical coercion and concentrate benefits while dispersing costs. But, in reality, politics is a realm of social morality too, which allows for non-market oriented moral types to operate. With liberal democracy, these moral types are mostly of the liberal kind because these polities constitutionally uphold such values and therefore create mechanisms, legal and cultural, to defend themselves against the participation of non-liberal agents (Loury, 1994, p. 430). These moral liberal types that take part in liberal democracies are a counter-balance to the operations of potential pecuniary rent-seekers that could highly restrict the satisfaction of preferences and destroy economic development, like Mancur Olson (1982) believed would inevitably happen. Yet, the complete collapse of economic growth did not happen and many market reforms took place (e.g. Margaret Thatcher). Even Hayek, who believed that economically interventionist democracies would end up under totalitarianism, did not understand the now acknowledged relative stability of liberal democracies under mixed economies (Alves & Meadowcroft, 2014). Hence, when considering the operation of liberal moral agents and the existence of liberal culture in democracies, it is possible to assert that, even though a straight comparison with free markets favours markets, liberal democracies can be relatively stable at creating a framework to maximise the satisfaction of preferences. Notably, evolutionary economist Paul Rubin comes to the same conclusion: "I believe that (western political systems) are the best systems that have existed, in the sense of being the most consistent with evolved human preferences and the best at satisfying these preferences" (Rubin, 2007, p. 53).

Yet, many evolved preferences can be maladaptive for groups, like free riding or the preference to conform to group moralities that uphold individual hedonism or economic production over large families and communitarian cohesion. And such a cohesion relies on non-economic rituals and beliefs. Thus, both free markets and liberal democracies can be considerably successful at satisfying preferences because they operate under the same liberal meta-morality, but the very own satisfaction of all individual preferences is detrimental to the group selectionist process of multilevel selection. Groups that act and think as units in the process of between-group selection displace groups that act and think merely as self-interested individuals uninterested in defending the larger collective (Sober & Wilson, 1998; Wilson & Wilson, 2007).

6.3.1.3 Market Liberalism: Success and Failure

In sum, from this evolutionary perspective, the answer to whether free markets can be a suitable replacement for the current model of liberal democracy regarding the capacity to satisfy preferences is "no". The answer is negative because both institutions operate under the evolutionarily problematic meta-morality of liberalism. Following the group selectionist logic of multilevel selection theory, moral individualism reveals maladaptive tendencies that have a negative impact on the evolutionary success of groups in inter-group competition. Furthermore, F. A. Hayek's social theory postulating evolutionary group success under market liberalism reveals empirical and theoretical problems. Contra Hayek's claim, market liberalism seems to contribute decisively to the fitness minimisation of groups in the long run because of the atomisation effects it creates, especially affecting reproduction and group identity. For instance, the western population explosion, which occurred after the industrial revolution, seems to support the Hayekian claim that the market creates the necessary wealth to raise more children. However, such a demographic explosion came from a temporary mix of traditional morality and better material conditions. When liberal morality replaced traditional morality, liberal values negatively affected reproduction. Hence, because of the importance that group morality has in shaping preferences, a certain degree of "tribal" collectiveness, which Hayek's market liberalism rejects, is fundamental for achieving fitness maximising groups. Moral tribalism is therefore fundamental for the sustainability and survival of institutions under cultural group selection pressures. Given that the liberal satisfaction of individual preferences reveals maladaptive tendencies for groups, the fact that markets seem to have a certain comparative advantage over liberal democracies in terms of preference satisfaction (Buchanan, 1999, p. 56; Buchanan & Vanberg, 2001) merely deepens the problem.

Ultimately, the meta-morality that underpins institutions is of crucial importance for the evolutionary success of groups. Hence, if liberal individualism reveals maladaptive tendencies, both markets and forms of democracy could become evolutionarily stronger if underpinned by more group-oriented meta-moralities. As Karl Polanyi (2001, p. 60) understood, markets require embeddedness. Markets need to be integrated and bounded by group cultural and moral norms. Particularly, it is of high importance that they become a part of society instead of society becoming a part of the markets. By the same token, Emile Durkheim equally understood that pre-industrial European economies "had its natural framework in the family (...), the life of the husbandman did not draw him away from his home. The family was at the same time a professional group" (Durkheim, 2001, p. 26). To keep this fitness wise fundamental connection between extended family and the economy, he proposed a system of professional guilds (Durkheim, 2001, pp. 37–38). This system might prevent the massive dislocation of individuals and the erasure of communities because of job market competitive pressures. Such a system of guilds would perhaps also allow for the enhancement of the characteristics of traditional societies, which, for Polanyi (1968), rely on reciprocity, kin-based leaderships, autonomy and morally patterned redistribution. These are contested solutions, and the analysis of their effectiveness would require another research project. However, following the logic of multilevel selection, a group meta-morality that shapes individual preferences and rests on an explicit collective seems to be of high importance for group cohesion, i.e. for working as adaptive units. This group moral underpinning is a process that Durkheim saw as a form of moral and collective discipline or punishment (Durkheim, 2001, p. 29). Because liberalism relies merely on the moral foundations of care, harm and liberty (Haidt, 2012, pp. 153–154), while mostly ignoring other important moral foundations for groups such as loyalty, sanctity or authority, liberalism reveals incompleteness as a group morality, which underpins its incapacity to make groups operate as adaptive units.

While market/social liberalism is a meta-morality of a western collective that is far from being universally accepted, much less politically and morally enforced everywhere, it is one that, with its emphasis on individualism, has the potential to dissolve, displace or reshuffle groups. By freeing individuals of a strong traditional collective discipline, new groups, identities, coalitions and associations arise. The relative freedom of association that liberalism upholds allows for the reshuffling of elements who will associate with other similar ones, allowing for those with minds that contain group-related adaptations (i.e. altruists) to join new winning groups. This reshuffling process of reorganisation of types (altruists, egoists, etc.) is what philosopher Samir Okasha calls multilevel selection two. In relation to multilevel selection one, which rests on the natural selection of stable and well-defined groups that exchange none or few elements with other groups, multilevel selection two is a reorganising process or a transitional phase that paves the way for new potentially stronger and more cohesive groups. This selection among shifting groups, i.e. multilevel selection two, will then lead to selection among stable groups at a later evolutionary stage, i.e. multilevel selection one (Okasha, 2006, Chapters II and VI). Hence, liberalism, whether of the market or of the social kind, is likely to be a transitional point that facilitates the rise of new collective identities under group selection forces.

This tension between reshuffling groups and the creation of stabler groups fits well with what Karl Polanyi regarded as a social "double movement". In his own words:

> The market expanded continuously, but this movement was met by a countermovement checking the expansion in definite directions. Vital though such a countermovement was for the protection of society, in the last analysis it was incompatible with the self-regulation of the market, and thus the market itself. (Polanyi, 2001, p. 136)

In other words, the protection of social groups impairs the capacity of the market to expand sustainably. Unlike Hayek's claim of market evolutionary superiority, which is a way of postulating the "end of history", market liberalism is evolutionarily unstable and transitional. Joseph Schumpeter (2008) also understood this process when he postulated that the success of market liberalism in achieving wealth creation and material comfort leads to corporatist counter-movements that aim at restricting the disruptions caused by market institutions on social groups (e.g. unemployment, mass dislocations, etc.). In the same way, the relatively high capacity of market liberalism to satisfy individual preferences, in particular of the material sort, collides with the evolutionary process of keeping cohesion within groups.

While market liberalism shows a great capacity to satisfy individual preferences, it does not, as if through an "invisible hand" in the group selection process, show enough strength to be an evolutionary winner at the meta-morality level. This market liberal maladaptation, at its core, makes it an unsuitable replacement for the shortcomings of liberal democracy. All in all, it is the ethic of the liberal satisfaction of preferences that is unsustainable in terms of evolution, and such an ethic underpins both market liberalism and liberal democracy.

References

Alves, A. A., & Meadowcroft, J. (2014). Hayek's Slipery Slope, the Stability of the Mixed Economy and the Dynamics of Rent Seeking. *Political Studies, 62*(4), 843–861.

Ariely, D. (2008). *Predictably Irrational: The Hidden Forces That Shape Our Decisions*. New York: HarperCollins.

Axelrod, R., & Hammond, R. A. (2006). The Evolution of Ethnocentrism. *Journal of Conflict Resolution, 50*(6), 926–936.

Beck, N. (2011). Be Fruitful and Multiply: Growth, Reason, and Cultural Group Selection in Hayek and Darwin. *Biological Theory, 6*, 413–423.

Beck, N. (2015). The Garden of Orderly Polity: F. A. Hayek and T. H. Huxley's Views on Social Evolution. *Journal of Bioeconomics, 17*(1), 83–96.

Boehm, C. (1999). *Hierarchy in the Forest: The Evolution of Egalitarian Behavior*. Cambridge, MA: Harvard University Press.

Boyd, R., & Richerson, P. (2005). *Not by Genes Alone: How Culture Transformed Human Evolution*. Chicago: The University of Chicago Press.

Brennan, G., & Hamlin, A. P. (2004). *Democratic Devices and Desires*. Cambridge, UK: Cambridge University Press.

Buchanan, J. M. (1999). Politics Without Romance: A Sketch of Positive Public Choice Theory and Its Normative Implications. In *The Logical Foundations of Constitutional Liberty* (Vol. 1, pp. 45–60). Indianapolis: Liberty Fund.

Chong, A., Duryea, S., & Ferrara, E. (2012). Soap Operas and Fertility: Evidence from Brazil. *American Economic Journal: Applied Economics, 4*(4), 1–31.

Demoscope.ru. (2009). *Russian Birth Rates 1950–2008*. Retrieved from http://demoscope.ru/weekly/ias/ias05.php?tim=0&cou=26&terr=1&ind=26&Submit=OK.

Durkheim, E. (2001). *Professional Ethics and Civic Morals*. New York: Routledge.

Durkheim, E. (2005). *Suicide: A Study in Sociology*. London: Taylor & Francis.

Durkheim, E. (2009). *Sociology and Philosophy*. New York: Taylor & Francis.

Fahim, K. (2013). *Egypt's Birthrate Rises as Population Control Policies Vanish*. Retrieved from http://www.nytimes.com/2013/05/03/world/middleeast/as-egypt-birthrate-rises-population-policy-vanishes.html?_r=2.

Feldmann, H. (2005). Hayek's Theory of Cultural Evolution: A Critique of the Critiques. In J. Backhaus (Ed.), *Entrepreneurship, Money and Coordination: Hayek's Theory of Cultural Evolution* (pp. 1–46). Cambridge, MA: Edward Elgar.

Frank, R. (2011). *The Darwin Economy: Liberty, Competition, and the Common Good*. Princeton, NJ: Princeton University Press.

Gneezy, U., & Rustichini, A. (2000). A Fine Is a Price. *Journal of Legal Studies, 29*(1), 1–17.

Haidt, J. (2012). *The Righteous Mind: Why Good People Are Divided by Politics and Religion*. London: Allen Lane.

Hamilton, B., Martin, J., & Ventura, S. (2013). Births: Preliminary Data for 2012. *National Vital Statistics Report, 62*(3).

Hardin, R. (2007). *David Hume: Moral & Political Theorist*. Oxford: Oxford University Press.

Hartshorn, M., Kaznatcheev, A., & Shultz, T. (2013). The Evolutionary Dominance of Ethnocentric Cooperation. *Journal of Artificial Societies and Social Simulation, 16*(3), 7.

Haub, C. (2012). *Fact Sheet: World Population Trends 2012*. Retrieved from http://www.prb.org/Publications/Datasheets/2012/world-population-data-sheet/fact-sheet-world-population.aspx.

Heckathorn, D. (1993). Collective Action and Group Heterogeneity: Voluntary Provision vs. *Selective Incentives. American Sociological Review, 58*, 366–384.

Hill, R. (2012). The Putin Era. In G. Gil (Ed.), *Routledge Handbook of Russian Politics and Society* (pp. 13–17). New York: Routledge.

Hobbes, T. (1975). *Leviathan*. London: Dent.

Hodgson, G. (1991). Hayek's Theory of Cultural Evolution: An Evaluation in the Light of Vanberg's Critique. *Economics and Philosophy, 7*, 67–82.

Hume, D. (1994). *Hume: Political Essays* (K. Haakonssen Ed.). Cambridge: Press Syndicate of the University of Cambridge.

Buchanan, J. M., & Vanberg, V. (2001). Constitutional Choice, Rational Ignorance and the Limits of Reason. In *Choice, Contract, and Constitutions* (pp. 127–148). Indianapolis, IN: Liberty Fund.

Jensen, R., & Oster, E. (2009). The Power of TV: Cable Television and Women's Status in India. *The Quarterly Journal of Economics, 124*(3), 1057–1094.

Kahneman, D., & Tversky, A. (1984). Choices, Values, and Frames. *American Psychologist, 39*, 341–350.

Locke, J. (1995). *An Essay Concerning Human Understanding*. New York: Prometheus Books.

Loury, G. C. (1994). Self-Censorship in Public Discourse: A Theory of Political Correctness and Related Phenomena. *Rationality and Society, 6*(4), 428–461.

MacIntyre, A. (2007). *After Virtue: A Study in Moral Theory*. Notre Dame, IN: University of Notre Dame Press.

Miller, D. (1989). The Fatalistic Conceit. *Critical Review: A Journal of Politics and Society, 3*(2), 310–323.

Norenzayan, A. (2014). Does Religion Make People Moral? In F. de Waal, P. Churchland, T. Pievani, & S. Parmigiani (Eds.), *Evolved Morality: The Biology and Philosophy of Human Conscience* (pp. 229–249). Leiden: Brill.

Okasha, S. (2006). *Evolution and the Levels of Selection*. Oxford: Oxford University Press.

Olson, M. (1982). *The Rise and Decline of Nations: Economic Growth, Stagflation, and Social Rigidities*. New Haven: Yale University Press.
Piketty, T. (2014). *Capital in the Twenty-First Century*. Cambridge, MA: The Belknap Press of Harvard University Press.
Pinker, S. (2002). *The Blank Slate: The Modern Denial of Human Nature*. New York: Viking.
Plumer, B. (2013). *Why Are Birthrates Falling Around the World? Blame Television*. Retrieved from http://www.washingtonpost.com/news/wonkblog/wp/2013/05/13/why-are-birthrates-falling-around-the-world-in-a-word-television/.
Polanyi, K. (1968). The Economy as Instituted Process. In H. Schneider & E. LeClair (Eds.), *Economic Anthropology*. New York: Holt, Rinehart and Winston.
Polanyi, K. (2001). *The Great Transformation*. Boston: Beacon Press Books.
Rawls, J. (1993). *Political liberalism*. New York: Columbia University Press.
Economic-Times. (2008). *Russian Policies Ignite Unprecedented Birth Rate in 2007*. Retrieved from http://articles.economictimes.indiatimes.com/2008-02-02/news/27716412_1_interfax-birth-rate-russian-policies.
Rubin, P. (2000). Group Selection and the Limits to Altruism. *Journal of Bioeconomics, 2*(1), 9–23.
Rubin, P. (2007). Utility, Fitness, and Immigration: Reply to Salter. *Journal of Bioeconomics, 9*, 53–67.
Rubin, P., & Gick, E. (2004). Hayek and Modern Evolutionary Theory. In R. Koppl (Ed.), *Advances in Austrian Economics* (Vol. 7, pp. 79–100). Bingley: Emerald Group Publishing.
Salter, F. (2004). Is Ethnic Globalism Adaptive for Americans? *Population and Environment, 25*(5), 501–527.
Salter, F. (2007). Proximate and Ultimate Utilities: A Rejoinder to Rubin. *Journal of Bioeconomics, 9*, 69–74.
Schumpeter, J. (2008). *Capitalism, Socialism and Democracy* (3rd ed.). New York: HarperCollins.
Skarbek, D. (2014). *The Social Order of the Underworld: How Prison Gangs Govern the American Penal System*. Oxford: Oxford University Press.
Sober, E., & Wilson, D. S. (1998). *Unto Others: The Evolution and Psychology of Unselfish Behavior*. Cambridge, MA: Harvard University Press.
Stone, B. (2010). The Current Evidence for Hayek's Cultural Group Selection Theory. *Libertarian Papers, 2*(45), 1–21.
Tullock, G., Seldon, A., & Brady, G. L. (2002). *Government Failure: A Primer in Public Choice*. Washington, DC: Cato Institute.
Turchin, P. (2006). *War and Peace and War: The Rise and Fall of Empires*. New York: Penguin Books.

Tversky, A., & Kahneman, D. (1981). The Framing of Decisions and the Psychology of Choice. *Science, 211*(4481), 453–458.

Uleman, J. (2010). *Kant's Moral Philosophy.* Cambridge: Cambridge University Press.

Vanberg, V. (1986). Spontaneous Market Order and Social Rules: A Critique of F.A. Hayek's Theory of Cultural Evolution. *Economics and Philosophy, 2,* 75–100.

von Hayek, F. A. (1945). The Use of Knowledge in Society. *The American Economic Review, 35*(4), 519–530.

von Hayek, F. A. (1979). *Law, Legislation and Liberty* (Vol. III). London: Routledge.

von Hayek, F. A. (1984). Competition as a Discovery Procedure. In K. Leube & C. Nishiyama (Eds.), *The Essence of Hayek* (pp. 254–265). Stanford: Hoover Institution Press.

von Hayek, F. A. (1988). *The Fatal Conceit: The Errors of Socialism.* Chicago: University of Chicago.

von Hayek, F. A. (2009). *The Pure Theory of Capital.* Auburn: The Ludwig von Mises Institute.

Wilson, D. S., & Wilson, E. O. (2007). Rethinking the Theoretical Foundation of Sociobiology. *The Quarterly Review of Biology, 82*(4), 327–348.

Witt, U. (1994). The Theory of Societal Evolution: Hayek's Unfinished Legacy. In J. Birner & R. Zijp (Eds.), *Hayek, Co-ordination and Evolution: His Legacy in Philosophy, Politics, Economics and the History of Ideas* (pp. 178–189). London: Routledge.

Yeager, L. (2001). *Ethics and Social Science: The Moral Philosophy of Social Cooperation.* Cheltenham: Edward Elgar.

Zywicki, T. (2000). Was Hayek Right About Group Selection After All? *Review of Austrian Economics, 13,* 81–95.

CHAPTER 7

Conclusion

This monograph took an evolutionary perspective to assess the sustainability of liberal institutions and the desirability of the liberal satisfaction of individual preferences on which these institutions rely. To evaluate the sustainability of liberal institutions, such as liberal democracy and free markets, the monograph scrutinised the impact of the liberal satisfaction of preferences on the evolutionary fitness of groups that promote such a liberal morality. In the process, the book also appraised the capacity of liberal institutions to maximise preference satisfaction. To do so, it reanalysed the classic public choice postulate that free markets are a more suitable institutional mechanism to satisfy individual preferences than current western liberal democracies—mostly because of the intrinsic shortcomings of the latter.

The evolutionary perspective rests on the group selectionist model of multilevel selection theory. From this multilevel selection perspective, the liberal satisfaction of individual preferences is undesirable because of the potential maladaptive tendencies that liberal morality creates for groups, especially concerning reproduction and collective cohesion. Hence, the free market is not a suitable alternative to liberal democracy's shortcomings because both institutions operate under a liberal meta-morality that is likely to be maladaptive for groups in the evolutionary process of intergroup competition.

By applying an evolutionary perspective to the study of preference satisfaction in markets and liberal democracy, this work concludes that both these institutions reveal a high potential for maximising the satisfaction

F. N. Faria, *The Evolutionary Limits of Liberalism*, Palgrave Studies in Classical Liberalism, https://doi.org/10.1007/978-3-030-31496-5_7

of individual preferences. More precisely, although free markets seem to have a higher relative potential to satisfy individual preferences, liberal democracy can be better at satisfying preferences than public choice theorists acknowledge. Yet, the maximisation of preferences is not synonymous with maximising the evolutionary fitness of individuals and groups. Institutions that undermine group fitness tend to be culturally selected against. Thus, the high potential to satisfy individual preferences that these two institutions reveal allows them to pursue and fulfil moral liberalism. But, from the perspective of multilevel selection, the fulfilment of moral liberalism is maladaptive, therefore making liberal institutions unsustainable over time.

In order to reach these conclusions, the monograph developed the main arguments throughout seven chapters. After the introduction, the second chapter discussed the key concepts and methodologies that are relevant for the over-arching argument. Chapter 2 focused on the behavioural assumptions of rational/public choice theory and its methods for comparing preference satisfaction in politics and markets, while also introducing the evolutionary model of multilevel selection theory along with essential clarifications of key concepts like preferences, fitness and morality. This chapter also reconsidered public choice theory's behavioural assumptions, suggesting a new set of assumptions based on multilevel selection theory with which to compare preference satisfaction in markets and politics. Most importantly, it was shown that multilevel selection theory is a group selectionist model which upholds that natural selection operates not only at the level of individuals but also at the level of groups. Further, classic public choice theory assumes that individuals are rational and self-interested/egoist and it uses a parity of assumptions when comparing preference satisfaction in markets and politics. Public choice theory thus assumes that individuals have the same behavioural motivations in both institutions. However, such assumptions may obscure real behaviour and should therefore be revised. From a multilevel selection perspective, behavioural assumptions should be pluralistic. Political theorists should assume that several evolved types might operate in politics and markets, from altruistic individuals to rational egoists. The evolutionary assumption with which to analyse social institutions like politics and markets is the "pluralism of types". Chapter 2 also discussed the connection between preferences and fitness to understand the social impact of a liberal satisfaction of individual preferences. This chapter showed that to have success in terms of preference satisfaction is not the same as having success in terms of evolutionary fitness and that fitness-enhancing institutions are more likely to be sustainable than the ones that diminish fitness, regardless of their ability to maximise preferences. Moreover, preferences result from innate tendencies and environmental framing, not being well defined a priori. Equally essential and related, Chapter 2 explored the importance of morality in the social analysis of preferences, highlighting morality's capacity to shape mass preferences. The moral sphere has a vital role in shaping individual preferences because of its function to create group cohesion and to make groups act more like adaptive units.

Subsequently, Chapter 3 put forward the fundamental arguments found in public choice literature regarding the shortcomings of liberal democracy and their potential solutions. According to classic public choice theory, these liberal democratic shortcomings prevent the satisfaction of individual preferences, but free markets are a suitable solution to maximise preference satisfaction. The third chapter analysed two potential market-enhancing solutions: market autocracy and the liberal contractarian solution. Within the public choice framework, this chapter assessed if a market autocracy could be an adequate solution to maximise preference satisfaction, while also revealing public choice theory's liberal-contractarian market solution, notably concentrating on the recognised market advantages over democratic choices. It was concluded that the shortcomings of liberal democracy connect to the problematic nature of collective choices. These collective choices are problematic for the purpose of maximising individual preferences because they are plagued by standard problems like Arrow's impossibility theorem, the principal–agent problem, rational ignorance or rational irrationality. Such shortcomings in liberal democracies are exploited by rationally egoistic rent-seekers who aim at acquiring wealth and privileges, thus frustrating the preference satisfaction of the ordinary voters. Regarding the viability of a market autocracy that aims at maximising individual preferences, the third chapter revealed the standard position within public choice literature. Namely, this chapter showed that public choice theorists rarely accept the viability of a benevolent autocracy committed to satisfying the preferences of the citizens because classic public choice rejects the assumption of altruistic/public-interested political agents. Thus, classic public choice theorists do not portray a market autocracy as a suitable alternative. They prefer to endorse the liberal-contractarian market solution. The liberal market solution relies on a social contract based on politics "as exchange". Here, politics is conceptualised as a system of voluntary exchange of individual preferences in the political "marketplace", which, through rational assessment, one can regard as optimal if kept to the minimum as much as possible, while leaving as many choices as possible to the economic (price-based) market. Because these public choice theorists think that current western liberal democracies are anarchic and coercive on individuals, their solution lies in re-founding the application of the liberal ideal via a constitutional/contractarian revolution. The solution of these contractarian theorists is then to regard markets as the right answer to maximise the satisfaction of individual preferences by also transforming politics into an exchange realm. Finally, this chapter presented the acknowledged advantages of choosing in markets over choosing in "majoritarian" democracies. Overall, Chapter 3 documented the essential public choice argument that free markets are a suitable and desirable alternative to the shortcomings of liberal democracy in respect of preference satisfaction.

Chapter 4 elaborated the evolutionary framework that, in Chapters 5 and 6, reassesses the postulates of public choice theory on markets and liberal democracy and judges the desirability of the liberal satisfaction of preferences. The fourth chapter further develops the notion of morality as an evolutionary mechanism for transforming competing groups into adaptive units of selection. In particular, it highlighted the mechanisms of punishment and social control of moral deviants as vital mechanisms to achieve group behavioural cohesion. This chapter also assessed how morality/culture can be adaptive or maladaptive for groups. Morality can be adaptive because it allows collective shifts in behaviour under circumstances of environmental change, allowing groups to adapt to new threats as cohesive units. Still, morality/culture is also potentially maladaptive because social collectives can adopt maladaptive moral practices. Based on gene-culture coevolution, morality/culture operates as a filter for individual selection within groups to maintain adaptive cohesiveness in competing groups. Moreover, the logic of the "pluralism of types", i.e. differently evolved behavioural types, analysed the production and internalisation of morality/culture. It was concluded that these types influence the morality one is likely to adhere to. Lastly, elitist moral/political framing is decisive in the shaping of mass preferences of individuals in their groups. Through collective punishment mechanisms that attempt to achieve moral homogeneity in groups, elites can therefore institutionalise morality from the top via moral framing to transform mass preferences. In sum, the fourth chapter highlighted the importance of morality and its strong effect on shaping preferences to understand how these preferences can be adaptive or maladaptive for groups and their institutions.

Chapter 5 reassessed public choice theory's explanation of the shortcomings of liberal democracy and of their market-enhancing institutional solutions from the evolutionary perspective developed in Chapter 4. By using the logic of the "pluralism of types", the fifth chapter showed that these shortcomings are less severe at preventing preference satisfaction than public choice scholars acknowledge. This is because morally driven types of a liberal democratic kind potentially operate in these systems along with rational egoists. These liberal moral types not only deepen liberal democratic values of free and equal utility maximisation but also frame a liberal morality, thereby shaping the preferences of the voters (principals) and aligning such preferences with the preferences of political representatives (agents). In that regard, the ability of successful political agents to shape mass preferences can broadly align general preference satisfaction with institutional representatives, allowing institutions to overcome or to minimise pathologies like the principal–agent problem or the problem of aggregation. Hence, the liberal democratic shortcomings can be a barrier to preference satisfaction of individuals if liberal democratic institutions are driven by exploitative/self-interested political agents; but, given the "right" altruistic types working in the system, institutions can overcome these problems (e.g. principal–agent and aggregation problem) or even develop mechanisms of modification and reform that allow for a better alignment of mass preferences with the political representatives (e.g. rent-seeking). Regarding the evolutionary assessment of the potential market-enhancing solutions, Chapter 5 concluded that the solution of autocracy as a framework for markets seems to be an unlikely evolutionary solution for the shortcomings of liberal democracy because autocracies require higher levels of loyalty. Such loyalty comes mostly via the capacity for autocracies to produce group identification and preferentialism. This in-group preferentialism favours anti-free market protectionist policies that aim at creating group autonomy and identity, which is the most likely reason why autocracies are more protectionist than liberal democracies. Finally, the fifth chapter considered the liberal-contractarian market solution, i.e. politics as exchange, to be incompatible with the logical workings of multilevel selection. This incompatibility comes from the fact that giving equal weight and respect to the maximisation of preferences of pro-group and anti-group behavioural types is not logically conducive to group cohesion. And because morality is a process of social pressure and collective punishment imposed by some on others, the aim of achieving "politics as exchange" of preferences runs counter to the very own nature of morality. The enduring logic of group competition is then incompatible with a contractual process where participants must negotiate, respect and maximise all preferences, including anti-group ones. To be group oriented or "altruistic" does not mean one is aiming at the good of all individuals in the group; it means that one enacts group-oriented actions for the good of the group, which implies the punishment and the preference minimisation of anti-group individuals. From an evolutionary angle, the social contract is an unsuitable solution. Finally, after reanalysing the advantages of markets over liberal democracies regarding preference satisfaction, Chapter 5 showed that markets have a high potential to maximise the satisfaction of individual preferences, especially because of avoiding the difficulties of collective choices. But liberal democracy reveals a higher capacity to satisfy preferences than public choice theorists usually put forward.

At last, Chapter 6 analysed the impact of the liberal market society on the evolutionary fitness of groups to understand if this free market solution is truly a sustainable and suitable alternative to the shortcomings of liberal democracy in respect of preference satisfaction. For this purpose, the sixth chapter revaluated F. A. Hayek's endorsement of market liberalism as evolutionarily superior regarding the fitness maximisation of groups under cultural group selection. Thus, this chapter examined the evolutionary fitness effect of the liberal satisfaction of preferences as a meta-morality in markets and democratic liberalism to recognise this morality's desirability for groups. Based on multilevel selection theory, moral (liberal) individualism produces maladaptive tendencies that are detrimental to the evolutionary success of groups in inter-group competition. In this sense, market liberalism seems to minimise the fitness of groups in the long run by atomising preferences, which impacts negatively on reproduction, group identity and cohesion, therefore negatively affecting group fitness. Because of the decisive role that group morality has in shaping preferences, a considerable degree of explicit "tribal" collectiveness is fundamental for achieving fitness-maximising groups with fitness maximising preferences. Thus, Hayek's argument that tribal moralities and their collective aims are detrimental for groups is erroneous. Market liberalism tends to erode non-market traditional moralities, and, when liberalism replaces these non-market traditional moralities, it harms groups in their cohesion and reproductive potential. Liberalism as a meta-morality does not use all the necessary moral foundations to make groups operate as adaptive units, relying merely on liberty, harm and fairness while neglecting important moral foundations for groups such as loyalty, sanctity or authority. Finally, while both free markets and liberal democracy seem to have a high capacity to maximise individual preferences, free markets are an unsuitable alternative to the shortcomings of liberal democracy regarding preference satisfaction. This unsuitability is due to the liberal satisfaction of individual preferences revealing maladaptive tendencies for the groups that promote such a morality. Thus, both in market and democratic liberalism, it is the ethic of the liberal satisfaction of preferences that reveals evolutionary unsustainability.

7.1 The Future Challenge

The acknowledgement of liberalism's evolutionary unsustainability suggests an obvious question: what should western societies do about liberal unsustainability? To answer such a question forces us to think about the meaning of moral and political institutions like democracy, government or freedom in non-liberal contexts. We should aim at constructing these traditional institutions in ways that are sustainable, ecological and intelligible. Although far from being complete, our knowledge of evolution is now robust enough to aid us in thinking about political institutions. In this sense, political theory benefits from evolutionary thinking. Evolution can show the limits of political ideas while offering new avenues. Because of liberalism's apparent unsustainability, we can expect non-liberal groups to challenge the liberal paradigm on a regular basis, which may lead to chaotic situations. Yet, with the knowledge coming from the evolutionary sciences, there is hope that we can manage these challenges and create a positive change, thus avoiding the worst turmoil. From here onwards, to discover sustainable new avenues in political thought becomes a much-needed challenge.

Index

F. N. Faria, *The Evolutionary Limits of Liberalism*, Palgrave Studies in Classical Liberalism, https://doi.org/10.1007/978-3-030-31496-5

The manufacturer's authorised representative in the EU is Springer Nature Customer Service Centre GmbH, Europaplatz 3, 69115 Heidelberg, Germany. If you have any concerns regarding our products, please contact ProductSafety@springernature.com

Printed and bound by CPI Group (UK) Ltd, Croydon, CR0 4YY
30/09/2026
02225661-0006